for

The Farrars from WHLL

TREASURES OF THE CHURCHES OF FRANCE

TREASURES OF THE CHURCHES OF FRANCE

JEAN TARALON

with the assistance of

ROSELINE MAITRE DEVALLON

GEORGE BRAZILLER   NEW YORK

Translated from the french by Mira Intrator.

Published 1966 by arrangement with
LIBRAIRIE HACHETTE - Paris.

George Braziller, Inc.

One Park Avenue, New York, N.Y. 10016

Library of Congress Catalog Card Number: 66-23097

Printed in France

CONTENTS

The Treasures and the Church

To unbolt the treasury doors is to step into a fabulous world that has remained remote from our daily life, but whose wonders glow mysteriously out of the darkness of the centuries and hold one spellbound with their luster. Originally, no distinction was made between the material value of the treasures and their spiritual significance, but as societies evolved the distinction grew. In every age, a treasure, whether secular or religious, adds to its artistic merit and archaeological interest the value of the rare materials of which it is made. The art of treasures is an art involving the use of precious materials whose value is expressed not only in aesthetic judgments but in current market prices. Whereas the cost of stretcher and canvas, or quantity of paint, has no bearing on the value of a picture by Rembrandt or Cézanne, the head of the Majesty of St. Foy at Conques would always fetch the going price of 800 grams of pure gold. It is this weight in gold or silver that was recorded in the chartularies and registers that listed the treasures of abbeys or cathedrals, and these treasures, like secular treasures, constituted a monetary reserve that could be drawn upon in case of need. On the other hand, the very preciousness of the materials used invests the treasure with a significance that transcends its formal aspect, giving it a mystical or magical quality. And this brings us to the distinctive features of church treasures. They were made in the first place as objects pertaining to worship, and only subsequently became works of art. In addition to their aesthetic value and their market value, they possessed a superior value derived from their consecration to liturgical use. The ciborium or the evangeliary were receptacles of divine reality or holy scripture. They were sacred objects. To the men who made them, the reliquaries came to be identified with the relics they enshrined and were accorded a like veneration, The Majesty of St. Foy (pl. 201) was granted the same devotion as the saint's head, which it enshrined. This held true for the saint herself, for it was in the form of the statue that she appeared to her worshipers in their dreams. Indeed, this identity between reliquary and relic has sometimes remained with unchanged religious significance even after the disappearance of the relic itself, as witness the pilgrimages that still continue to the Virgin of Orcival (pl. 66) or the Virgin of Evron (pl. 161).

These remarks explain why and how the church treasures came into being, and why they disappeared or were dispersed. And also why those that remain still possess so much evocative power.

Religious significance and material value—this dual aspect of the church treasures brings both religious and economic factors into play, the former corresponding to the demands of the liturgy and developing along with it, the latter bound up with events of a political nature. The two factors constantly overlapped. The financial conditions of states, their relations with one another, periods of peace or of trouble, religious crises, the degree of attachment of the people and their rulers to matters of religion, the place occupied by the clergy in the social hierarchy—all these were relevant factors at various periods of history. Related circumstances had repercussions in this sphere of church treasures: the preponderant part played by Eastern monasticism at the time of the emergence of Christian art in the West; the development of trade and pilgrimage routes, along which these easily portable precious objects—textiles, manuscripts, ivories, goldsmithery—were circulated, with constant exchanges between one province and another all over Europe and between East and West; ambassadors carrying gifts, as for instance, those of the

Empress Irene of Constantinople, of Alfonso II, conqueror of the Arabs, of Harun al-Rashid, caliph of Baghdad, to Charlemagne; imperial alliances, and royal; conquests, that is, plunder—the Franks in Italy in the eighth century with Charlemagne, or, at the dawn of the Renaissance, the French with Charles VIII and Louis XII; crusades—the sack of Constantinople in 1204 was to provide an example of the violent transfer of treasures from which St. Mark's in Venice profited. So many incidents—among so many others—where vainglory, greed, and religious fervor combined to promote a circulation of goods that contributed to the formation—and transformation—of the riches that made up the treasuries.

This building up of treasures made of rare and expensive materials was dependent upon the wealth of the clergy and its readiness to invest a part of that wealth in works that, by exalting the glory of God and his saints, would affirm the pre-eminence of the Church. This combination occurs primarily in the kind of theocratic society that prevailed during the Middle Ages, and that is why this period is par excellence the period of church treasures. The clergy—enriched by private gifts, supported by the sovereign power which obtained its investiture from the Church and in return showered its largesse upon it—was at the pinnacle of the social hierarchy. Treasuries were built up in flourishing abbeys, in cathedrals whose generously endowed chapters were placed under the authority of powerful bishops, but also in more unassuming churches, ordinary parish or collegiate churches or priories enriched by the attachment of the faithful or the furor of a particular devotion.

The creation of treasuries had been endorsed by the Council of Aachen in 836, although a part of ecclesiastical opinion disapproved of the consecration of precious materials to God. We know of the contents of the treasuries from detailed descriptions in the records. Up to the end of the ninth century, churches were required by royal decree to make periodic inventories (*descriptio* or *somma*) of their possessions, both immovable and movable, which were recorded in registers. This custom then fell into disuse and was replaced by that of censuses, records of benefices, chartularies, etc., scrupulously kept up to date, especially from the twelfth century onward, in which the precious objects in the treasuries were included among the other possessions. The treasury itself was divided into two categories: the *ministerium*, comprising the consecrated furnishings used in the celebration of the liturgy, and the *ornamentum,* which included whatever was used for church adornment. The monies, or *ergastulum,* of the prelate and the religious community were distinct from the treasury and was kept in separate coffers. This monetary reserve was extremely important in the early Middle Ages, when workshops for striking coins were attached to churches and monasteries. It was supplied by the offerings and ground rents received by the religious house, and was used for the purchase of real estate, for work and improvements on the church, and for current expenditures. Before the Carolingian period, the prelate's *ergastulum* was at his discretion, but remained separate from his personal possessions. Subsequently, however, the revenues of the see or abbey became the property of the prelate and he could use it as he wished. Generally, he allocated a part to augment the treasury and for the needs of the community. In the thirteenth century, the bishop was supposed to set aside one fourth of his income for the construction of the cathedral in his diocese. Sometimes, however, conflicts arose between the bishop and his chapter, or the monasteries of his diocese. In the Carolingian period, for example, the monks of Saint-Calais, at odds with St. Aldric, bishop of Le Mans, fled in a body, taking the treasures of the abbey with them. And the abuses that arose, at the beginning of the fourteenth century, from the institution of the *commendam* are well known.

Texts prior to the ninth century make no mention of the existence of a special place known as the treasury. Priestly vestments and other objects used during services were stored in chests which stood in the *sacrarium* (sacristy). Valuables were stored in secret repositories. Other chests, intended for the receipt of offerings, were placed in the church. Later, however, a treasury chamber came to be a normal feature of most big secular and regular houses, with wall closets, as at the Cathedral of Saint-Jean-de-Maurienne or the Abbey of Saint-Antoine-en-Viennois, or immense cupboards, as at Bayeux, Obazine, or Sallanches. Closets and cupboards were locked by heavy bolts fastened with complicated locks. In the seventeenth century, cupboards appeared in which vestments were laid flat. Sometimes, as at Clairvaux from the twelfth century, the "great treasure" was stored in a separate chamber reserved for very precious objects used in solemn ceremonies. The "small treasure," consisting of church furnishings for everyday use, was kept in the sacristy.

A *custos sacrarii* (custodian of the sacristy), watched over the treasures. But the sanctuary, too, was guarded. We read in the *Livre des Miracles de Sainte Foy* (Book of the Miracles of St. Foy), written in the first quarter of the eleventh century, that the custodian of the gold statue at Conques was named Gimon, and that the saint took pleasure in waking him up at night. When the sanctuary light went out, he would "hear the gold of the statue ring." At this signal he would make ready to relight the lamp, but it would relight itself. "Boiling with rage, the old man, who was very quick-tempered, would begin to revile St. Foy and accuse her of making fun of him." At Chartres, the custodian's room was on top of the thirteenth-century rood loft, which was destroyed at the end of the eighteenth century.

Indeed, particularly in the early periods, the vestments and the pieces of gold- and silverwork permanently located in the church itself were no less sumptuous than the objects stored in the treasury. In the Merovingian period, churches were hung with rich stuffs, for the most part from Byzantium or Persia, and later, beginning with Carolingian times, from western territories under Islamic rule, Sicily and Spain. These stuffs were hung at the entrance doors and between the columns of the basilica, concealing the altar from the faithful in the side aisles, save at certain points during the service when they were drawn aside (Lesson, Sermon, Communion). They were draped on the altar, which was also surrounded by hangings. The most precious of these textiles were wrapped about the bodies of saints (whence the word "shroud": Shroud of St. Calais, Shroud of St. Polycarp, etc.), or were made over into liturgical vestments, as were those of St. Cesarius of Arles. The names of some of these churches—La Daurade (the chrysophrys, i.e., a fish with gold and silver highlights), Les Saints d'or (the golden saints), now Saint-Germain-des-Prés—give us some idea of how highly valued—among the many brightly colored ornaments—were the mosaics and metalware that contained some portion of that most precious substance, gold. Indeed, the altar with its antependium, its retable, the ciborium, or the large cross surmounting them—all those fittings which, in present legal terminology, belong to the category of fixtures rather than furnishings—were made of the rarest materials, not only silver and silver gilt, but gold. These metals sparkled in the candlelight, with a brilliance and splendor enhanced by jewels set in filigree, by precious stones, by enamels.

The imagination is staggered by the unbelievable sumptuousness of the early medieval churches as described in the old texts. Altars covered with precious metals existed in the seventh century at Stavelot, in the eighth century at Saint-Riquier, in the ninth century at Besançon, Saint-Germain-des-Prés, Auxerre, Reims. In 834, St. Aldric had a "marvelously wrought altar surmounted by a ciborium of gold and silver," constructed in the center of the apse of his cathedral at Le Mans. In the same cathedral, the Altar of the Blessed Trinity was surmounted by a cross of gold and silver. The retable of the altar in the chapel of SS. Gervasius and Protasius was also of gold and silver. Innumerable other examples come to mind. The fifteenth-century painting of the Mass of St. Giles (p. 10) shows us the golden retable at Saint-Denis given by Charles the Bald surmounted by a great cross of gold and garnets made, according to tradition, by St. Eligius. From the story in the Book of the Miracles of St. Foy of the theft of a fragment of gold at the time the great altar frontal at Conques was made, we know that it contained gold. All that remains in France of these marvels is what is believed to be the fragment of a tenth-century silver and silver-gilt antependium at Conques (pl. 203), and the gold Ottonian antependium from Basel at the Musée de Cluny. The ninth-century altar frontal (*paliotto*) in Milan at Sant'Ambrogio, and the antependium at Aachen, dating from the year 1000, both of gold and still in their original locations, remain famous testimony of a period when the primacy of art was expressed in work in precious materials placed at the service of a society organized on an essentially religious foundation. The tradition was to be maintained in succeeding periods with works such as the Pala d'Oro at St. Mark's in Venice, a twelfth-century Byzantine work remodeled in the fourteenth century; the silver antependium at Verona; the altar frontals of Pistoia, Florence, and Gerona in the Gothic period; the sixteenth-century retable of the Hofkirche at Innsbruck and, right up to the eighteenth century, with the silver-gilt antependium that until recently could still be seen on the high altar at Saint-Denis. But by the Romanesque period these techniques were no longer to be used exclusively. They were quickly to be supplanted by sculpture and painting. In the sixteenth century, alabaster replaced ivory in the retables of Juignettes or Ecaquelon. And after the Counter Reformation, great retables made of wood gilded in imitation of metal almost everywhere replaced metal itself.

Clearly, if a store of treasures made of precious metals was to be built up, sufficient funds had to be available. Such funds varied according to period and place, and were derived from various sources. The principal source always remained the offerings of the faithful (although the church did not accept all such offerings; it refused those of public sinners and excommunicated persons). The offerings (*oblationes*) were sometimes placed at the doors of monasteries or churches. More often they were handed to the *custos* or left on the tomb of the saint to whom the donor had come to pray. Sometimes a special chest, which enshrined the saint's relics, was placed near the altar. In ninth-century texts the high altar at Saint-Denis is normally called "the treasury," because Dagobert had arranged for a silver chest to be placed at one of the corners (*ante cornu altaris*) to receive the *oblationes* of the faithful. At Saint-Martial in Limoges, a *fenestra* (that is, an aperture through which the faithful might see the sarcophagus) had been made over the saint's tomb and into this, pilgrims threw their offerings. Offerings could also be made by a deed instead of being brought to the place of pilgrimage. The wills of abbots, bishops, kings, nobles, and—after the advent of a middle class—burghers often contained such clauses. The one most frequently cited is Charlemagne's will which divided two thirds of his movable estate among the twenty-one metropolitan churches of his empire— on the basis of which the monasteries of Aquitaine fabricated a legend in the eleventh century to the effect that the emperor had founded

MASTER OF ST. GILES. *The Mass of St. Giles*
The National Gallery, London

CRESPIN. Monstrance reliquary

SAINT-BERTRAND-DE-COMMINGES. Casket

twenty-four abbeys and given to each of them a reliquary in the form of a letter of the alphabet, the first being the "A" of Charlemagne in the Conques Treasury (pl. 212).

In every period, the nature of the offerings—made by kings, nobles, and common people—varied from the most sophisticated to the most simple, from objects made of the humblest materials to those made of the most precious. (The clergy, we might note, always showed a marked preference for the latter; but the practice of ex-votos shows the lasting character of the former.) Prisoners who had invoked St. Foy to deliver them—for it was one of her "specialties" to deliver captives—would bring their chains to her at Conques. And these chains were used in the twelfth century to forge the magnificent grills of the abbey church. For the most part, however, offerings were articles of value—precious textiles, goldsmithery—or money. Among the offerings we must distinguish between pieces made especially for the Treasury—votive crowns, which may have been the origin of the crown on the statue of St. Foy, or that of the Abbey of Le Paraclet in the thirteenth century (pl. 108); reliquaries like the one of the Precious Blood which Philip the Fair is supposed to have given to the church of Notre-Dame in Boulogne in 1308 (pl. 111); crosses, like the great rock crystal cross given by Etienne Gueffier to the Cathedral of Le Mans in 1626 (pl. 165)—and precious objects that were mainly secular in character. Some of these were preserved unchanged, in memory of the illustrious donor—the iron crown given by Bérenger to the Treasury of Monza, or the knife of St. Louis at the Abbey of Longpoint—or simply by reason of their usefulness, the small casket at Saint-Bertrand-de-Comminges, for example (p. 11 below). Others were re-used as parts of new pieces—ancient intaglios or cameos from Imperial or royal treasuries; necklace beads or plaques detached from crowns, which were used to decorate goldsmithery up to Romanesque times; pieces of military equipment, such as the Arab saddle that Count Roger of Toulouse gave to the Treasury of Conques; maces, such as the one of rock crystal, whose pommel was used to fashion the Crespin reliquary (p. 11 above), etc. Still others were melted down for various purposes, in which case they were asssessed in the inventories at their weight in metal. Thus the Book of the Miracles of St. Foy tells us (Book II, chapter 10) under the heading, "Of the miracle of the gold fibula which Countess Richarde refused to give to St. Foy," that this fibula had been lost, and was then found "pinned to the head of the statue of the saint," and, we read further, "this gold was subsequently used for some necessary work." This would mean that the fibula had been melted down, the "necessary work" perhaps being the antependium of the high altar, for which St. Foy "collected gold" from pilgrims ("How St. Foy collected gold everywhere for the fashioning of an altar," Book of the Miracles, Book I, chapter 17).

Ingots and coins were also brought as offerings, and, at the most profitable seasons of pilgrimage, these would be piled pell-mell with gifts in kind. Mgr. Lesne, in his work on ecclesiastical property in France from the ninth to the eleventh centuries, notes that in the ninth century the gifts made to the relics of St. Sebastian at Saint-Médard of Soissons were such that "the heaps of jewels, masculine and feminine finery, gems and vessels, produced a sum of 900 livres of gold," and that "the pile of silver pieces exceeded the capacity of 85 hogsheads."

It should be borne in mind that one of the characteristic traits of the Catholic religion is that along with the veneration paid to everything connected with Christ and his Passion—the True Cross, the Column of the Flagellation (a fragment of which was venerated at

Conques), tiles from the Holy Sepulcher (as at Villers-Saint-Sépulcre, p. 51 left center), etc.—there was also the cult of the Virgin and the saints, and consequently of their relics, too, that is, of their mortal remains or clothing that had touched them. Such relics came to be divided up, and even multiplied, as evidence by the numerous hairs of the Virgin, fingers of John the Baptist, etc., distributed throughout the Christian world. In the Middle Ages this characteristic underlies the whole subject of church treasures. The importance of the treasures was proportionate to that of the relics that were being venerated. The practice of dividing up saints' bodies in order to distribute their benefits, and of preserving these fragments in reliquaries, gave to Christian treasuries a character not found in any other religion: a wealth created by the multitude of caskets and reliquaries alongside the properly liturgical objects such as chalices and ciboria; and as a result of this practice, the creation of unusual categories of forms that corresponded to the purpose of the reliquary or casket. This purpose was not only to protect a saint's body, or a fragment of it, and to honor it by the quality and luster of the materials used, but also to make the saint's presence felt. This was achieved by means of symbols or an iconography pertaining to the saint, or by showing the relic itself in the caskets by means of a fenestella, or monstrance reliquaries, or, lastly, by recalling the shapes of the relic itself. Relics which were part of a human body—a finger, a foot, a leg, an arm, a shoulder blade, a rib, a head—gave rise to the series of foot reliquaries, arm reliquaries, rib reliquaries, etc. (p. 50), whose appearance might seem peculiar were they not intended, by their shape, to "exalt" the relics themselves, which were sacred because they were parts of bodies of saints who would one day rise again.

And one can ask, as Bréhier does, whether the custom of statue reliquaries which spread throughout southwestern France from the ninth century did not correspond with the desire of the theologians of these regions to link the two concepts of veneration of relics and veneration of images, the latter finding its justification in the former. The veneration of images had taken on so vast a scope in the East that, during the iconoclastic controversy of the eighth and ninth centuries, the Byzantine emperor and higher clergy turned all their energies to destroying them. In the West, the clergy did not take part in the controversy; they confined themselves to "condemning alike those who adored and those who destroyed images," recalling that only the image of God should be venerated, whereas "the images of saints are made to recall their deeds, not to be worshiped in their own right." Beginning with Carolingian times, there was an aversion in the ecclesiastical schools of northern France for "images of veneration," which were also known as "effigies" or "statues of Majesty"; if they represented saints rather than Christ or the Virgin, they were felt to be idolatrous. This attitude was exemplified by Bernard of Angers, pupil of the great Fulbert of Chartres and official grammarian of his cathedral chapter, who subsequently wrote the Book of the Miracles of St. Foy, on visiting Conques early in the eleventh century: "It appears unseemly," he wrote, "to fashion statues, save to represent Our Lord on the Cross." This intellectual point of view did not correspond with the religion of the common people. In all religions, popular belief, in which superstition sometimes plays as large a part as faith, has usually centered around tangible forms of worship. Among pagan peoples whose art is non-figurative, men worship stones; among others, an idol fashioned in human form. In the Christian religion, the saint is preferably entreated through his individualized representation; the personality behind the image remains vague if it is only imagined. This process of identification between the image and the saint it represented was an unconscious

Head of the Majesty of St. Foy at Conques

one. The image came to be venerated on a par with its subject, and supernatural powers were imputed to it. It was this that Bernard of Angers termed idolatry. "What do you say, brother, of this idol?" he asks his companion, Bernier, before the statue reliquary of St. Gerald of Aurillac. But if the image contained a relic, whose form it represented, it was from the relic that it derived its power. It might then be regarded as miraculous, and the taint of idolatry was averted. Bernard, in any event, soon repented before St. Foy: "I contemptuously labeled this statue Venus or Diana . . . Later I felt the most sincere regret for my insensate conduct regarding this holy friend of God."

It so happens—a circumstance Bernard could not have guessed—that the head of St. Foy of Conques, the oldest medieval statue in the West, and the only surviving pre-Romanesque "Majesty," is a pagan head fitted into a tree stump carved in human likeness, in the millenial tradition of the Celtic divinities, like the Pyrenean god at Tarbes, whose mask of bronze sheets should, according to Lantier, "be linked with the group of statues of the wooden herma type." This technical, as well as formal and religious, continuity gives the statue of St. Foy of Conques an indefinable power that has left an unexplainable impression on all those who have described it since Merimée. And one can understand the astonishment of the grammarian of Angers, already prejudiced against what he regarded—before his conversion—as "a practice that educated men consider superstition," "a relic of the worship of heathen gods," the astonishment of a northerner unaccustomed to "images," at the unexpected sight of this "golden statue laden with gems like a pagan idol," as Bédier has described it, to which offerings were made and prayers ascended.

An "idol" in its inhumanity—and thus fundamentally contrary to the spirit of Christian humanism that was to develop some centuries later, in Gothic times—it nevertheless constitutes not only the oldest but also the loftiest surviving example of the symbolic exaltation of the body of a saint as personified by its relic, in this case, the martyr's head. Crowned, clothed in a dalmatic, she is seated in Majesty upon her throne—the throne of triumphant martyrs—which had been a feature of Early Christian funerary furnishings and was subsequently used in Byzantine iconography. It is both the throne of Christ's glory—similar to that occupied by the deified emperors of the Roman pantheon—and "the seat of honor which Christ will prepare for the faithful in his paradise," on which as Christ's representative, the martyr, "who by his sacrifice partakes in the Passion of the Saviour which is renewed through the mystical agapae of each Mass," presides over these agapae from behind the altar, at his own tomb.

In no other work is the formal aspect so permeated with its mystical significance. There is something supernatural about the "presence" of this golden St. Foy. It is the effect of the holy immobility of one lost in prayer, of the haunting fixity of the enamel-and-glass eyes, of the barbaric splendor of the dazzling gold adornment, from which emanates a mysterious power that explains the awed veneration of the crowds who came to pray to her. When we read in the Book of the Miracles of St. Foy that the Majesty was carried in procession by monks through lands that she claimed on their behalf, that a girl was paralyzed because she did not rise when the Majesty passed by, that Vuitbert "the enlightened" recovered his eyes after invoking St. Foy, it is no longer very clear whether the reference is to the holy martyr, to her relic enshrined within the statue, or to the statue itself. But the saint herself clarifies the issue. A cleric "who considered himself more learned than the rest" (once again we have the opposition between the "intellectual" and the "popular" approach to the faith) indulged in "unseemly remarks against the

Eyes of the Majesty of St. Foy at Conques

image of the saint," whereupon St. Foy comes in person to chastise the foolhardy critic. "Wretch," she says to him, "how dare you abuse my statue?" In a word, the statue seems really to have been identified with the saint through the medium of the relic. The cult of the statue reliquary of St. Foy took the place of the cult of St. Foy herself.

This outcome, which corresponded to the deepest popular instincts, was the result of a concerted theological plan. The idea of a saintly body, and of its relics, begot the idea of miracle, and miraculous powers were deliberately imputed to the statue reliquary. (In fact, the statue retained its miraculous character even after the disappearance of the relic. This is true of many Virgins that were the objects of pilgrimage.) In the latter part of the tenth century, Stephen II, bishop of Clermont, ordered Alléaume, his clerk, to fashion a gold Virgin for his cathedral. Robert, abbot of Mozat, was inspired by a vision: he saw swarms of flies descending upon the workshop, disturbing Alléaume and his brother Adam, who was helping him. Since flies represented the forces of the evil one, the workshop was exorcised, whereupon the flies departed, to be replaced by 300 bees, which alighted on the precious stones of the Majesty. The bees, being virginal insects, symbolized the Virgin. Thus it was under the personal protection of the Virgin that the statue was completed. The statue had become miraculous. This vision of the abbot of Mozat shows that the fashioning of a statue reliquary was surrounded by ritual ceremonial, designed to communicate to the image a supernatural power emanating liturgically from the supraterrestrial being that it represented. Through this legendary hallowing of a recently made object, we perceive, as Shrade has pointed out, the process of the "invention" of miracles.

Miracles did in fact originate from the presence of the bodies of saints. Even the oil burning over the altars where they lay possessed a power that it derived from their proximity. As early as the fourth century, Syrian monks in the great sanctuaries had established a circulatory system whereby oil was poured through a funnel placed over the saint's tomb and drawn off by means of a spigot below the tomb. The oil, thus impregnated with the virtue of the relic, was collected and distributed among the pilgrims. This pious custom had had antecedents in the time of the catacombs. A few drops of perfume poured over the venerated remains and collected in phials—known as phials of praise—were regarded as a substitute for the body of the martyr itself. This phenomenon of "belonging," which is to be found in many primitive religions, was very marked in the Middle Ages. Oil collected in the manner just described, "milk of the Virgin," that is, white dust or torta from the cave of Bethlehem, possessed sovereign prophylactic powers against maladies of soul and body. They were carried off in terra-cotta phials or encolpia like those in the treasuries at Bobbio and Monza in Italy— the shape of which is reproduced in gold in the Talisman of Charlemagne (pl. 83) and the reliquary of the Charroux treasury (pl. 183) —or in little bags that could be hung about the neck, like the one in the Sens Treasury (p. 16).

The inventories and chartularies listing the riches of the treasuries do not fail to mention the most precious objects among them, namely, the relics possessed by the abbey or cathedral. In case of war or other danger, the monks' first thought in the midst of flight was to take their relics with them. And if so many Byzantine reliquaries were brought back to the West by the crusaders, it was because of the relics they contained. Oaths were sworn on relics. The Bayeux Tapestry depicts Harold's false oath (p. 17), which was the source of all his subsequent misfortunes. Unwittingly, he had taken his oath on "important relics." For there was a hierarchy in the importance and efficacy of saints' bodies. Some saints had only a local clientele, but others, like the great wonder-workers St. James of Compostela, St. Martin of Tours, St. John of Ephesus, were renowned to the ends of the Christian world. In some cases, contemporaries were honored from the day of their canonization, and their iconography was immediately established. Scenes depicting the murder of Thomas à Becket, which took place in 1170, became one of the most commonly reproduced themes in the thirteenth-century enamel casket reliquaries of Limoges because they were most in demand (e.g., the casket reliquaries in the treasuries of Sens, Le Vigean, etc.). The body of St. Stephen of Muret, founder of the Order of Grandmont, who died in 1124, was placed in a casket over the high altar of the abbey church in the very year of his canonization, 1189 (fig. 44), and he is represented on one of the two plaques made at about that period, now in the Musée de Cluny. And while the sumptuousness of the caskets enshrining the relics was proportionate to the wealth of the abbeys and churches concerned, it was usually from these relics that their prosperity was derived in the first place, since it was the fame of the relics that drew the crowds of pilgrims who came to implore the healing of their maladies and the salvation of their souls by touching the miraculous shrine before which they kept prayerful vigil through the night. At Saint-Riquier, for instance, the "yield of the altar" was larger than all other revenues of the abbey, and exceeded 15,000 livres.

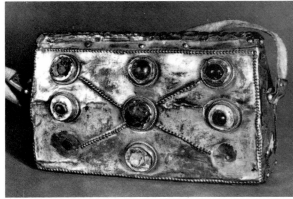

SENS. Portable reliquary

The extraordinary spiritual attraction of the great pilgrimages, whose routes persisted throughout the Middle Ages—to the Holy Land from the fourth century, which were to exert a paramount influence on the development of a Christian iconography, to Rome from the eleventh century, to Santiago de Compostela and Mont-Saint-Michel, punctuated by halts at sanctuaries dedicated to the mortal remains of saints (St. Martin of Tours, St. Martial of Limoges, St. Foy of Conques, St. Saturninus of Toulouse)—was accompanied by benefits of an altogether material nature. The pilgrimage roads were the tourist routes of the Middle Ages. There were rivalries among sanctuaries. The bishop of Laon, angered at seeing the stream of pilgrims diverted to Soissons, exhorted the faithful not to take their alms to churches other than his. And in order to attract gifts, some monasteries sought to obtain possession of relics even at the cost of distant and often perilous journeys. Sometimes, even, legends were fabricated in order to authenticate relics. In the eleventh century there was the one spread by the monks of Vézelay who claimed to possess the body of Mary Magdalen, and in order to justify its presence among them, invented the story of her sea voyage to the shores of Provence where they discovered her body in a sarcophagus. Sometimes, too, legends grew up of themselves, by some mysterious process. Thus the "Holy Lance" of the Vienna Schatzkammer, which King Rudolph of Burgundy gave in the tenth century to Henry the Fowler, an ancestor of the Ottonian emperors, was at first venerated as the lance of St. Maurice, but after the thirteenth century as the lance with which Longinus had pierced Christ's side.

And sometimes pious thefts were committed at the expense of other religious houses. One of the most famous of these, known as the "furtive translation" of St. Foy, of which we have two eleventh-century accounts, one in verse, the other in prose, secured the prosperity of Conques. The abbey, founded in the eighth century, led a humble and precarious existence in its solitary wilderness of Rouergue until, in the ninth century, the monks decided to appropriate the body of a saint. At first they set their sights on the body of St. Vincent of Saragossa. But their emissary was arrested and thrown into prison, so

BAYEUX. The Oath of Harold,
detail of the Bayeux Tapestry

they had to be satisfied with another St. Vincent, a martyr of the diocese of Agen. It was at this point that it occurred to the monks to secure the body of St. Foy, a young third-century martyr who was held in great veneration at a church in Agen. One of them proceeded to this church, and after gaining the confidence of the clergy, took up residence among them. He stayed for ten years. At the end of this period, on the Feast of the Epiphany, while the community was at dinner, he broke open the saint's tomb, wrapped the body in a sack, and managed to get back to his monastery despite the horsemen sent out in pursuit. From that day, pilgrims flocked to the gold statue containing the head of St. Foy (pl. 201), and the monastery prospered. A century later a miracle took place which made a tremendous impression throughout the West and carried the saint's reputation beyond the frontiers: the restoration of sight to Vuitbert, "the enlightened," through the intervention of St. Foy as personified in her statue. Conques, a halting place on the way to Santiago de Compostela and a place of pilgrimage in its own right, became one of the most frequented spots in Christendom. A magnificent church was built. The golden Majesty received sumptuous adornments. Priories under the patronage of St. Foy were founded as far as England, Germany, Spain, and Italy. The Treasury, one of the most considerable still in existence, was enriched by many and splendid pieces of precious metalwork. Then the decline of pilgrimages led to the decline of the abbey, while the priories, grown too powerful, detached themselves from the mother house, thereby depriving it of substantial revenues. We can follow its history in the history of the Treasury, to which only less valuable pieces were now added. Conques returned to its obscure existence around an abbey church now much too large for it, an existence reduced to the dimensions and devotion of a village, the only reminder of its ancient splendor its marvelous Treasury, buried in its former solitude.

Thus the great waves of religious fervor, fluctuating over the centuries, influenced the building up of church treasures, their increase or—as at Conques—their stagnation resulting from a form of disaffection. The causes of the dispersal and disappearance of these treasures were of the same kind as those which had led to their establishment. They were the counterparts of the former and, like them, were economic, historical, and religious in character. The commercial value of the materials of which the treasures were made rendered them an obvious prey to theft and pillage. Thefts took place in every period. One of Charlemagne's capitularies, dated 806, urged bishops, abbots, and abbesses to guard their treasures and watch their custodians, whose negligence or venality enabled "Jewish or other" merchants to boast that they could buy from them whatever they wanted, and other capitularies recalled that it was prohibited to dispose of sacred vessels. In the ninth century, Bishop Hincmar of Laon was deposed by a synod that accused him of having traded in his church's treasures. "Gold and silver reliquaries estimated at 30,000 livres" were stolen from the Evron Treasury in 1508. In 1564, four malefactors, including a woman, carried off the great reliquary of St. Taurinus of Evreux (fig. 30). They were caught and broken on the wheel. The reliquary was returned, but it had been damaged. Early in the present century, the "Black Gang" plundered the treasures of Corrèze. Among other fine pieces that disappeared at that time were the Eucharistic doves of Obazine and La Guienne. As a provisional conclusion to this series, we might recall the recent theft of the eighteenth-century silver-gilt antependium from the high altar at Saint-Denis.

As for looting, this was the concomitant of invasion, war, and revolution. In the ninth century the Normans occupied the monastery of Saint-Denis for twenty days and carried off innumerable pieces of gold and silver plate. In 953, it was the turn of the Hungarians at Saint-Géry of Cambrai. In those turbulent times, the king himself pillaged his own territories. In 841 Lothair invaded the provinces of Maine and Sens and seized the treasures of the churches of those dioceses, which had been stored in the two cathedrals. A half century later King Odo obtained 8 livres for the gold-bound Gospel Book and 4 livres for the gold chalice from the Treasury of Saint-Denis. In 1562, Protestants plundered the Treasury of Rouen of "more than 50 livres of gold and 300 livres of silver in a single day," which included the silver ledge from the high altar. In the same year the monks of Evron removed the "sheets of gold weighing 2 livres 8 ounces" from their great statue of Christ, as a precautionary measure against the arrival of the Huguenots. The Treasury of Notre-Dame of Paris, one of the most considerable in France, was plundered in 1792, then sacked during the revolution of 1830. Nothing remains of the magnificent pieces it contained—the silver-gilt crown enshrining relics of the Passion given by St. Louis, the gold arm of St. Andrew given by Louis XI, the great reliquary studded with rubies, sapphires, emeralds, and fine pearls given by duc Jean de Berry, the large gold ostensory adorned with rubies and diamonds known as "the great sun," fashioned in 1718 by Thomas Germain, unequaled in sumptuousness save by another by the same master which still survives in Lisbon. It is less surprising, indeed, that so many treasures should have disappeared—for in periods of religious wars or revolution their religious character increased the fury with which they were destroyed —than that even a relatively few should have been preserved, their survival being due, for the most part, only to the attachment of the faithful to "their treasure." This explains why more treasures disappeared in cities than in rural areas, in cathedrals than in village churches. When the emissaries of the Convention arrived in Conques, they found nothing; the villagers had hidden everything during the night.

To such thefts and lootings, we may add, in our own day, substitutions of skillful copies for originals, for instance, the original silver and silver-gilt head of St. Yrieix in Haute-Vienne which has been at the Metropolitan Museum in New York since World War I, the original of the Soudeilles piece at the Louvre, or the original of the statue reliquary of Saint-Christophe-de-Lasbordes in Aude, also at the Metropolitan; even the marks are faked on the piece now at Lasbordes. Cupidity has also been the cause of certain mutilations. For instance, the oval stone on one of the faces of the Talisman of Charlemagne was replaced in the nineteenth century by a glass lens. Several small statuettes of repoussé copper-gilt from the Casket of St. Romanus in Rouen (pl. 156) have been replaced by electrotype copies (p. 25). The descriptions in the best works on the Majesty of St. Foy assume that the precious stones and intaglios that adorn the bodice and robe, as well as the added silver-gilt plaques, were embellishments. In point of fact, under each intaglio and under each silver-gilt plaque, the gold of the original foil has been cut away, and these additions were made only to cover up thefts.

Finally, the role of the treasures, whether religious or secular, as a monetary reserve must be included among the principal reasons for their disappearance. Here, economic considerations outweigh both aesthetic and religious ones. Such use of church treasures was always deemed justified in certain cases. For instance, it was authorized by canon law for the ransoming of captives. In 858, Louis, abbot of Saint-Denis, ordered his abbey treasury to pay his ransom, amounting to 688 livres of gold and 3,250 livres of silver. Often, in periods of invasion, a whole abbey would pay ransom to avoid pillage. In 857, the Normans set fire to all the churches in the neighborhood of Paris with the exception of Saint-Etienne, Saint-Germain-des-Prés, and Saint-Denis, which had bought themselves off. The treasuries of all the churches in the kingdom were made to contribute to the ransom of Saint-Denis, this being a royal abbey. In the last quarter of the tenth century, Bego II, bishop of Clermont and secular abbot of Conques, forcibly removed from his abbey treasury "the four most precious copes, a large silver censer, and a large chalice of the same substance" to pay ransom for his nephew Hugh, who was imprisoned in the castle of Gourdon—but fortunately, St. Foy was on the alert and the objects were returned. The disposal of a part of the treasures was also permitted when the regular sources of income no longer sufficed to support the community. Thus, Loup de Ferrières was obliged to sell some of his abbey's sacred vessels and vestments in 845. The treasures constituted a last resource especially during periods of public calamity. Around the year 1000, at a time of food scarcity, William of Volpiano sold the gold and silver covering of the casket reliquary of St. Benignus and a gold casket reliquary adorned with precious stones, and distributed the proceeds to the poor. Again, it was to feed the poor during a famine that Archbishop Rotrou sold the ancient *fierte,* or Casket of St. Romanus of the Cathedral of Rouen. But it was for other—political—reasons that the Rouen chapter sold a part of their treasures at about the same period, to assist Henry II in his struggle against Stephen of Blois for the throne of England. And it was both political and economic reasons that motivated sovereigns, after emptying the public treasury, to call upon the treasuries of the churches. Thus, in the ninth century, Charles the Fat collected the church treasures that had been hidden for fear of the Normans and used them to pay the Normans a tribute of 2,412 livres. At the other end of the line, in 1760, Louis XV ordered the Carolingian gold retable of the Cathedral of Sens to be melted down.

Another characteristic peculiar to the pieces included in the treasuries, and especially in church treasuries, which must be taken into account as a factor contributing to their disappearance or deterioration, is their use: these are objects that serve a purpose. The pages of an Evangeliary are turned. A miter, a cope, a dalmatic, are worn. A chalice or a ewer are held in a man's hands. A reliquary is carried in procession. While stained glass, paintings, or statues suffered the ravages of the elements, of time, or of deliberate spoliation, the pieces in the treasuries suffered the further ravages of wear and tear. Such wear and tear, which was proportionate to the degree of usage —crosses were often dented, bowls of chalices had sometimes to be replaced, as in the case of the Chalice of St. Rémy in the Reims Treasury (fig. 7) —varied also according to the workmanship and degree of fragility of the materials used. Textiles wore threadbare and broke at folds. Gold and silver thread used in embroideries tore and the material frayed. Rock crystal was less breakable than glass. Ivory was more durable than enamel. Champlevé enamel spread on a thick plaque was stronger than cloisonné enamel set between thin, ribbon-like partitions soldered to lightweight plaques. Cast metal was stronger than repoussé metal, and, in the latter medium, sheets of precious metal, such as gold and silver, which were often extremely fine and assembled with fragile soldering, were the least durable of all. They might be crushed or broken, particularly those of the very early periods when the thinness of the sheets had a twofold cause: first, the scarcity of precious metals, and secondly, the problems involved in trying to work on thick sheets with the rudimentary techniques in use then, such as the repoussé executed with a punching tool at Conques. And where the coating was so thin, it shared the fate of its wooden core. That fate in turn depended on the quality of the wood. The Majesty of St. Foy of Conques was carved out of a yew root, the Evron Virgin (pl. 161) out of an oak trunk, both hard woods that have been little affected by time. On the other hand, at Saint-Antoine-en-Viennois, the pearwood of the big casket reliquary of repoussé silver (fig. 12) fashioned in the seventeenth century had to be replaced in 1956. At Conques, the wood of the base of Bego's lantern (pl. 214) had shrunk, causing buckling and cracks in the silver-gilt plaques, which sprung at the soldered seams. At Rouen, the twelfth-century *fierte,* or casket reliquary of St. Romanus, was in such poor condition in 1776 that the chapter decided to transfer the relics to another casket, of the fourteenth century. Technical advances made it possible, from the Gothic period, to create a whole series of works related to statuary, such as the angel of Saint-Pavace (pl. 168) or the reliquary of St. Aldegundis of Maubeuge (pl. 114); thicker plaques and more expert soldering of cramp-set joints permitted the fashioning of independent figures in the round, thereby relieving the sheet of repoussé metal of its dependence on a wooden core, and hence of the consequences of its disintegration.

Carolingian crown of the Majesty of St. Foy at Conques

The wear and tear on the materials composing the individual pieces in the treasuries is another reason for the changes that many of them have suffered through the centuries. When a reliquary was in very poor condition, the damaged portions might be restored with pieces from another, still more damaged or less venerated reliquary. There are many examples of this practice, particularly at Conques, where reliquaries were treated with a respect bordering on veneration at least until the end of the sixteenth century. The removal of portions of some to repair others was carried out with such devotion that the unused parts, even when they were unusable, were also preserved. In 1875, the demolition of a wall erected behind the high altar of the abbey church led to the discovery of a large twelfth-century chest (pl. 219) covered with leather and decorated with enamel medallions which had been concealed there at the time of the wars of religion, and which contained not only relics and ancient textiles but also many fragments of reliquaries. Among these fragments were bits of wax that had been used to fill and thus strengthen, the hollows in figured repoussé metal plaques from an old reliquary, and which had retained the shapes of those figures. These plaques were re-used on the base of the Reliquary of Pope Pascal (pl. 216) where, after having been hammered flat, they were used to complete an inscription. At Conques, again, the two phylacteries (pls. 210, 211) were made of heterogeneous elements, the oldest of which date back to Merovingian times. And still at Conques, a fragment of a silver-gilt plaque in repoussé had been placed on the back of the statue of St. Foy (pl. 203), which Darcel described a century ago as "the head of Christ . . . whose crudeness . . . reminds us of the appalling miniatures that one finds from time to time in eighth- or ninth-century manuscripts." This plaque had been cut out on the back of the hexagonal phylactery, which had served as a cutting block, on which the knife marks are still visible.

Sometimes, too, a reliquary was fashioned entirely out of pieces that came from various places, taken from outworn reliquaries, such as the Reliquary of St. Romanus in the Rouen Treasury (fig. 31), formerly at Saint-Denis, where two early-fourteenth-century ivory angels were reset in the seventeenth century on a copper-gilt base dating from 1340. At Conques, the filigree cross was made up of strips from a number of reliquaries.

Changes of style also played their part in these remodelings. The most typical example, perhaps, is the Virgin of Bernard of Hildesheim of the year 1000, which was so completely remodeled in the seven-

Detail of Antependium at Conques

Detail of Lantern reliquary at Conques

MORTAIN. Chrismal

teenth century as to become unrecognizable, and whose original aspect has only recently been rediscovered by Wesemberg. In France, too, examples abound. The Carolingian crown adorning the statue of St. Foy (p. 20) originally consisted of only a single band. When it was placed on the head of the gold Majesty, another was added in order to bring it into line with the then prevailing fashion in crowns. In the sixteenth century, or seven centuries after it was made, the Cope of Charlemagne in the Metz Treasury (pl. 119) was decorated with sumptuous orphreys. Again in the sixteenth century, the thirteenth-century Reliquary of the True Cross in the Treasury of Saint-Sernin at Toulouse (pl. 240) made of Limoges enamel was mounted on bronze legs in classical style. In the eighteenth century, alterations were made on the fourteenth-century *fierte* of the Rouen Treasury. The resulting additions were replaced in the nineteenth century by others in neo-Gothic style, which were removed in their turn a few years ago, during the latest restoration.

These alterations, additions, or eliminations frequently led to the juxtaposition, on a single piece, of elements of different periods and origins, a heterogeneity favored by the multiple possibilities to which metalwork lends itself through the combination of different materials and techniques. When the combination is a skillful one, it can cause even experts to hesitate to distinguish the successive stages of a work. This is sufficiently attested by the debate on the possible "ages" of St. Foy, or the dates of various parts of the Reliquary of Pepin in the Treasury of Conques (pls. 206, 207). In some cases, additions were made to existing pieces, as on the silver-gilt repoussé plaque representing Samson overcoming the lion (p. 21 center) on the base of the Lantern Reliquary in the Conques Treasury (pl. 214); in others, a piece was composite from the time of its fashioning, either because an element of different origin was used to enrich the composition, e.g., the ancient cameo adorning the center of the front cover of the Evangeliary at Gannat (pl. 63), or because the design was conceived specifically to enhance that element, e.g., the reliquary from the church of Jaucourt, now at the Louvre, where two fourteenth-century silver-gilt angels support an eleventh-century Byzantine reliquary of the True Cross. Or again, as in the previously cited case of the Reliquary of St. Romanus at Rouen, disparate elements from earlier works might be assembled to produce a new object. The little casket at Mortain (p. 21 bottom), before becoming a reliquary had been a chrismal used to carry the viaticum.

Thus the treasures had their own life, in the course of which they grew old, died, and were reborn in other forms, sometimes with other meanings. Thus a reliquary of St. Placidus in the Treasury of Saint-Denis might be transmuted into the Reliquary of St. Romanus in Rouen, or plaques of cloisonné originally belonging to the crown of a Byzantine empress might be affixed to the cover of the so-called Evangeliary of Theophano now in the Munich library. The process of transmutation went even further; precious remnants of pagan, antique, barbarian, or Oriental treasures, and, in general, secular valuables in the form of coins or jewelry, were adapted to religious ends. A famous example is that of the Avar treasure which fell into the hands of Charlemagne, who proceeded to distribute it among his intimates, and among churches and monasteries. Traces of it are to be found, re-used, on various pieces of Carolingian goldsmithery: the gold ewer in the Treasury of Saint-Maurice d'Agaune, in Switzerland, is an example. There are many others: antique intaglios, as at Conques, Grandselve, etc.; cameos, such as the famous intaglio of Julia, now in the Cabinet des Médailles, which surmounted the screen of Charlemagne at Saint-Denis, or the one that occupies the center of the Evangeliary cover at Gannat; Fatimid rock crystals, as at Reims, Saint-Riquier, Milhaguet, Sens. Charles V ordered a fourth-century sardonyx bust of a Roman emperor to be mounted on the top of the precentor's staff at the Sainte-Chapelle, which had originally adorned a consular scepter and had been brought from Constantinople. The head of St. Foy of Conques dates back from the late Roman Imperial period and may have been the head of a statue of a Roman emperor. The head of the Christ of the twelfth-century Heriman cross in Cologne had been the head of an antique Venus. Of the ivories, some were of pagan origin and acquired a sacred character from their use for liturgical purposes. Such was the case with the consular diptychs, whose dates we know from the names of the consuls, and which cover a period from the beginning of the fifth to the middle of the sixth centuries: for instance, the diptych of the consul Felix, formerly at the church of Saint-Junien, or the diptych of Anastasius at Bourges Cathedral. On the latter was inscribed the list of archbishops and bishops up to the fourteenth century. Sometimes, as at Milan or Monza, the consul's name was replaced by that of a saint. Some pyxes were originally jewel boxes, such as the one in the Sens Treasury on which is represented a lion hunt (p. 22). Another, formerly in the Brioude Treasury, represents Orpheus, a figure adopted in Early Christian art as a symbolic representation of Christ; here the transition from a pagan to a Christian significance is clear.

This continuity with paganism, which Mâle emphasized, is found in the church treasures just as it is in other areas: churches replacing temples and constructed on the same sites (Notre-Dame-des-Fontaines erected at the sources of the Seine over the temple of the goddess Sequana); re-use of stelae and ancient sculptures (as at Valcabrère, or in so many small Pyrenean churches); pagan sarcophagi used to enshrine the body of a saint (St. Ludre at Déols), or even to serve as altars (Belloc Saint-Clamens); Celtic lechs, Druidic stones, around which legends persisted, and which the Church exorcised; the cult of the divinities of springs, trees, and mountains, hallowed by the erection of an oratory or the statue of a saint and to which pilgrimages have wended their way to this day—witness the many "pilgrimage springs" in Brittany; cathedrals, like that of Chartres, raised over a well held sacred by the Gauls, or that of Le Mans, whose façade rises against a menhir, or that of Le Puy, whose narthex houses a dolmen. As regards treasures, the adaptation of secular pieces to religious ends has persisted traditionally from ancient times to our own: necklaces, such as the one adorning the neck of the Chambon bust reliquary (pl. 180); silver-gilt belts adorned with pearls and enamels; brooches, as on the Majesty of St. Foy of Conques; all kinds of jewels and rings, as on the nineteenth-century Reliquary of the True Cross in the Lyons Treasury; diamonds, as on the Dunkirk ostensory, whose worldly brilliance enhances the magnificence of the caskets and reliquaries.

So many causes have conspired to wear out, transform or destroy the treasures that we have less reason for astonishment at what has disappeared than at what remains. Despite large gaps, most periods are represented. And this remarkable continuity enables us to appreciate the part played in the history of societies and the history of forms by that branch of the arts that worked with precious materials.

SENS. PYX

Detail of the Majesty of St. Foy at Conques

The Treasures and Society

A society might be defined by the essential purposes to which it dedicates its precious works of art. In a theocratic society, that purpose is the glory of God through the exaltation of the spiritual power. In a strongly hierarchical society, that purpose is the exaltation of the temporal power. In the very early periods of European history, the two notions of spiritual and temporal power were linked and given expression in the whole of the religious art of the times. Subsequently, however, they were separated through the emergence, with the restructuring of society, of secular goldsmithery, ivory work, enamel work, etc. The process of the reversal of values comes to a climax under Louis XIV, when the preponderance of the temporal imposed the pomp and circumstance of its ceremonial upon religious art. We come, finally, to a society where the accent is no longer on the spiritual or the temporal power, but on the individual in his private life, in a pursuit of luxury and pleasure within the framework of that life, and the objects ministering to it. The entire history of the church treasures might be said to consist, in brief, in the transition from the twofold spiritual and temporal function reflected in a symbol-laden art, whose significance in some way transcended the materiality of its appearance, to a decorative, sumptuary, or utilitarian art, whose principal objective is to achieve elegance of forms or their usefulness; the other element in that history is, of course, the development of techniques in the uses of precious materials.

This sociological aspect of the church treasures applies principally to goldsmithery, which was the most important of the techniques using precious materials; so important, indeed, that, under Louis the Pious, "treasures" were sometimes identified as gold- and silver-work alone, to the exclusion of vessels, vestments, or manuscripts. It is reflected, in particular, in the goldsmith's place in the social hierarchy. His art, employing fire to transform at will the raw metal drawn from the bowels of the earth, conferred on him the mysterious and somber power that the ancients ascribed to his ancestor, Vulcan. In Mediterranean societies, which were more interested in monumental art, goldsmiths and silversmiths were slaves, or belonged to the lowest class. In Celtic and Germanic societies, where the metal industry—for adornment and armament—enjoyed particular honor and constituted the very expression of art itself, they were notables. This was the rank and tradition, with the prestige attached to their marvelous science, that the early medieval gold- and silversmiths inherited. The most illustrious of them was St. Eligius, a minister of King Dagobert. A capitulary of Charles the Bald in 868 recognized the privileges of the goldsmiths of Paris. St. Louis organized them in corporations, with the motto, *In sacra inque coronas* (For altar and throne), which illustrates what we have said concerning an art devoted to exalting jointly the spiritual and temporal powers. Philip of Valois, for his part, awarded goldsmiths letters of semi-nobility: *"Orfèvre ne déroge pas"* (The goldsmith shall not derogate from his rank). Goldsmiths always enjoyed a privileged position. Yves Le Brailler, goldsmith to John the Good, held the office of valet to the king. In the eighteenth century, great goldsmiths like Bernier, Balzac, or Thomas Germain were ennobled. When Germain died, his royal client, John V of Portugal, had funeral services celebrated for him in Lisbon.

The goldsmith's place in society, then, was determined by the role of his art in that society's life. His art, in turn, provided a brilliant reflection on the society in which he lived through the manner in which it translated that society's aspirations, and also its humblest ways—eating habits, modes of lighting—as well as by its emphasis, according to the period, on the sacred or the profane, on the taste for display or the preference for discretion and refinement. Goldsmithery cannot be studied in isolation from the contemporary movement of art as a whole, even where it was not a determining factor in the development of forms and merely reproduced a style developed in other media, for it expressed a certain human condition, the social and spiritual as well as the artistic aspirations of a society.

Goldsmithery owed this special character to the diversity of uses to which it could be put, the limits of which are not easy to determine. Similar tools were used by craftsmen to carve the silver or copper-gilt colonnettes of reliquaries and the bronze appliqués on furniture, to chase the gold and silver plaques of toilet articles or table centerpieces or bust reliquaries, to set stones in metal bands laced with filigree, or to mount them in rings. It is sometimes hard to distinguish between the work of the coppersmith, the armorer, the blacksmith, and the goldsmith, between the casting of the sculptor and that of the goldsmith. At what point did the goldsmith turn sculptor, designer, cabinetmaker, architect, jeweler, painter, or enameler? The Virgin of Hildesheim, made in the year 1000, is a wooden statue. Sheathed as it was originally with precious metal, it could be regarded as a piece of precious metalwork, in the same way as the Majesty of St. Foy at Conques. As to the other statue of St. Foy in the Conques Treasury (fig. 50), fashioned of silver in the fifteenth century, should it be regarded as goldsmithery or as sculpture?

The reason the goldsmith's art can adapt its effects to mediums as diverse as painting, sculpture, or architecture lies in the very quality of the material it uses. For metal is a substance that is both malleable and hard, lending itself to every combination of shape and dimension, and which, through the use of alloys, can pass from the rare to the common, from gold to tin; from the malleable to the rigid, from lead to bronze. It is so ductile that it can be reduced to an infinitesimal thinness, and the gold leaf applied on wood or combined with mercury is no thicker than a coat of paint. The magic of its luster gave this semblance of opulence its greater popularity. The gilded wooden cross of Alos-Sibar-Aheuse imitates bronze gilt; the Romanesque crucifixes of Catalonia, Rousillon, or Cerdagne are decorated with scrolls and cabochons in gilded stucco imitating repoussé metal; and that other substitute for goldsmithery, retables with backgrounds of painted gold, silver, or tin, in mountainous regions too poor to use metal led to the development of a genuine art of painting.

The diversity of these methods was accompanied by an infinite variety of juxtapositions of metals either with one another—gold and silver, silver gilt, copper, tin, steel—or with other substances, such as ivory, mother-of-pearl, enamel, niello, rare wood, crystal, jewels. The result was a diversity of uses, from the rarest to the humblest articles, from objects made for display—an imperial crown or luxurious trinket—to objects made for everyday needs, such as silver or pewter ladles, gilded bronze clocks, or copper lamps. No other medium, by reason of its adaptability to both the precious and the utilitarian, is closer to man in his private life and as a member of society. It is the only one that can be understood and loved without any particular artistic taste. Only an experienced art lover—and even he would need an expert's confirmation—could distinguish the genuine piece from the copy, the fourteenth-century copper-gilt statuette of an Apostle in repoussé on the casket reliquary of St. Romanus in the Rouen Treasury (pl. 156) from its eighteenth-century cast or its nineteenth-century electrotype copy (p. 25); or the thirteenth-century bust reliquary of silver parcel-gilt of St. Yrieix, now in the Metropolitan Museum in New York, from the copy that has been substituted for it in the church. While the monetary value of the

Apostles, details of the Casket of
St. Romanus at Rouen

piece depends on its genuineness—and that is a matter for the expert —the unbiased viewer, unconcerned with such problems, will pause before this casket or that statuette because its luster, its substance, its value—even the commercial value, at which he guesses—will have cast some sort of spell upon him, the spell that captivated the Barbarians as they adorned their cloisonné inlays indifferently with garnets and glass beads.

Side by side with this twofold capacity for the sumptuous and the utilitarian, there is thus another feature that emphasizes the social character of goldsmithery: the brilliance inherent in the material used is experienced almost physically, quite independently of any aesthetic considerations. Among people of primitive mentality this sensation is externalized by a taste for apparel, one of the nobler concepts of which appears in the insignia of power—plumes, a crown, gold braid. But this brilliance also confers on precious materials— stones and metals—a transcendental quality to which, according to the beliefs involved, a magical or purely mystical power is attached. The two ideas are not always distinct, as we see from the term "amulet" or "talisman" of Charlemagne, used to designate the jewel which, according to legend, was worn by the emperor (pl. 83). The second idea prevailed, thanks to the efforts of the theologians and often despite popular sentiment, throughout the Middle Ages. And it is this idea that gives the church treasures their true significance. Without its adornment of gold and gems, the Majesty of St. Foy of Conques would be no more than a scarecrow. As a number of authors, and in particular H. Swarzenski, have pointed out, it was not out of a taste for luxury and ostentation but for the greater glory of God, that the most precious materials were used to enshrine that which was most highly revered: the divine symbol of the cross, the Eucharistic Species to be contained in the sacred vessels, a martyr's relic, a book of Gospels. Swarzenski observes, incidentally, that only in the Christian religion is God represented with book in hand. The church itself is no more than the place of worship, celebrated on the altar it protects, of the precious relic preciously preserved within its casket. And this casket came to enjoy the same reverence as its content; not only because of that content but because of its own symbolism. This is expressed in Suger's famous words [as translated by Erwin Panofsky]: "Bright is the noble work; but being nobly bright, the work should brighten the minds, so that they may travel, through the true lights." The true light, that is, in the neo-Platonic vision, God. The symbol, therefore, transcending the reality of the object, may be represented in its own right, and translated into another material with effects imitating those of the precious material. The sculptured marble slab of the eighth-century pilgrims' church at Narbonne, the seventh-century Shirt of St. Bathildis at Chelles (p. 26), reproduce a jeweled cross of the kind that surmounted the retable of Charles the Bald at Saint-Denis. A thousand years later, and for the same reason, a great gold ostensory was painted in silver-oxide yellow on the axial window of the apse of Saint-Sulpice in Paris.

This symbolism achieves its highest expression in the use of precious stones to which is imputed a virtue bordering on magic; transposed into religious language, each one of them acquires a mystical significance related to a mystery of the faith. Thus jewelry, which would seem to be the most secular aspect of goldsmithery, causes it, on the contrary, to attain to the very essence of its sacred character, even when pagan elements—ancient intaglios or Fatimid crystals—are used to enhance that luster. Let us quote Suger again: "The loveliness of the many-colored gems has called me away from external cares, and

CHELLES. Detail of the Shirt of St. Bathildis

Detail of the cover of the Evangeliary of St. Gauzelin at Nancy

worthy meditation has induced me to reflect, transferring that which is material to that which is immaterial . . ." [translation Erwin Panofsky]. In Carolingian and Ottonian goldsmithery the symbolism attaching to gems is brought out by the way in which they are set in filigree, supported by arcades that constitute a form of glorious pedestal for them (p. 27). Set on a single band, as on the Reliquary of Pepin at Conques (pl. 207) or on a medallion, as the central motif of the Evangeliary cover of St. Gauzelin, they symbolize the heavenly Jerusalem. When they are mounted separately and as on a chalice, as on the Codex Aureus of St. Emmeran at Ratisbon, or the Metz Evangeliary, they symbolize the blood of the martyrs. The transcendental value of this symbolism, which confers its true meaning upon the object, "transferring that which is material to that which is immaterial," is stressed in the character of a whole series of crosses fashioned in the style of the triumphal art of the Church during the first centuries, the prototype of which was the immense jeweled cross that Constantine had suspended from the vault of the basilica of the Holy Sepulcher, and the tradition of which continued up to Gothic times. In the case of those crosses where one side is jeweled and filigreed and the other bears the carved figure of Christ, the front is not, as one would have expected, the face representing Christ, but the one resplendent with the symbolic luster of jewels and filigree (e.g., the imperial cross at Aachen, the cross of Bernard of Hildesheim, the cross on the crown of the Holy Roman Empire in Vienna, all fashioned around the year 1000, and, as late as the thirteenth century, the crosses of Le Paraclet (pl. 105) and Blanchefosse (pp. 28, 29). Precious stones seem to be fashioned with light, and it is understandable that jewel effects should have been sought in the medium that comes alive through light, namely, stained glass. The thirteenth-century window of St. Eustace at Chartres was made to resemble multicolored gems, by a design composed of very small pieces of glass; the multiplicity of whites in marked contrasts of tone brings out the sparkle in the other colors. The concept was carried even further in the chapel of the imperial palace of Karlstein, in Bohemia: the windows were made of genuine stones, as in a translucent cloisonné enamel. The process used for the Merovingian cross at Saint-Denis, that celebrated piece attributed to St. Eligius, of which count de Montesquiou-Fézensac has identified a fragment in the Cabinet des Médailles, would appear to belong both to stained glass work and cloisonné precious metalwork, since the "pieces of glass resembling hyacinths, garnets, emeralds, and sapphires," set in a network of gold tracery, were not placed on a ground of foil, and their transparency, as in stained glass, brought out their colors through the play of light. All these processes converge in a single purpose and a single spirit.

While this symbolism was essentially religious, it was not confined to liturgical objects alone. It applied also to the insignia of authority, merging their twofold temporal and religious character in a single concept. This identification took place through the convergence of two ideas originating in different spheres, a process that took place during the period when the declining world of antiquity gave way before a Christian society: the idea of the primacy of the arts of apparel, and the idea of the religious coronation of kings. During the first turbulent centuries of our era, when the West, disrupted by the great Germanic invasions, recovered its equilibrium only through the authority exercised by the Church, a new civilization developed on the basis of other spiritual, sociological, and aesthetic values. From the remote reaches of the steppes, the Barbarians brought with them jewels, apparel, sumptuously decorated weapons—the valuables of nomads whose perpetual mobility cuts them off from any

BLANCHEFOSSE. Cross (rear view)

BLANCHEFOSSE. Cross (front view)

concern with building. This primacy of apparel and the metal arts, which continued in theory up to the Romanesque period, is apparent in the treasures found in graves. Childeric, king of the Franks and father of Clovis, who died in the fifth century, was buried with his gold sword with cloisonné inlay of garnets. This sword, wrought by a goldsmith, precious as a jewel, betokened the authority of the chief. Such a concept was unknown in antiquity; Achilles' shield, as Homer describes it, did not signify his power. The scepter and the crown, on the other hand, did present such a character. As the insignia of office, they had their place in the celebration of the coronation ceremony. And this gave them a religious purpose. The Roman *imperator* was borne to the highest function by the acclamation of his soldiers, and the Senate ratified the decision without any ritual involving the use of objects especially consecrated to that purpose. The Christian king or emperor, on the other hand, received his investiture from God, through the agency of an ecclesiastic who annointed him with the holy oil and placed the crown upon his head. Legitimate investiture required the possession of the insignia of office, the vesting in the robes of office. And participation in the coronation ceremonies conferred upon these objects a religious character. Up to the sixteenth century, the insignia of the Holy Roman Empire, which were in the safekeeping of the imperial city of Nuremberg, were solemnly presented for the people's veneration, and such presentation had the same spiritual significance as a presentation of relics.

The imperial sword that was carried in procession, point up, before the sovereign was engraved with an inscription to the glory of Christ. The Hand of Justice of the Frankish kings, the so-called Sword of Charlemagne, the spurs used at coronations—these belonged to the Treasury of Saint-Denis, as the Holy Ampulla belonged to the Treasury of Reims, or Charlemagne's saber to the Treasury of Aachen. This ideology and this social structure explain the homogeneity of medieval art up to the time when, with the emergence of new ideas, a gradual development took place in the direction of an art aspiring to an ideal of beauty in which the divine would yield to the human, the religious to the secular. Until then, the same themes had been used in secular and sacred objects. The crowns of Otto I, St. Stephen, or the Holy Roman Empire, the imperial bracelets (one of which is at the Louvre) were decorated with enamel plaques on which religious subjects are represented. The courtly hierarchy, inspired by that of Byzantium, was a transposition of the celestial hierarchy. Votive crowns, crowns of saints and crowns of emperors and kings were so similar that their origin is hard to determine. The crown of the gold Virgin of Essen, from the year 1000, was the one used at the coronation of Otto III, who was crowned emperor at the age of three. The crown of St. Foy of Conques was also re-used, although it is not clear whether it had originally been a votive or an imperial crown. Martyrs like St. Foy were shown seated in majesty on thrones—those symbols of their glory—fashioned in imitation of imperial thrones, and whose dazzling adornment of gold bands enriched with gems is reproduced in the same forms in Carolingian manuscripts; Charles the Bald and Lothair are represented on similar thrones in Bibles or psalters dedicated to them. The type was perpetuated, with the same significance, in the Virgins in Majesty, the *sedes sapientiae*, like that of Orcival (pl. 66), where cabochons embossed in metal simulate jewels. The prestige attaching to precious metals or to their representation was to ensure the survival of this device up to the end of the Gothic period, although by then it had lost all iconographical significance; in manuscript illumination and in painting—the King David in the Psalter of the duc de Berry, Fouquet's Virgin represented with the features of Agnes Sorel—are shown on jewel-work thrones.

This union of spiritual and temporal, which reflected the sociological and psychological conditions of the West up to Romanesque times, was long and fully expressed in the religious treasures that constitute the "art of church treasures," as Swarzenski so happily defines it. This art, its unity based on the same religious concepts and the same symbolism, used the same devices in the area of form as in that of ideas, whatever the object to which they applied. The Sacred Lance, for instance, was the symbol of imperial sovereignty; it therefore possessed a temporal character. Its spiritual significance was emphasized when it was carried into battle before the enemy, placed on the transverse beam of the imperial cross, and when victory was attributed to its power. Or again, the plaques of the royal crown of St. Oswald, dating from the tenth century, were reset on a twelfth-century bust reliquary belonging to the Hildesheim Treasury. The unity prevailing during this period made possible such equivalences and interchanges. In the Gothic period, when the royal power came to rely increasingly on the middle class and to be secularized, the emphasis in art changed. Monastic and clerical workshops were replaced by lay workshops serving an expanding secular clientele. This development, corresponding to a fundamental transformation of manners, tastes, and social structures, gave the techniques in precious materials a different function, and hence a new significance. An idea emerged which had been altogether unknown in times when all art was religious, namely, that of a work of art made solely for the pleasure of the eyes. Courtly art, born in a Parisian environment, and which was to become the art of the whole of Europe in the fourteenth century, sounded the note of sophistication that was to be found even in objects relating to worship, such as the Reliquary of the Precious Blood at Boulogne (pl. 111), or the fifteenth-century *Roessel* —the little gold horse of Altoetting. As far back as the end of the thirteenth century, we find the charming enamels of the crown of Le Paraclet decorated with secular subjects (pl. 108). The Renaissance accentuated these effects in exquisitely lavish works, such as the Reliquary of St. Ursula in the Reims Treasury (pl. 90). The trend reached its apex in the ostentatious pomp of the seventeenth century, expressed in the "glories" of the great retables of gilded wood, as much as in those of the ostensories, and in the aristocratic elegance of the eighteenth century, which gave episcopal "chapels" like that of Saint-Sever, or candelabra like that at Lillers, a worldly character typical of the *salons* of the day. All this gave rise to forms created for public ceremony or the pleasures of daily living, which imprinted their style and ornamental vocabulary on the most sacred pieces in the treasuries. The mask on the Poitiers ewer (p. 30 above) might have come from the same mold as the bronze on a chest of drawers; the candlesticks of the altar furnishings at Marsat (p. 31) might have decorated a mantel; the motifs of the Fromentières chalice (p. 30 below) or the Strasbourg ostensory might have been borrowed from rich paneling.

Thus the overriding preoccupations of societies, fluctuating as they do in the course of the centuries, become a determining factor in the development of art forms. This social aspect of the treasures, which is apparent throughout their history, is also apparent in the difference that has always existed between religious and secular treasures as regards their make-up and preservation. Of all the techniques concerned with precious materials, the most important, by its continuity, is goldsmithery. But this continuity is not equal in religious and secular goldsmithery. It would be possible to describe the development of goldsmithery exclusively in terms of what remains of the church treasures. It would not be possible to do the same on the basis of the surviving pieces intended for secular purposes. For secu-

POITIERS. Detail of ewer

FROMENTIERES. Detail of chalice

MARSAT. Altar furnishings

lar precious metalwork, which was virtually nonexistent before the Gothic period, has almost entirely disappeared, especially anything earlier than the seventeenth or eighteenth centuries. Of the 906 pieces of tableware belonging to Charles V, weighing 8,879 gold marks, only one piece has survived, the single enameled gold cup decorated with religious subjects which is now known as the Chalice of Charles V. And all that remains of the treasure of Charles VI is a religious piece, the "little gold horse" of Altoetting.

Another difference between secular and religious treasures is that the latter were at all times fed by what might be termed an average stream of artistic production, corresponding to the demands of a larger clientele. Where the most characteristic pieces of a category of religious objects are lacking, it is unusual for these lacunae not to be filled by other, less ornate pieces whose forms imitate the vanished models of a higher art; thus the great "sun" of Notre-Dame of Paris, for instance, was melted down, but other "suns," containing less gold, and fewer diamonds and rubies, have been preserved in other churches. There was no counterpart in secular goldsmithery to this average stream. There were no humbler substitutes for the marvelous objects collected by sophisticated art patrons. When gold and silver plate was melted down, all that remained was pewter or china. The history of the goldsmithery of the Crown exemplifies these remarks. For the most part, any knowledge we have of it is gleaned from stories, illuminated manuscripts, or paintings. And no piece of lesser value can conjure up for us the splendor surrounding princes such as the duc de Berry, which we can only guess at now from the illuminations of the *Très Riches Heures*. Only portraits like those of Elizabeth of Austria, which, with their enamel-like glossiness, are at the same time portraits of dazzling jewels, pearls, and precious stones, can still revive for us the luxury and refinement of the court of the Valois in the sixteenth century. As Babelon has pointed out, all that remains of the incredible splendor of the entertainments given by

Louis XIV in his triumphant youth, with their sideboards laden with silverware and their magnificent lighting fixtures, is their reflection in a medal struck for the embassy of Siam.

The reason why no average stream of production existed in secular goldsmithery is that the latter was an art of extreme luxury and essentially aristocratic. Its patrons were always drawn from the upper classes of society. During the Middle Ages and a part of the sixteenth century, only the courts and the great princely families were wealthy enough to surround themselves with objects fashioned of the most expensive materials. The scarcity of gold and silver made it impossible for the lesser gentry and the burgher class to provide themselves with objects of this kind on any large scale. Their valuables never amounted to more than a few goblets, silver spoons, and jewels, the weight of which was carefully recorded in marriage contracts and wills. The influx of precious metals that followed the discovery of America, and the emergence of new social classes, were to enlarge the secular market from the sixteenth century onward. Now, however, the appetite for luxury became so strong that this market absorbed too large a quantity of metal, at the expense of currency; indeed, the money supply was depleted to the point where it was insufficient for public and private commerce. Under Louis XII, and again under Henry IV, sumptuary laws had to be enacted to restrict the manufacture of objects of silver and gold. Hence it was the monetary reserve aspect of goldsmithery which was to outweigh all others during economic crises, particularly when the public finances could no longer defray the costs of war. In 1529, Francis I requisitioned all the gold plate in the kingdom. And under Louis XIV, as Saint-Simon recalls, "a great many precious furnishings of massive silver which adorned the gallery and the large and small chambers of Versailles were sent to the mint during the war of 1688, even the silver throne." He refers to the "inestimable loss of these admirable designs, even more beautiful than the material of which they were made, and which luxurious living had since introduced into tableware." Louis XV, after the disasters of the Seven Years' War, "exhorted his subjects," by letters patent of 1759, "even ecclesiastical workshops and communities . . . to take their plate and silver to his minting agencies."

Religious ideals, social structures, economic conditions—all these factors help to explain the treasures, both those that existed and have perished, and those that have survived, and to define the connection and the contrasts between secular and religious treasures. The objects comprising them belong to the sphere of forms. Because they followed the general development of art in the particular sphere of precious materials, they reflect stylistic tendencies that varied according to period and circumstances. But the aesthetic factor is not the only one that must be taken into account in connection with religious treasures. As objects created for purposes of worship, they corresponded to the requirements of the liturgy.

The Treasures and the Liturgy: Forms

The forms of the objects pertaining to worship corresponded to the purposes for which they were intended. In a sense, we might say that the treasures were the product of the liturgy, changing in character as the liturgy evolved. Various considerations, some doctrinal, some purely practical, entered into these changes. Some resulted in the emergence of new religious articles: statue reliquaries after the ninth century, the ostensory after the fourteenth. Others resulted in the disappearance of earlier ones, such as the liturgical comb and episcopal sandals, which vanish after the fifteenth century. Others, again, resulted in the substitution of one object for another: the ciborium for the pyx, for example, or the tabernacle for the system of suspending the Reserved Sacrament over the altar.

Without pretending to give a complete picture of the connection between the liturgy and religious articles, it might be useful to cite some aspects of it as illustration of the role of the liturgy in the formation and development of religious art. That role was, in the first place, to initiate the various categories of objects fashioned of precious materials which we find listed in the inventories of the treasures, and which take their place in the over-all development of art forms, and, secondly, to adapt them to the needs of worship. The tabernacle took the place of the suspended Reserved Sacrament because the ciborium could be more conveniently placed inside it. And the lunula soon replaced the vertical glass tube of the first ostensories because its shape was more functional, the purpose of the ostensory being to expose the Host.

Our examples will be selected from objects grouped under two headings: the ceremonial of the Mass and the administration of the sacraments; and the veneration of relics.

Under the first group, we have the sacred vessels, that is, the chalice and paten, as well as other blessed objects such as the ciborium, the ostensory, the cruets, the censer, the incense boat. We might add to these the objects placed on the altar: the canon, the cross, the candlesticks, the evangeliary, as well as priestly vestments with crosier, sandals, and liturgical comb.

The chalice and paten, with their accessories, the cruets and plate, form a set. The earliest example we know, the small gold chalice of Gourdon that dates from the sixth century, was dug up with its plate. The only complete sets that have survived belong to the rich episcopal chapels of the seventeenth and eighteenth centuries (La Daurade of Toulouse, Narbonne, etc.). Some of the early cruets were of ivory (those at Saint-Riquier, for instance, which date from the ninth century). For the most part, however, they were of silver or silver gilt. The earliest surviving in the treasuries of France appear to be those of Sallanches (sixteenth century), which in shape are reminiscent of contemporary drinking bottles with spouts (p. 33 above). In any case, whether with a lid or without, cruets were the pieces most similar to secular utensils used for comparable purposes. And in the periods when religious art adopted secular forms, such forms are apparent in the oil cruets and ewers (for instance, at the Colbert de Villacerf chapel at Troyes, p. 33 below).

Out of humility, St. Benedict of Aniane, in the ninth century, wanted no chalices of silver, but only of wood or glass. Reluctantly, he agreed to use pewter. After the middle of the ninth century, an interdict of Leo IV forbade the use of chalices made of base materials. Theoretically, even in our own day, the inside of the cup should be either of gold, or at least gilded. Nevertheless, particularly precious materials other than gold or silver gilt continued to be used. The ancient cantharus known as the Cup of the Ptolemies, which Charles

SALLANCHES. Cruets

TROYES. Furnishings from the Chapel of Colbert de Villacerf

ANGERS. Chalice   ECOUIS. Chalice   PERPIGNAN. Chalice

the Bald presented to the Treasury of Saint-Denis, was of onyx. And the twelfth-century cup of the so-called Suger Chalice of Saint-Denis, now in the National Gallery of Art in Washington, D. C., is of agate, the cup of the chalice in the Reiche Kapelle in Munich, of rock crystal, etc. In all these cases, it seems that the rarity of the material conferred on it a value that made it precious enough to be used for consecrating the Blood of Christ.

At first, two types of chalices coexisted, one with handles, the other without; only the second type was to survive. Both were derived from very ancient models. To the first type belong antique vessels such as the one of glass in the Wallraf-Richartz Museum in Cologne, or those vases from which the waters of the Fountain of Life gush forth, found on representations engraved or sculptured in stone, such as the one at Charenton-sur-Cher on the sarcophagus of Calentius who died in 660. The oldest surviving chalices in France are of this shape (the sixth-century chalice at Gourdon, or the tenth-century gold chalice of St. Gauzelin in the Nancy Treasury, pl. 122); and also the Suger Chalice made in the twelfth century.

The seventh-century Chelles chalice belonged to the type without handles; it was ascribed to St. Eligius and is known to us from a drawing which shows it as resembling a beaker with flared mouth, tall and straight. The oldest surviving examples of this type are the eighth-century piece of the Werden Treasury, and the chalice presented to the church of Kreutzmünster around 780 by Duke Tassilo of Bavaria, the unfortunate foe of Charlemagne, who ended his days in exile at Jumièges. These already have the three parts that were henceforth to characterize the chalice: foot, knop, and cup with ovoid base. The two oldest French chalices of this type are the twelfth-century funerary chalice found in the tomb of Bishop Ulger, which is in the Angers Treasury, and the Coronation Chalice, or Chalice of St. Rémy, fashioned around the year 1200, which is in the Reims Treasury (fig. 7). The upper portion of the Reims piece is in two parts, an ornamental outer cup, and an inner cup with a smooth surface. (Few examples of this type exist earlier than the fifteenth century; in the sixteenth century, the cup with an outer shell be-

NOZEROY. Chalice

CHATEAU-GONTHIER. Detail of chalice

comes more frequent, and is fairly customary after the seventeenth.) In the thirteenth century come the chalices of the treasuries of Troyes and Orléans, the one in the latter having been dug up with its paten. They are of very simple design, squat in outline, with a circular foot and a gadrooned knop; the same design occurs in the fourteenth century, on the chalice in the Bordeaux Treasury. Not many more fourteenth-century pieces survive. The Ecouis chalice (p. 34 center), found in the tomb of Bishop Jean de Marigny, and those of Guarriguiers and Larré, are more elongated. The sides of the hexagonal foot are concave, as are the stem and the knop. Each of the facets of the knop is diamond-shaped and decorated with an engraved motif. This type was to continue into the fifteenth century (Cahanès) and up to the beginning of the sixteenth, with a foot that might be circular (Pexiora) or polylobed (Salsigne).

Alongside these straightforward forms, other more complex ones emerged in the fifteenth century and continued into the sixteenth, while the decoration, engraved (as at Pexiora) or in repoussé, covered the whole piece. The outer shell, at first barely indicated (Chaudron) or silhouetted in openwork against the inner cup (Perpignan), in the sixteenth century assumed the dimensions (Saint-Jean-du-Doigt, pl. 79, Chartres, fig. 28, etc.) that were to characterize it in the seventeenth. In the fifteenth and sixteenth centuries the foot was circular (Brétignolles) or curvilinear (Palestron, Palau-del-Vidre, pl. 249) but usually polylobed (Sin-le-Noble, Narbonne, Rodez). The combination of the two processes gave the outline of the foot a complex design of concave and convex curves, as in flamboyant architecture (Besançon, Chaudron, Perpignan, p. 34 right). The foot was sometimes raised on an openwork gallery (Perpignan, Locronan). The knop became more massive. It was sometimes accompanied by a secondary knop over the foot (Chaudron), and assumed the most varied forms: sometimes a thick torus, decorated with medallions instead of the lozenges of the fourteenth century, and often adorned with busts, engraved (Flagnac), embossed (Chaudron), or enameled (Damvilliers), with sometimes a hexagonal architectural structure occupying a part of the stem (Perpignan). This architectural element was enriched with elements borrowed from sculpture, the oldest example of which seems to be the fifteenth-century chalice of Palau-del-Vidre, with its half-length cherubs and its foliated decoration. Pieces of this type were made throughout the sixteenth century and up to the beginning of the seventeenth, with full-length figures placed in the niches of the knop (Saint-Jean-du-Doigt, pl. 79, Château-Gonthier, p. 35 below), on a secondary knop (Chaudron), or on the stem and the outer cup (Nantes). A design of undulating flames was common in the fifteenth century (Argentière), and especially in the sixteenth. Polylobe bases were rare in the seventeenth century (Nancy). As a rule, they had become circular again. The principal knop tended increasingly to take the form of a baluster between two very flattened secondary knops, usually decorated with heads of winged cherubs or beading. The ornamentation, which from now on was very elaborate, usually consisted of Gospel scenes in repoussé, accompanied by the instruments of the Passion. In the seventeenth and eighteenth centuries, their decorative themes were borrowed from the secular ornamental vocabulary, or from floral designs (Nozeroy p. 35 above).

Patens were bare or decorated, in a circular or polylobed border, with engraved or embossed scenes or symbols, such as the Crucifixion (Halberstadt), the Lamb (Louvre), the Hand of God (Argentière), the crown of thorns (Fromentières), flames (Bazoche-Montpinçon). The decoration was sometimes extremely ornate, as on the paten of Silos in Spain, the rim of which is entirely covered with filigree.

On patens fashioned at the end of the sixteenth century and in the seventeenth, the decoration sometimes covered the entire piece (La Bigottière, Trinité de Château-Gonthier).

Before going on to discuss the ciborium, we have to recall the original arrangements made for the Reserved Sacrament in relation to the altar. Carolingian texts frequently refer to the existence of a ciborium (or tegurium) placed over the high altar, whose vault symbolized the heavens. It was of gold and silver in the Cathedral of Le Mans under St. Aldric, and also in Auxerre during Charlemagne's time. This arrangement is preserved with regard to the *paliotto* of Sant'Ambrogio at Milan and, in miniature, the tenth-century portable altar of Arnulf in the Munich Schatzkammer. The receptacle for the Reserved Sacrament was suspended from this ciborium or, failing that, from a crosier. It might be in the form of a dove (like those at La Guienne or Obazine, both of which were stolen at the turn of the present century), or of a closed vessel (like the Holy Ampulla at Sens, pl. 73), or again of a miniature shrine (which was the case in the Cathedral of Arras, as we see from one of the wings of the sixteenth-century triptych of the Holy Candle (p. 37). Although this practice had become infrequent, it continued up to the seventeenth century (good examples are the dove at Saint-Yrieix, p. 36 above, preserved together with the canopy of embroidered material, or *cincellium,* in which it was wrapped, and the suspension crosier of wrought iron and chased sheet iron of the church of Cossé-en-Champagne). In these receptacles were placed round boxes known as pyxes *(custodes, capsae, buxtae)* of boxwood or ivory, similar to those of secular origin in the treasuries of Sens (p. 22) or La Voûte-Chillac, in which the consecrated Hosts were kept. This practice was maintained until the thirteenth century, with enameled pyxes originating in the Limoges workshops. Once ciboria, as we know them, came into use, it became inconvenient to place them in these receptacles. At first, they were placed in wall tabernacles, in niches (as in the church of Gemeaux) or, in the fifteenth and sixteenth centuries, in "Sacrament Houses" or "repositories," sometimes also called "monstrances." These were independent of the altar and were surmounted by tall, pyramidal structures with gables and pinnacles, either of stone (as at Saint-Jean-de-Maurienne, Grenoble, Semur-en-Auxois), or of gilded wood (as at Saint-Antoine-en-Viennois). Then, in the fifteenth century, the practice spread of placing pyramid-shaped tabernacles in the rear of the altar (Lasson, Foissy). Finally, in the sixteenth century, these tabernacles were incorporated in retables constructed around them. This is the arrangement that we know.

The first ciboria in the form familiar to us date back to the thirteenth century. They resembled a chalice with a semispherical lid. The earliest pieces, of which very few remain (at Prunet and Belpuig, dating from the thirteenth century; at Argelès, Le Vigeois, and Avranches, p. 36 below, originating at Mont-Saint-Michel, dating from the fourteenth century), are enameled. The cup, surmounted by a cross, is supported by a tall foot, the stem of which includes a knop. After the sixteenth century (Seix, Coursegoule), the shape and ornamentation are similar to those of chalices, but are more ample and with a larger cup. Those of the seventeenth and eighteenth century are generally topped by a cross (Arras, Entremont), and sometimes by a symbolical pelican (Nozeroy). The proportions are beautifully balanced, and the design of foliate scrolls (Fangeaux, Arras), of representations of the Last Supper (Saint-Antoine), or of symbolical grains of wheat and grape clusters (Nozeroy), is very elaborate.

Of all religious articles, the ostensory is probably the one where it is possible to specify, if not the date, then at least the period of

SAINT-YRIEIX. Eucharistic dove

AVRANCHES. Ciborium

ARRAS. Detail of the Triptych of the Holy Candle

its emergence. The rite of exposing the Host was instituted in 1264 by Urban IV, following the miracle of the Mass at Bolsena. And the practice was definitively confirmed in 1317, under John XXII, with the insertion of the Feast of Corpus Christi in the liturgical calendar. Nevertheless, as Darcel points out, there is no proof that the Blessed Sacrament was originally exposed unveiled. The first reference to such a practice dates from the provincial council of Cologne in 1542. The ostensory must therefore have originated earlier. This hypothesis is borne out by an examination of the surviving pieces. Ciboria seem originally to have been used to expose the Blessed Sacrament or to carry it in procession. Then monstrances came to be used for the purpose. It is not clear, however, whether they were actually designed to expose the Host, or whether they were originally monstrance reliquaries; they consisted of a glass or crystal cylinder set into and surmounted by a structure made of precious metals (Rouen, p. 38 above, Mailley, etc.). But by the end of the fourteenth century, and prior to the creation of the finest monstrances, which date from the fifteenth century, a device was being sought to enable the faithful to view the Host. Of these halting experiments, the earliest surviving example seems to be one originating in the workshop of Guillaume Ito, a goldsmith of Rodez active around the year 1400. It is a reliquary consisting of a horizontal cylinder surmounted by a lunula flanked by two angels; the Host was placed in the lunula. The solution was a hybrid one; a reliquary was provided with a device whereby it could be used for exposing the Host. We know of other applications of the same principle dating from the fifteenth century; for instance, at Flagnac, where the monstrance reliquary with lunula, fashioned in the Provins workshop at Rodez, is most gracefully conceived, the two angels supported by brackets, and the lunula more closely associated with the cylindrical reliquary by means of a triangular framework. At Darazac or Prudhomat, again in the fifteenth century, we find this leading to the creation of a very simple type of monstrance, but one which had no sequel. It is a square panel surmounted by a blind arch, with a circular aperture for the Host. It is the generally accepted view that the solution found at Conques (p. 39 above) is the definitive one as regards a vessel especially intended, instead of incidentally employed, for exposing the Blessed Sacrament. The great disk embellished by *fleurons,* placed at the summit of a tall architectural stem that rises from a foot engraved with scenes from the Passion, and flanked by two angels supported on brackets, is believed to be the first example of an ostensory. For this was the form in use from that time forth. It should be pointed out, however, that here again it was associated with a reliquary—which this time, however, took second place—in the shape of a short vertical cylinder of rock crystal which served as the base for the edifice of the stem. The disk alone, considered now not as the principal but as the exclusive element, appears in the fifteenth century in pieces such as the Lucéram ostensory, where it is supported by a foot similar to those of chalices (polylobe base and knop with lozenge-shaped facets). It is one of the first to display a feature that was to characterize ostensories: the very large disk is surrounded by concentric strips of metal, short and undulating, representing rays, the effect of which is still similar to that of the Conques ostensory, surrounded by foliated crockets, of which only the stems are retained in the Lucéram piece.

But this systematization of forms, as applied to a novel idea, which was not merely to display the Host but to make the divine presence that it signifies felt by the visual exaltation of the power and glory radiating from it, was to lead to an extreme development of these rays. Embryonic at first, they were to develop into the dazzling coronas of the majestic "suns" of the seventeenth and eighteenth

ROUEN. Monstrance

LILLERS. Monstrance (disassembled)

CONQUES. Ostensory

LILLERS. Monstrance

centuries, accompanied by a symbolic decoration of ears of wheat and grape clusters, and thronged with angels gamboling in the clouds. Some were to be quite monumental. The one in the Perpignan Cathedral weighed 400 silver marks. Eight priests were needed to carry the one in Narbonne Cathedral. The one in the cathedral of Toledo is some 14 feet high.

The "sun" type, however, was not exclusive, and in some regions, such as northern France, the Netherlands, Germany, Spain, or Poland, there was a parallel development, as for monstrance reliquaries, of a vertical cylinder fitted with a crescent into which the Host could be inserted, and usually surrounded by a complicated structure of gables, flying buttresses, and pinnacles, rising pyramidally to a high central tower. Examples survive from the fifteenth century (Rouen), and from the seventeenth and eighteenth centuries (Saint-Omer, Boulogne, etc.). The best examples, however, are to be found in treasuries outside France. In most cases the monstrance was mounted on a foot (Paderborn, Düsseldorf, Madrid). In some cases, particularly in Spain in the fifteenth and sixteenth centuries (Cordova, Cadiz), it had no foot. It would then be known as a *custode,* and was allied in form as well as in purpose to the "repositories" of the churches. Sometimes the vertical cylinder in the center of the edifice was replaced by a broad lunula (Cologne in the fifteenth century, Oporto in the sixteenth) identical with that of the "suns" whose rays are represented in certain instances (Wielierka, Münster). Here the sun type and the monstrance type are combined.

As a last point in connection with chalices, ciboria, and monstrances, we should draw attention to the curious seventeenth-century piece of silver gilt at Lillers (p. 39 below), which is a composite of all three. Taken apart, or put together in a certain way, it can be used as any one of them (p. 38 below). The lower part is a chalice which becomes a ciborium if the upper part, consisting of a lid surmounted by a cross, is fitted directly over it. If the middle section is inserted between the two—it is a vertical glass cylinder mounted at either end in rings held in a circular frame in the form of handles enclosing two angels—the piece is complete, forming an ostensory, or monstrance, in which the crescent designed to support the Host rests on the head of a winged cherub. In this part of northern France, where seventeenth-century goldsmithery is so abundant, nineteenth-century restorations that substituted a lunula for the cylinder often impaired the originals (as at Boulogne, for instance).

The structure of the Lillers monstrance denotes a practical turn of mind, and it is by no means unique. The little cruet at Saint-Menoux (p. 40 above) opens up like a pomegranate or a flower whose petals are compartments for the storing of grains of incense. This type of object, all the more readily transportable since it could be turned to several different uses, brings us to the consideration of a category of objects which were not intended to be kept permanently in a church, but rather to be used for the administration of the sacraments outside the church, or on journeys.

For the sacraments administered to the sick—Communion, Extreme Unction—small pyxes or circular *custodes* were used to carry the Host; they were either similar to those which we have mentioned above, or, as at Béziers in the seventeenth century, in the form of a ciborium with a low foot, less than 4 inches high, which could hold one or two Hosts. Inside the Prunet-Belpuig ciborium, for instance, there is fitted a small pyx which could be removed in order to carry the viaticum. Before being used as a reliquary, the small seventh-century casket at Mortain (p. 21 bottom), of Anglo-Saxon origin, had been a "chrismal," or small box suspended from the neck, which Irish priests or monks took with them on their journeys. The holy oils were kept in special boxes of the most varied types. The one in the church of Saint-Viance, dating from the thirteenth century (p. 40 below) is oblong in shape, of Limoges enamel, with a conical lid; it has a double bottom consisting of a copper plaque pierced with three circular holes for the vials of holy oils. There were three kinds of oils: holy chrism, the oil of the catechumens, and the oil for the anointing of the sick. The vial containing the oil for the sick would be removed from the box for the administration of Extreme Unction. All the "holy oil boxes" were arranged this way inside. Usually they were very simple: a rectangular box with a roof surmounted by a cross. The metal used was either silver, as at Béziers or Minerve (seventeenth century), or pewter, as in the Angers Treasury (seventeenth century). In the eighteenth century, at Saint-Chinian, the holy oils were kept in a silver dove whose tail, which could be opened, was divided into three compartments. Often the three oils were kept in separate boxes that were carried on a plate with a handle. The set was then known as a chrismal (Plouenan). In episcopal chapels (Narbonne Treasury), there were only two boxes, one for the holy chrism, the other for the oil of the catechumens.

Portable altars, which are believed to have been first used in times of persecution, were used on journeys. They became much more frequent as a result of the crusades. By the end of the thirteenth century they were few and far between, there being less need for them since the cessation of expeditions to far-off countries, and they were virtually prohibited by the Council of Trent. They were small (their longest side rarely exceeded 20 inches), and consisted of a consecrated stone, usually of precious substance (alabaster and porphyry at Conques at the end of the eleventh century, pl. 218, amethyst in the Byzantine altar at Lyons, fig. 19, in the thirteenth century), mounted in an elaborate frame. The French treasuries possess few examples of these apart from the ones just cited.

In the sphere of decoration, the portable altars with their richly ornamented frames present many analogies with the book covers of evangeliaries and psalters. Indeed, it is a moot point whether the alabaster portable altar at Conques, surrounded by filigree and cloisonné enamels, was not originally an evangeliary cover whose central plaque of ivory or embossed or engraved metal had been replaced by this alabaster plaque. The extreme liturgical importance of the sacred books, and particularly of the book containing the Holy Gospels—on a closed copy of which both laymen and ecclesiastics would bind themselves by oath—explains the veneration surrounding them. This veneration was expressed in the lavishness of the precious materials used to adorn them. The most sumptuous bindings are those of Carolingian and Romanesque times (St. Gauzelin at Nancy, Gannat, Morienval, and especially from Saint-Denis and other treasuries, now in the Bibliothèque Nationale—the evangeliaries of Charles the Bald, of Metz, etc.). They rank among the most remarkable expressions of the precious arts. The tradition was to be maintained into the Gothic period, up to the fourteenth century. At that point, however, the decoration began to borrow its effects from sculpture rather than from goldsmithery, in contrast to the earlier periods. From the sixteenth century, wood and leather, sometimes with silver or copper appliqués at the corners or in the middle (as at Saint-Antoine), were to take the place of metal, ivory, and enamel; there were a few exceptions to this rule in the sixteenth (Conques) and seventeenth centuries (Saint-Riquier), and fewer in the eighteenth (Sallanches).

Another analogy in the area of design may be found in respect of altar canons. In the picture of the Mass of St. Giles (p. 10), the Gospels are open on the altar; indeed, there is nothing else on the

SAINT-MENOUX. Cruet

SAINT-VIANCE. Box for Holy Oils

altar. After the sixteenth century, however, it became customary to frame the texts read during the Mass separately. The frames of the altar canons at Saint-Riquier bear the same designs as those of the evangeliary cover. For the most part, in the seventeenth and eighteenth centuries, these frames of gilded wood (Valloire) or metal (Saint-Antoine) recall those of pictures or mirrors.

Other liturgical objects used during religious services were censers and incense boats. Censers consisted of two interlocking capsules; the lower one was a brazier for burning incense and the upper one was pierced with holes through which the smoke escaped. A chain made it possible to give the device the swinging motion implied by the term, "censing." We do not know at what point censing became a part of the ritual. The tenth-century censers at Verdun and Saint-Benoît-sur-Loire were of gold. Most of those known to us are of bronze, silver, or silver-plated copper. The earliest known types are neither in treasuries nor in museums but are depicted in manuscripts (eleventh-century Apocalypse at Saint-Sever), wall paintings (Saint-Savin), reliefs (twelfth-century tympanum of Conques), goldsmithery (angels bearing censers on the A of Charlemagne, pl. 213). They are spherical in form. Rupin mentions a twelfth-century censer that had belonged to the Treasury of Rocamadour and is now in a private collection, the upper part of which represents an edifice with loopholes. The necessity of making openings in this part of the object led to the idea of an architectural structure, which immediately assumed a symbolic significance: the bronze censer in the Trier Treasury (c. 1000) represents the temple of Solomon as it is described in the Bible. The decoration of censers usually followed the development of the architectural style of the period. In the Gothic period they were pyramidal and the base became more prominent. The Ur censer, dating from the fifteenth century, is a central plan monument made entirely of windows. The sixteenth-century censer of the chapel of the Order of the Holy Spirit was in the form of a small temple. But Gothic forms sometimes continued very late in the provinces, as evidenced by the Montferrer censer (p. 41 below right) dated 1687, and originating in a Perpignan workshop, whereas at about the same date that of Cesseras (p. 41 below left) bearing a Toulouse stamp, was shaped like a vase with a rounded, bell-shaped lid in the Louis XIV style. This vase type was maintained in the eighteenth century in the elegant and worldly style of the day (Narbonne).

The incense boat was a necessary accessory of the censer. It held the grains of incense, which were scooped out with a spoon. Because of the symbolism attached to the boat, the Church gave this object the shape of a hull. Sometimes, when it was made of a shell, as at Chartres in the sixteenth century (pl. 152), the incense boat achieved a natural and marine form perfectly adapted to the idea it represented. Its form did not change until the eighteenth century. At that time, under the influence of secular goldsmithery, one of the ends was lengthened, raised and curved back, like a gravy boat. Here, again, the earliest incense boats are known to us only through representations in other media, such as stained glass (the St. Nicholas window in the Cathedral of Le Mans), sculpture (door of St. Anne, Notre-Dame, Paris, or the tomb of St. Stephen at Obazine). The thirteenth-century incense boat at Soudeilles, of Limoges enamel, is one of the earliest in the French treasuries.

Finally, on the altar, there is a cross. As we saw before, the records frequently refer to extremely sumptuous crosses suspended over the high altar in the Carolingian period. And the arrangement reproduced at the end of the fifteenth century in the painting of the Mass of St. Giles (p. 10) shows the cross not exactly on the altar, but

PLOUENAN. Chrismals

left: CESSERAS. Censer
right: MONTFERRER. Censer

standing back, above the retable. The altar cross proper did not appear before the eleventh century. We possess altar crosses of the twelfth century, similar to those which used to be at Saint-Bertin and Obazine, and of which only the richly decorated bases remain. But frequently in the Middle Ages, the cross did not stand on the altar permanently. The celebration of the Mass was preceded by a procession at the close of which a cleric would detach the processional cross from its shaft and place it on the altar. The acolytes would place their candlesticks upon the altar too. Cross and candlesticks constituted the altar furnishings. In the seventeenth century (Sées) and in the eighteenth (Bayeux), it became customary to make sets of these pieces, with identical bases and ornamentation. In the eighteenth century (Embrun) and the beginning of the nineteenth (Amiens), these sets achieved monumental and very elegant proportions, in harmony with the altars, which had become very impressive.

The origins of the representation of the cross go back to the fourth century. When the news spread through the Christian world that the True Cross had been discovered in the course of excavations undertaken at the order of Constantine and his mother, St. Helena, pilgrimages to the Holy Places, which had begun in the age of the persecutions, became increasingly popular. The pilgrims climbed up to Golgotha, and, when they entered the basilica of the Holy Sepulcher, erected by the emperor in all the magnificence of a triumphal art, they saw an immense gold cross studded with sparkling jewels above the high altar. This gold cross of Golgotha, the memory of which is preserved in the sixth-century mosaic of the church of Santa Pudenziana in Rome, was the first glorification of the cross; Christian iconography had previously not dared represent it. It was the model, as we pointed out earlier, for all the non-figurative medieval crosses, whose symbolism sprang from the transcendental luster of the precious materials of which they were fashioned. The largest and most beautiful of these crosses, of which we know now only from literary sources, were made of gold, filigree, and jewels, and were situated in the eastern apses of churches, in the direction of the tomb of Christ, to announce the second coming of the Supreme Judge. As Frolow has shown, the cross was to become the symbol of the Christian faith. As the instrument of sacrifice, it was to become identified with the Redeemer to the point where the two terms, cross and Christ, became synonymous. And the wood of the True Cross, bathed in the blood of the Divine Victim, was regarded as a relic.

There was no figure of Christ on the triumphal cross of Golgotha. And it was in Jesus' own country, again, that the theme of Christ crucified was to originate. The walls of the Holy Sepulcher were decorated with mosaics representing scenes from the Gospels and these are reproduced on the famous silver ampullas in the treasuries of Monza and Bobbio, presented around the year 600 to Theodolinda, queen of the Lombards. The pilgrims found in these pious representations a note of realism very different from the Early Christian formulas of Hellenistic art to which they were accustomed. The Christ they looked upon was no longer a beardless adolescent, but a man of Syrian type, bearded and long-haired. This iconography, so different in character, was soon to supplant that which had preceded it in the West. We know from Gregory of Tours that in the sixth century the church of Narbonne already possessed an icon of the Crucifixion. The faithful, however, were shocked by it, since they were accustomed to a symbolical representation of the cross, and the icon had to be veiled.

The shapes of the various categories of crosses—altar crosses, portable crosses, suspended crosses, processional crosses—were similar. The

MONETIER-LES-BAINS. Detail of processional cross

examples in France do not go as far back as those in Spain (cross of Oviedo cathedral, dating from the ninth century), in Italy (cross of Justin II, dating from the sixth century, in the Sancta Sanctorum), or in Germany (Carolingian crosses such as the imperial cross at Aachen, or Ottonian crosses in the Essen Treasury). Apart from the fragment of the seventh-century cross of Saint-Denis in the Cabinet des Médailles and crosses represented on reliquaries (Reliquary of Pepin at Conques, pl. 207), the earliest in France date from the end of the eleventh century or from the twelfth. They are small—even the processional crosses—and for the most part of cast copper (Saint-Mars-sous-la-Futaye, pl. 175) or enamel, either Limoges enamel (Nancy) or Mosan enamel (Liessies). They became larger in the thirteenth century (as illustrated by the cross of Limoges enamel in the Cathedral of Lyons).

The most widespread type of processional crosses, their designs varying according to region and workshop, consisted of embossed silver or copper plaques nailed on a wooden core. The earliest known examples date from the fourteenth century. The embossed design, consisting at first of very simple foliate scrolls (Oreilla, Parisot), became increasingly crowded and elaborate, developing plant themes up to the end of the Gothic period (Conques, pl. 224, Nauviale), then, in the sixteenth century, Renaissance motifs (Ahetze, p. 44 top). Often, however, the process of change was delayed by the traditionalism of the workshops, which continued to use their time-honored dies (sixteenth century, Mayra, Saint-Symphorien). The figures in the seventeenth and eighteenth centuries—of Christ on one side, and usually of the Virgin or the patron saint of the church on the other, as at Saint-Thégonnec or Bellentre (fig. 21)—stand out against smooth plaques, and the decoration is confined to *fleurons* at the extremities (as at Béziers); in other cases, the arms continue to be ornamented (as at Saint-Chaffrey). The appliqué figures were usually cast in a mold, seldom embossed, as at Conques. The ends of the arms were usually embellished with symbols or figures of the Evangelists, enameled (Parisot), embossed (Monetier, p. 43), or of cast metal (Lyons). In the sixteenth and seventeenth centuries, this decoration was usually replaced by cherubs' heads, as at Formiguères. Such heads sometimes decorated the knop (Hauteville-Gondon); or again, angels might stand full-length on the base (Moutiers d'Ahun). Sometimes the figure of Christ was flanked by the figures of the Virgin and St. John on the arms (Carliha, fifteenth century). In some regions, the figures of the Virgin and St. John were supported by a double bracket placed under the arms (Guingat, Salles-Curan, sixteenth-century agate cross in the Lyons Treasury, pl. 134). The ends of the arms might terminate in squares extending beyond the arms, thus creating the outline of a cross potent (Lyons), but usually they terminated in trefoils (Prévinquières) or quatrefoils (Salles-Curan, p. 44 below), the tips of which were sometimes adorned with globules (Bruejols) which at Conques took the form of acorns (pl. 224). In the fifteenth and sixteenth centuries, the arms sometimes ended in large fluted globes (Guingat); in the seventeenth and eighteenth centuries, the ends of the arms had the shape of *fleurons* (Cesseras) or baskets (Béziers) with a shell (Saint-Julien-d'Olargues) or *rocaille* design (Fraisse-sur-Agout). The fleur-de-lis appears as a distortion of the trefoil (Angers Treasury, fifteenth century). It is common in the seventeenth century (Le Mans, pl. 165). In some regions, particularly Roussillon, the arms were bordered with small *fleurons* (Rigarda). In Britanny (Locronan) and the Basque country (Ahetze, p. 44 above), small bells were sometimes suspended from the transverse arm. Special mention should be made of the *lignum vitae* (Tree of Life) crosses (twelfth-century cross at Saint-Julien-aux-Bois, fifteenth-

AHETZE. Cross

SALLES-CURAN. Cross

SENS. Cross of Nailly

century cross at Mayran) which were not flat but are circular in cross-section, bristling with stubs, like a tree trunk whose branches have been lopped off.

Crosses with filigree form a group apart. Up to the Gothic period they continued the tradition of the triumphal crosses of very early times. Filigree work covered the entire surface (Le Valasse, Nailly, p. 45, Najac) or was used in association with enamels (Cross of Le Paraclet, pl. 105), or with precious stones and intaglios (Castelnau-de-Montmiral). Sometimes gems continued to be mounted in arcaded settings as in pre-Romanesque times (Eymoutiers). Fine examples exist of rock crystal crosses dating from the fourteenth century (Labessière-Candeil) and the sixteenth (Joué-Etiau, Thonon, fig. 26), as well as those in the Cathedral of Grenoble, of Meurcé, fig. 36, Le Mans, pl. 165, and Angers which are of the seventeenth century.

All these crosses, with the exception of some that are overlaid with filigree, had a single transverse arm. Another fairly large category had two transverse arms. It is generally accepted that this form was a continuation in the West of a Byzantine type derived from *staurothecae,* or reliquaries of the True Cross, and that the second transverse arm was an effect derived either from the titulus over the head of the Christ figure, or from the support under the feet. It is a fact that most of the crosses with two transverse arms were reliquaries, enshrining relics of the True Cross. They date mainly from the thirteenth century. Some had pedestals, in which case they were altar or "stational" crosses, as at Saint-Priest-Taurion, Les Cars, Corre, Sens; some were processional crosses, as at Eymoutiers and Rouvres; some were suspended, like the small cross at Conques in its original form. All were of precious metal, silver or silver gilt, some composed of smooth plaques decorated with cabochons (Saint-Priest, Brageac, Obazine) or rosettes (Conques), others richly overlaid with filigree (Blanchefosse, Clairmarais, pl. 116, Rouvres, Eymoutiers, Corre). It should be noted, however, that whereas all crosses with two transverse arms are reliquary crosses, not all reliquary crosses have two transverse arms. We have an illustration of this point in the seventeenth-century piece in the Montreuil Treasury with its fine fleur-de-lis design, which was a reliquary of the True Cross but designed to be suspended. In very rare cases, relics of the True Cross were placed in casket reliquaries (Saint-Sernin at Toulouse, pl. 240), or panel reliquaries (Ardus).

The contribution of the textile arts to the treasures of the churches is represented by embroidered altar frontals (parements of the comtesse d'Etampes in the Sens Treasury, in the Hôtel-Dieu of Château-Thierry, dating from the fourteenth century, at Beaune-la-Rolande, from the seventeenth century, etc.), and embroidered alms-purses (such as those in the treasuries of Montpezat or Sens, dating from the fourteenth century); also by embroidered or woven sacerdotal vestments. From the seventeenth century, embroidery on rochets and albs (Sens) was replaced by lace (treasuries of Lyons, Embrun, Eu, p. 46); and lace was also used to decorate altar cloths (the one in *point de France* presented by Madame de Montpensier to the collegiate church of Eu).

The rules governing the use of sacerdotal vestments had been laid down by the councils. The cope was a voluminous mantle originally worn outdoors for processions and provided with a hood as protection against rain. For that reason, it was called a "pluvial." The hood soon took on a purely ornamental role in the form of a rectangular piece of cloth on the back below the neck. Copes retained their ample proportions (sixteenth-century cope at Béhuard, p. 47) without substantial change (the Restoration cope in the Amiens Treasury has the same form and dimensions as the fourteenth-century copes at

Saint-Bertrand-de-Comminges). They were fastened by a morse, or jeweled clasp (Arras Treasury). The base of the Egletons reliquary, with its horizontal cylinder, had previously been an enameled cope morse.

The chasubles worn by priests to celebrate Mass were originally bell-shaped (twelfth-century chasuble of St. Regnobertus in the Bayeux Treasury, thirteenth-century chasuble of Blessed Thomas Elye at Biville, fourteenth-century chasuble known as the Chasuble of St. Dominic at Saint-Sernin at Toulouse). Some, retaining this early shape, were cut from materials of earlier eras (Chasuble of St. Ebbo in the Sens Treasury, originating in Fatamid Egypt). In the seventeenth century the shape changed; it was cut lower at the neck and the oval was narrowed. The fine chasubles of the late fifteenth and early sixteenth centuries in the Embrun Treasury were unfortunately remodeled in this style. The dalmatic was the vestment worn by the deacon during services. Its sleeves were originally very short (thirteenth-century piece at Ambazac, fig. 45). They were subsequently lengthened (Saint-Mars-sous-la-Futaye, seventeenth century).

The bishop wore a miter. This consisted basically of a horizontal band, or *circulus,* and a vertical band, or *titulus.* In its primitive form it was a round cap, as shown in manuscripts such as the "Letters of St. Gregory" of about 1160 from the Abbey of Saint-Amand. One such miter is in the Sens Treasury. A new style appeared in the middle of the twelfth century and lasted until the end of the century, namely, that of a cap with two lateral points, as may be seen in certain wall paintings (Saint-Jacques-des-Guérets). But is was also at this time that the triangular form appeared, with the two points placed directly in front and at the back; and after the thirteenth century, all miters were of this type. In the window of Le Mans Cathedral which depicts the vision of St. Ambrose (c. 1190), we see the bishop wearing this miter; its form is the same as that of the miters in the treasuries of Saint-Bertrand-de-Comminges, Saint-Sernin at Toulouse, and Sens. The miter at Saint-Bertrand-de-Comminges has retained a feature that was to become characteristic, namely, lappets, or long ribbons hanging down from the back. The triangle formed by this type of miter was quite low. By the thirteenth century (casket reliquary of St. Taurinus at Evreux), a taller shape had developed. From the sixteenth century, miters were very tall and flared under the triangle surmounting them. Their decoration also developed. The decoration of the miter of Saint-Sernin of Toulouse, of purely geometrical design, was made up of circles in imitation of bezels into which stones were to be fitted, and the decoration of the Sens miter consisted of broad foliate scrolls suggesting wrought ironwork. In the thirteenth century, in embroidery as in all branches of art—in the monumental sculpture of buildings as in filigree work—the ornamental stems blossomed into flowers. Decorative themes borrowed from the metal arts, whether precious metal or iron, were to be succeeded in the fourteenth century by themes adapted from illumination, as we see from the Sixtus miter, or from the miter of Jean de Marigny at Evreux. The imitation went so far that the silk on the miter of the abbey of Oignies, or on the fourteenth-century miter known as the Miter of the Old Temple, in the Archives Nationales, was not embroidered but painted. In the fifteenth century there was a return to the effects of precious metalwork, with miters adorned with cabochons, as on the St. Denis window in the Cathedral of Tours (c. 1460), or embroidered with gold thread.

Crosiers and tau crosiers were other insignia of bishops and abbots. As regards crosiers, the development begins with the Crosier of St. Austreberta in the Montreuil Treasury (pl. 112), the top of which is curved in the manner of a cant hook, like a shepherd's crook; it

EU. Detail of alb

BEHUARD. Cope

appears to be the earliest of its kind, together with the crosier in the Abbey of Quedlimburg (end of the eleventh century) which has a slightly more accentuated curve. Even before the year 1000 there appeared what was to become the standard type of the crosier ending in a volute. The crosier of Bernard of Hildesheim was decorated with figures modeled in the round, as were the subsequent Gothic crosiers. In the Romanesque period the crosier heads consisted of a simple spiral volute ending with a flower (Rouen museum) or an animal head (Reims museum) or human heads (twelfth-century crosier of Ulger in the Angers Treasury, fig. 32). A scene is already depicted on the crosier of St. Cesarius of Arles (p. 48 left). Most crosiers were of ivory or engraved metal. The staffs of this period, which were of wood, were sometimes carved with scenes (Crosier of St. Aldegundis at Maubeuge, Crosier of St. Cyprian at Reims). In the Gothic period ivory became more rare (fifteenth-century crosier of Bishop Hardouin du Bueil, in the Angers Treasury). Rock crystal was sometimes used (Le Lys Abbey) and also silver gilt (Crosier of St. Aldegundis, pl. 113), but most are of enamel, especially in the thirteenth century. The series of extremely elegant Gothic crosiers includes an endless variety of floral themes, as at Orléans or Poitiers, as well as scenes from the Gospels, the Paschal Lamb, zoomorphic themes, etc. In the thirteenth century, as in the preceding period, the socket of the volute fits directly onto the extension of the staff. From the fourteenth century, it bulges at this point (crosiers of Maubuisson Abbey, p. 48 center, of Bishop Hardouin du Bueil, etc.). The convexity became more pronounced from the sixteenth century, and cast and chased metal were used exclusively. In the seventeenth and eighteenth centuries, and right into the nineteenth, as in the Treasury of Carcassonne, the volute developed into a spiral without figured ornament.

Up to the Gothic period, abbots and abbesses, like Bernard of Hildesheim and St. Austreberta, usually carried a tau crosier, not a crosier proper. These taus were very varied in form. Sometimes they were of rock crystal (Chemillé), but usually they were of ivory, carved with figures, architectural motifs, foliate scrolls, plant and zoomorphic themes. At Moutiers (pl. 136) or Sixt, the tau was triangular. That of Morard, abbot of Saint-Germain-des-Prés (c. 1000), was a horizontal cylinder. This simple form was frequently embellished with terminal volutes (eleventh century tau from Jumièges Abbey, now at the Rouen museum, p. 49 above), and eventually developed into the tau of St. Anthony, with patté ends, which became the emblem of the Antonine order.

At his consecration, and in token of his investiture, the bishop received special gloves and sandals. Both were embroidered (gloves and sandals of St. Bertrand of Comminges). Gloves were often decorated with plaques of enamel (Orléans, fig. 38, Cahors) or of chased silver (Moutiers). Up to the fifteenth century this ceremony also included the use of the liturgical comb (comb in the Sens Treasury, fig. 6). This practice is mentioned in the pontifical of William of Mende: before officiating, the bishop would put on his sandals and sit down on his throne, while the deacon would "comb him respectfully and gently."

We must mention, finally, the oliphants, of which there are some eleventh-century examples (Horn of Roland at Toulouse, p. 49 below), as well as from the fourteenth century (Sallanches). They were sounded during processions to announce the passage of the cortège. There is reference to them in the Book of the Miracles of St. Foy.

Another group of objects in the treasuries which we shall mention only briefly consists of the insignia of office and the instruments used at imperial and royal coronations. The most illustrious example occurs in Austria, in the treasury of Vienna (insignia of the Holy

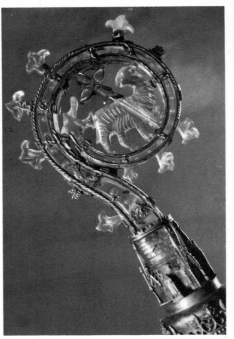

ARLES. Volute of crosier

VERSAILLES.
Crosier of the Abbey of Maubuisson

REIMS. Detail of the
so-called Staff of St. Gibrien

Roman Empire: crown, orb, scepter, sword, Holy Lance, coronation cope, insignia of homage, etc.). No complete set remains in France. The sword and the Hand of Justice, both greatly restored, are in the Louvre; like the spurs and an epaulet, they come from Saint-Denis. The Holy Ampulla, in the Reims Treasury, was mounted in a small shrine dating from the reign of Charles X. In this category we should also include the insignia of the sovereign Order of Malta and the great Orders of the west (Golden Fleece, Holy Spirit) worn by laymen, but having a religious significance. The Order of the Holy Spirit was founded by Henry III. The sword, the dagger of the grand master, the herald's mace, as well as the sumptuous cloaks of the knights embroidered with flames of gold, are in the Louvre. The knights attended the king during the coronation and took part in the banquet ceremonial. And the forms of the objects peculiar to the coronation liturgy, the flasks or *ferrières,* and the great goblet, now in the Louvre, were retained up to the time of Charles X (offertory vase for the wine, offertory dishes for the bread, in the Reims Treasury).

Reliquaries are another group of objects that enriched the treasuries. They present an infinite variety of features. In the Middle Ages, the altar itself was a reliquary. The Council of Carthage, in 401, defined the portable altar as a consecrated stone enshrining relics. And in a church, Mass was celebrated over the martyr's tomb. At Saint-Germain of Auxerre, the high altar of the upper church was directly over the crypt in which the saint's body reposed. The *paliotto* of Sant'Ambrogio in Milan is both an altar and a reliquary, as its dedicatory inscription indicates. The enormous growth of the cult of relics—relics from the Holy Land and related to Christ's Passion, such as the True Cross, nails, "milk of the Virgin," and relics of saints—made it necessary to enshrine them in a manner that both recalled and honored their presence; and this, as we have pointed out above, produced a whole variety of forms peculiar to the Catholic religion. In no other religion is it conceivable that an object in the shape of a foot should be the subject of veneration (Thonon, p. 50 right below), or of a thigh (Saint-Gildas-de-Rhuys, pl. 78), or of a leg (Montreuil), or of an arm (Crespin, fig. 14), or of a rib (Saint-Laurent-de-la-Côte, p. 50 right above), or of a heart (Angers,

ROUEN. Tau from Jumièges

TOULOUSE. Oliphant called the Horn of Roland

p. 50 left), or of a shoulder blade (Saint-Paul-de-Vence, p. 50 center). This world is so varied that it is difficult to classify reliquaries in distinct categories. They range from the very large (the casket reliquary of the Three Kings at Cologne Cathedral is some 67 inches high and 71 inches long) to the very small (the cylindrical reliquary in the Amiens Treasury is pencil thin); from the simplest shapes (casket of St. Louis in the Louvre containing some of the king's bones and his hair shirt, which Philip the Fair presented to the Abbey of Le Lys) to the most elaborate (reliquary in the Chapel of the Holy Spirit); from the most straightforward (monstrance at Saint-Georges-des-Landes, which is a crystal ampulla mounted on a tall base with a knop decorated with turquoises and a lid topped by a knob) to the most strange, whether such strangeness be the effect of a contrived form (the Charroux Reliquary, pl. 181, which opens up) or the unexpected sight of an ordinary object, sometimes utilitarian in appearance (the Beaulieu Lantern, which looks like a miner's lamp, p. 51 left top; or the reliquary of Saint-Aignan of Orléans, which is a small sprung carriage of rock crystal and copper gilt with engraving and openwork, p. 51 left bottom). Or there is the singular "relief plan" at the Cathedral of Soissons (p. 51 right) representing an entire city enclosed behind its ramparts, with every one of its parish churches indicated. The relic at Villers-Saint-Sépulcre is a humble paving stone (p. 51 left center). But this stone, mounted in a Gothic frame with two angels and a scene of Christ in the tomb, had been brought back from Jerusalem, and its legendary origin gave the village its name. The Holy Sepulcher itself, a haunting memory throughout the Middle Ages, was reproduced on ivories (buckle of St. Cesarius of Arles, pl. 101), in illuminations (Evangeliary of Drogo), in precious metalwork (casket reliquary of Entremont). It was to give rise to a type of central plan reliquary (the Bego lantern in the Conques treasury, dating from the late eleventh century, pl. 214; the reliquary in the Berlin museum, dating from the end of the twelfth).

ANGERS. Heart reliquary

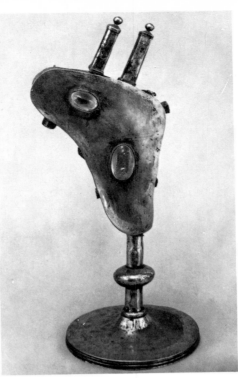

SAINT-PAUL-DE-VENCE.
Shoulder blade reliquary

SAINT-LAURENT-DE-LA-COTE.
Rib reliquary

THONON. Foot reliquary

The increasing diversity of forms was emphasized in the Gothic age thanks to technical advances that released the goldsmith from his dependence on the basic volumes prescribed by the wooden support, and permitted him to indulge the most extraordinary flights of fantasy. The diversity was accompanied by a variety of terms—reliquaries, caskets, phylacteries, monstrances. But these different terms do not always correspond to precisely defined categories, giving rise to typical forms. The heading, "reliquary," covers all the rest.

Under "casket," we may classify what the ancient records describe as *arca, capsa, chapse, theca, tumba,* or *feretrum* (whence the French word, *fierte,* which is still applied, for instance, to the casket of St. Romanus in the Cathedral of Rouen). The earliest types of caskets, dating from the seventh century, were either in the form of a purse, as at Saint-Bonnet-Avalouze (pl. 197), which could be suspended from the neck, or in the form of a sarcophagus, perhaps derived from Jewish ossuaries, as at Saint-Benoît-sur-Loire (fig. 37). Of the two types, only the second survived. From the twelfth century on it was often supplanted by a casket in the form of a church. The casket in Cologne by Nicholas of Verdun combined the two ideas of church and sarcophagus; from the gabled side, it looks like a church, but the two side aisles with the nave rising above them formed three tombs, for the casket enshrined the bodies of three saints. In the Gothic period, caskets became real miniature churches (thirteenth-century casket of Saint Taurinus at Evreux).

In pre-Romanesque times, according to Mgr. Lesne, a phylactery was a jewel enshrining a small relic which kings and princes wore about their necks; an example is the Talisman of Charlemagne. It was in the form of an encolpion. The small ninth-century phylactery of the tooth of the Child Jesus, of Saint-Médard in Soissons, since vanished, was probably of this type, a small relic enshrined in a jewel. It was to continue into Gothic times; an example is the phylactery of the tooth of St. Nicholas of Arras (pl. 109) in the form of a cope morse. But of the two elements of the phylactery, one soon disappeared, and Mgr. Barbier de Montault defines it as a "reliquary of indeterminate form and material used exclusively for the preservation

BEAULIEU. Lantern reliquary

SOISSONS. Relief plan of the city of Soissons

VILLERS-SAINT-SEPULCRE. Reliquary of the paving stone of the Holy Sepulcher

ORLEANS. Reliquary in the shape of a carriage

of fragments of relics." The reliquary of Arnac-la-Poste (pl. 191), with its numerous vials designed to hold small relics, is a phylactery. And, by this definition, the Conques triptych (pl. 222) pierced with a multitude of cells, was also one, although it was not termed such. On the other hand, the term phylactery is used for reliquaries such as those of Saint-Sylvestre or Saint-Goussaud which contained fragments of relics of several saints, and whose form, namely, a single cylinder of rock crystal on a foot, was akin to those of the monstrances of Eymoutiers, Beaumont, or Saint-Georges-des-Landes.

A monstrance, as its name implies, was conceived to display the relic. But under this definition, the caskets with apertures of the earlier periods were monstrances; for instance, the Reliquary of Pepin of Aquitaine (pls. 206, 207) if its windows were uncovered, or the eleventh-century lantern of Bego of Conques (pl. 214), or again, the thirteenth-century openwork casket of Gimel. The term would apply especially to the series of footed reliquaries of the Gothic period, consisting of a vertical or horizontal cylinder of glass or rock crystal. Here again, there is confusion as regards forms and terms. For not only reliquaries of this type have similar forms and are similarly designated, but also the ostensories which, in northern France and other parts of Europe, continued to be used up to the seventeenth century to display the Host in a vertical cylinder of transparent material. At the same time, the monstrance type reliquaries had changed in form; the vertical part was usually discarded, and the glass cylinder was replaced by a closed metal container—rather like a small casket mounted on a foot—with the relic visible only through a narrow window (Treasury of Montreuil).

The forms of reliquaries designed to preserve parts of a human body—head, arm, etc.—in most cases corresponded to the part concerned, but this was not always the rule. The reliquary of Charlemagne's arm (c. 1170) at the Louvre is an oblong casket, decorated with figures under an arcade. And many reliquaries of heads, even in the Gothic periods, were not head reliquaries. They were central plan, often octagonal, structures, large enough to hold a skull (head of St. Regnobertus at Varzy, fig. 39, of St. Susanna at Avranches, p. 52 above, from Mont-Saint-Michel, of St. Austreberta at Montreuil). Conversely, not all central plan reliquaries (apart from monstrances with vertical cylinders) were head reliquaries. They reflect another idea, as we saw earlier, that of the Holy Sepulcher. And this notion of an ideal church, which entered into the conception of the great Gothic caskets representing the heavenly Jerusalem, is to be found again in the central plan objects that represent buildings, such as the Spanish *custodes* at Cadiz or Cordova, or the Reliquary of Our Lady's Milk at Evron (fig. 34).

Thus reliquaries cannot be classified in distinct categories according to nomenclature, purpose, or form. There is constant overlapping among the different headings, and also among the various tendencies governing forms, whether in the direction of monumental architecture (as in caskets shaped like churches), furnishings (triptychs, polyptychs in the Gothic period), sculpture (the extreme form of which is the statuette or individual statue), adornment (belt reliquaries as at Grand, p. 53, and pendants, such as the one in the Amiens Treasury, p. 52 below), or an art purely of precious metalwork (votive crowns such as that from Le Paraclet, pl. 108). Polylobed phylacteries in the form of cope morses, like those at Saint-Nicolas in Arras (pl. 109) or of St. Mary of Oignies, might well be regarded as adornments. When the same forms are mounted on pedestals, their character changes and instead of a portable jewel, we have an object resting on a support (reliquary of St. Sixtus at Reims, pl. 85, reliquaries of Langres and Saint-Menoux). And with panel- and triptych- and polyptych-reliquaries, a relationship is established between goldsmithery and other techniques, among them painting and embroidery.

In the earlier periods, the various types of reliquaries were more differentiated; the objects at Conques provide a kind of sampling. From the end of the twelfth century they tended increasingly to merge and, as architectural and sculptural forms mastered the element of space, constitute a single work. The stage of this mastery and this merging might be analyzed by following the evolution of certain themes during the Gothic period. For instance, the individual architectonic elements of a piece such as the gabled panel reliquary, mounted on a foot, of St. Samson in Reims (pl. 84) begin to develop independently. The triangle of the roof is detached from the central portion to form, first, a perforated triangle (Fanjaux), then a gable (Rigarda, pl. 250), and finally a bell tower (Millas), while the two knobs at the bottom of the slopes of the roof will stretch out into pinnacles. The pattern of the reliquaries at Sallanches, Saint-Etienne of Sens, and Saint-Riquier, is that of a central and two lateral towers. Through the multiplicity of verticals played off against the diagonals of the flying buttresses that connect them, a fairy tale architecture eventually comes to surround the horizontal or vertical cylinders of the monstrances.

The polylobed jewel mounted in the footed reliquary of St. Sixtus of Reims is set in a square frame at Langres. At Charroux (pl. 181) the square frame festooned with filigree is an independent form. When it is opened, it shows two kneeling angels holding the container of the relic. This theme of angels facing each other on either side of a reliquary (Salles-Curan), a cross (Moutiers d'Ahun), or an ostensory (Sées, pl. 138, Beaupréau), is one of the most charming conceits of religious goldsmithery. At first, as in the A of Charlemagne at Conques (pl. 212), their figures are clumsily adapted to a rudimentary composition. With wings outspread (Rigarda, pl. 250), or folded (Saint-Polycarpe, pl. 252), kneeling (Jaucourt) or standing (Oust, pl. 234), supported on brackets (Serdinya) or placed at the foot of the reliquary (Coulomb), they are no more than a graceful accompaniment. At Egletons, however, where one of the angels is replaced by the Virgin, the two figures support the horizontal cylinder of the reliquary on their heads, like atlantes. At Saint-

AVRANCHES.
Reliquary of the head of St. Susanna

AMIENS. Pendant

GRAND. Belt reliquary

Polycarpe, Montpezat, and Montreuil, the angels devoutly hold the container of the relic in their hands, or raise it in a glorious gesture with outstretched arms; their plasticity becomes an essential element in the architecture of the reliquary. In the Reliquary of St. Aldegundis of Maubeuge (pl. 114), sculpture and architecture achieve so perfect a balance that it may be regarded as the crowning masterpiece of its kind.

The purpose of the reliquary was to protect the relic and at the same time to honor it by enclosing it in a precious receptacle designed to emphasize the sacred character of the trust. To this end, the reliquary bore an inscription or an iconographical representation explaining the subject, or it displayed the relic, or it called the relic to mind through its shape. Caskets, and closed reliquaries generally, corresponded to the first of these purposes. The second was expressed by monstrances, which reached their full stature in Gothic times. The third, which goes back to very early medieval times, would correspond to reliquaries that reproduced the shape of the relic, particularly of the human body or a part of it.

As we have shown from examples of arm and head reliquaries, the practice of shaping reliquaries to represent the human body, in whole or in part, did not exclude other practices. Thus the Reliquary of the Finger of St. Julian in the Treasury of Le Mans was a closed vertical piece bearing the inscription, "Le doy de Mons. S. Julien" while the reliquary of the hand of St. Attala in the church of La Madeleine in Strasbourg (p. 55) shows the skeleton of the hand in a monstrance, and at Brienne, the relic is in the shape of a finger, which is held by John the Baptist (p. 54). But this type of mimesis between subject and object is not peculiar to human forms. There is a general tendency to translate the idea represented by the relics by a shape suggestive of that idea. The Reliquary of the Holy Candle at Arras recalls the shape of a candle. At Trier, the Holy Nail is enclosed in a tenth-century case of gold and cloisonné enamel in the shape of a nail. And it was rare for relics of the True Cross—the casket reliquary in the Treasury of Toulouse (pl. 240) and the Reliquary at Bouillac (pl. 226) are exceptional in this respect—not to be placed in reliquaries in the form of a cross or in reliquaries on which the cross is represented (*staurothecae,* panel reliquaries such as the Floreffe polyptych, or votive crowns like that of St. Louis in the Louvre).

Now that we have made these points, the question arises as to when these representations of the human body began, and in what order. Did the part precede the whole? Were fragments attempted —head, arm, foot—before the statue as a whole? This problem, related to that of the return to figurative art and sculpture in the round which begins in the Carolingian period, concerns religion to the same degree as it concerns art, as we noted earlier in connection with "Majesties."

The relic was deemed a miraculous object; indeed, it was often believed to have healing powers. This belief is evidenced by the use of encolpia—humble phials of earthenware for pilgrims, sumptuous gold jewels for kings and princes—worn upon the breast as a protection against evil spells or maladies of one kind or another. Only one such piece, the Talisman of Charlemagne, has survived of a series of "amulets" mentioned in ninth-century wills such as those of King Bérenger or Count Everard. By association of ideas, words, or forms between the nature of the relic and the purpose and shape of the reliquary enshrining it, this virtue was sometimes attached to specific cases, a phenomenon corresponding to what in our own day we call specialization (indeed, Bernard of Angers uses that term when he says that St. Foy's "specialty" was the deliverance of

BRIENNE. Statuette reliquary of the finger of John the Baptist

prisoners). At Evron, a relic was venerated which had been brought back from the Holy Land; it consisted of particles of white limestone from the cave of Bethlehem known as *tortae* or, on account of its whiteness and its origin, "milk of the Virgin." By analogy, this Holy Milk became beneficent: "Women whose breasts dried up for lack of milk," wrote the historian of the bishops of Le Mans in the seventeenth century, experienced "great relief from their infirmities . . . after fulfilling their vows." The devotion to the "belt of the Virgin" of Le-Puy-Notre-Dame illustrates a similar principle. Sterile women would gird themselves with it. Anne of Austria had it brought to St.-Germain. And in thanksgiving after the birth of Louis XIV, she presented the Treasury of Chartres with some small silver-gilt dolls which probably resembled those curious, swaddled infants, fashioned in the nineteenth century, which are preserved in the Treasury of Angers (p. 56). Such ancient beliefs have at all times found a very direct means of requesting favors and expressing thanks for favors received in the practice of ex-votos, by reason of the figurative nature of the latter. There is a striking resemblance, indeed, between the group of reliquaries which might be called "orthopedic" (shoulder blades, ribs, legs, etc.) and their plaster equivalents, brought by the beneficiaries of miraculous cures to the pilgrimage shrines.

As Shrade has pointed out, the "power" of the relic, as reflected in the idea of miracle, achieves a "presence" through its figured representation in the reliquary which has always especially attracted popular devotion, and against which intellectuals have protested since the days of Bernard of Angers, regarding it as a survival of idolatry. The form of this category of reliquaries was derived from the idea that they represented. And to explain the process whereby Carolingian craftsmen succeeded in rediscovering the concept of the three-dimensional human form in space, it might be tempting to theorize that they passed from the idea of a finger, foot, or arm suggested by the relic, which they sought to "express" in order to honor it and render it present to the faithful, to the form of that finger, foot, or arm. From there they went on to the idea and form of a bust and a head and, finally, having thus learned to represent each individual part of the body, they were able to fashion complete statues.

This theory has been developed in particular by Keller, who cites very early examples of limb reliquaries. Although the earliest surviving examples date from the tenth century (foot of St. Andrew at Trier), and the beginning of the eleventh (arm in the Varzy Treasury, fig. 40), the records mention some in existence in the ninth century, both in the treasuries of the North and in those of the South (contrary to the opinion of Molinier, who believed that they were localized in Aquitaine, that is, in the region par excellence of the "Majesties"). At Saint-Denis, Abbot Fardulf ordered a finger to be enshrined in a reliquary shaped like a hand. And there are references to head reliquaries at Langres (bust of St. Mamas), at Nevers, and at Vienne, where Boso, first king of Provence, who died in 887, presented the cathedral with a crowned bust reliquary of St. Maurice, the appearance of which has been preserved in a seventeenth-century sketch. These examples, and particularly the last, would seem to confirm Keller's view, since limb or bust reliquaries were earlier in date than statue reliquaries, provided that we agree with Bréhier that the statue of St. Foy of Conques, may be dated to the end of the tenth century, as also the gold Virgin of Clermont. But if we date it in the last quarter of the ninth century, as we have suggested, our oldest statue reliquary—and we have pointed out that it was probably not a prototype—would be contemporary with the Vienne bust.

STRASBOURG.
Reliquary of the hand of St. Attala

If this is the case, it becomes difficult to believe that the reliquaries in the shape of limbs preceded statue reliquaries and led gradually through an improved knowledge of forms to the creation of statues. The problem is not the same, however, in the North as in the South, since the principle of limb-shaped reliquaries, as well as that of bust reliquaries, seems to have been accepted by the northern clergy, whereas that of a complete and realistic statue was rejected; the practice in Aquitaine, on the other hand, as related by Bernard of Angers, was to divide the body of the saint into two parts, as had been done in the case of St. Foy, one part being placed in a *theca*, or casket, and the other—the head—in a reliquary in the form of a statue.

But the misgivings evinced by the northern clergy up to about the year 1000 on the subject of *imagines,* that is, images of saints made in human proportions and aspect which Bernard of Angers at first called idols when he discovered them on his journey to Conques, did not apply to two particular types of human representation, that of "Our Lord on the Cross," and that of the Virgin, who had been proclaimed Theotokos, or Mother of God, at the council of Ephesus in 431. It is therefore not surprising that such representations should have apeared long before those of saints, whether fragmentary or complete. This is where the theory we have described appears weakest. Moreover, since the hostility to images did not extend to the representation of certain human forms which were in no danger of being worshiped, there was no objection, from a religious point of view, to the fashioning of statuettes such as the one of bronze, inspired by an ancient model, representing Charlemagne, now in the Louvre. But such works were probably few, and technical inadequacies made possible only small-scale pieces. The example is still sometimes cited of an equestrian statue of gilded wood that Salomon, duke of Britanny, was believed to have ordered made in his image, toward the close of the ninth century, and to have sent to Pope Adrian II, in the naïve hope that he would thus be absolved from fulfilling his vow to journey to Rome. However, the text relating this marvelous tale may be apocryphal.

The earliest representation we possess of a crucified Christ is a fifth-century Byzantine ivory now in the British Museum, where Christ is still beardless, in the Hellenistic tradition. The tradition lingered in rare examples up to the tenth century, as in the ivory in the Narbonne Treasury (pl. 245). In the sixth century, we find the Syrian type of bearded Christ on the door of Santa Sabina in Rome, and on the Syriac Evangeliary of Rabula; this type was to become the rule. We know from literary sources that representations of Christ executed in the round had existed previously to those now surviving, among which we might cite the ninth-century stone Christ in the church of Saint-Pantaléon-lès-Autun (of which only the head remains), and the wood Christ of Gero, in Cologne Cathedral, of the Ottonian period. And it is logical to assume that representations of the human figure in the round began with representations of Christ. At first, the faithful were disconcerted by them, as we saw from the incident of the icon placed in the Cathedral of Narbonne in the sixth century. Two centuries later, however, Bishop Théodard had a great gold crucifix placed in the entrance to the choir of the same Cathedral enshrining a relic of the True Cross, and this time there was no outcry. At Conques, Bernard of Angers saw "a crucifix of considerable dimensions, entirely of fine silver, with the exception of the crown and the loin cloth, which were of gold." These figured representations of Christ, already frequent in the eighth century, abounded in the ninth. C. Beutler has shown that the bronze Christ in St. Peter's at Rome is a sixteenth-century copy of a Carolingian Christ. The

ANGERS. Dolls

type of Ottonian Christs which succeeded that of Gero, and of which Wesemberg has made a study, namely, the silver one of Bernard of Hildesheim or the bronze one of Ringelheim, was developed in France in a series of bronze Christs of which that of Saint-Mars-sous-la-Futaye (pl. 175) is one. These figures of Christ are interesting not only because they attempt to define the volume of the human body, but also because they attempt for the first time to express feelings. Suffering and resignation appear on the features. This is very apparent in the figures on the crosses of precious metalwork of the Ottonian period, that of Archbishop Heribert in the Treasury of Milan, that on the Reliquary of Pepin in the Treasury of Conques (pl. 207).

This concern with psychology, this attempt to translate human feelings, is not apparent in the series of statue reliquaries of the Virgin Mother holding her Child in her lap, with the Child giving his blessing. From literary sources we know of eighth-century statues of this kind; for instance, the gold Virgin that Pope Gregory III presented to the church of Santa Maria Maggiore in Rome. They were *sedes sapientiae,* thrones of wisdom, grave and impassible sovereigns, the rigorous symbolism of which was not abandoned until the beginning of the Gothic period. The great silvered Virgin of the Evron Treasury (pl. 161) made around the year 1200 was still in that tradition. The Virgin in the Roncevaux Treasury also belongs to this series, but here another conception is already discernible, a more human one, in which there is apparent that air of graciousness which was to characterize Marian statuary in the fourteenth century.

All these religious representations—Christ crucified, *sedes sapientiae,* Majesties, limbs, busts—whose emergence corresponded to the development of doctrine or the liturgy, were reliquaries. This sacred origin of the renaissance of plastic art in the medieval West, achieved by craftsmen working with precious materials, is confirmation of the primordial role played by the treasures of the churches in the over-all history of art.

PLANCHES

AUVERGNE

CANNAT Ivory plaque on back cover of an Evangeliary (detail)

GANNAT Jeweled front cover of an Evangeliary

LE MONASTIER Textile with griffins (detail)

64 MAURS Crosier (detail of volute)

MAURS Bust reliquary of St. Cesarius

SAINT-NECTAIRE
Bust reliquary of
St. Baudimus ▶

BURGUNDY

SAULIEU Ivory plaque on the cover of the so-called Evangeliary of Charlemagne

69

70 SAULIEU Ivory plaque on the cover of the so-called Evangeliary of Charlemagne

72 Detail of plate 71

SENS Ciboruim

AUTUN Shroud of St. Lazarus (detail)

BRITTANY

PLOURGOURVEST Reliquary

SAINT-GILDAS-DE-RHUYS Knee and thigh reliquary of St. Gildas

80 VANNES Marriage casket (details)

CHAMPAGNE

84 REIMS Reliquary of Samson

REIMS Reliquary of SS. Sixtus and Sinicius

REIMS Reliquary of the Holy Thorn

Deta
of reliquar
on plate 88

REIMS Reliquary of the Resurrection, and deta

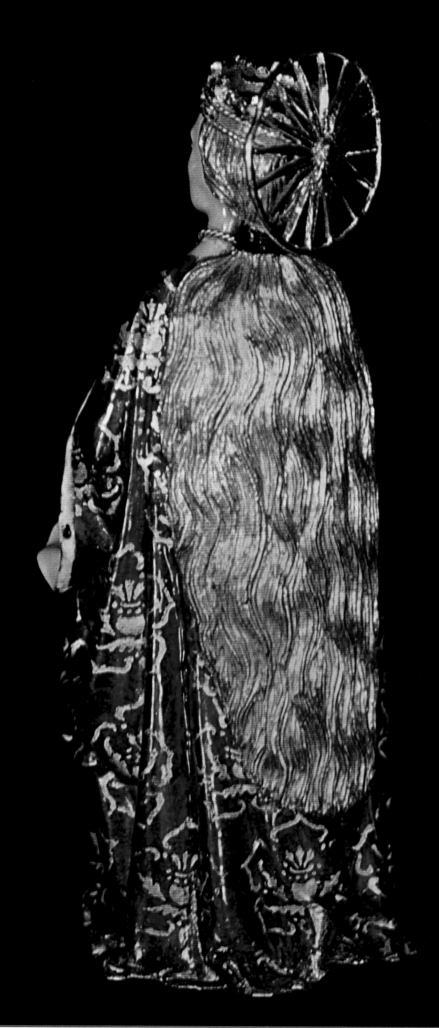

TROYES Ivory casket

TROYES Cloisonné enamel medallions

TROYES Champlevé enamel plaques

DAUPHINE
PROVENCE

LUCERAM St. Margaret and the Dragon

ARLES Ivory belt buckle of St. Cesarius

102   SAINT-ANTOINE-EN-VIENNOIS Crucifix (detail)

FLANDERS
ARTOIS
PICARDY

106 AMIENS Ciborium from the Abbey of Le Paraclet

AMIENS Crown reliquary from the Abbey of Le Paraclet

RAS Phylactery reliquary of the tooth of St. Nicholas
109

BOULOGNE-SUR-MER Reliquary of the Precious Blood

112 **MONTREUIL-SUR-MER** Crosier of St. Austreberta (detail)

MUBEUGE Crosier of St. Aldegundis (detail)

Reliquary of the veil of St. Aldegundis, and detail

SAINT-OMER Cross reliquary from the Abbey of Clairmarais

LORRAINE
ALSACE

METZ Embroidered silk, called the Cope of Charlemagne (detail)

120   METZ Ivory crosier (detail)

REININGUE Casket of St. Romanus (detail)

NANCY Chalice and paten of St. Gauzelin ▶

NANCY Back and front covers of the Evangeliary of St. Gauzeli

125

126 SAINT-NICOLAS-DU-PORT The Boat of the Cardinal of Lorraine

LYONNAIS
SAVOIE

ELLENTRE Processional cross (detail)   CHAMBERY Ivory diptych (detail) ▶

132 LYONS Plaque of a book cover showing Christ in Majesty

ons Gemellione (detail)

LYONS Agate cross   MOUTIERS Champlevé enamel casket (detail)

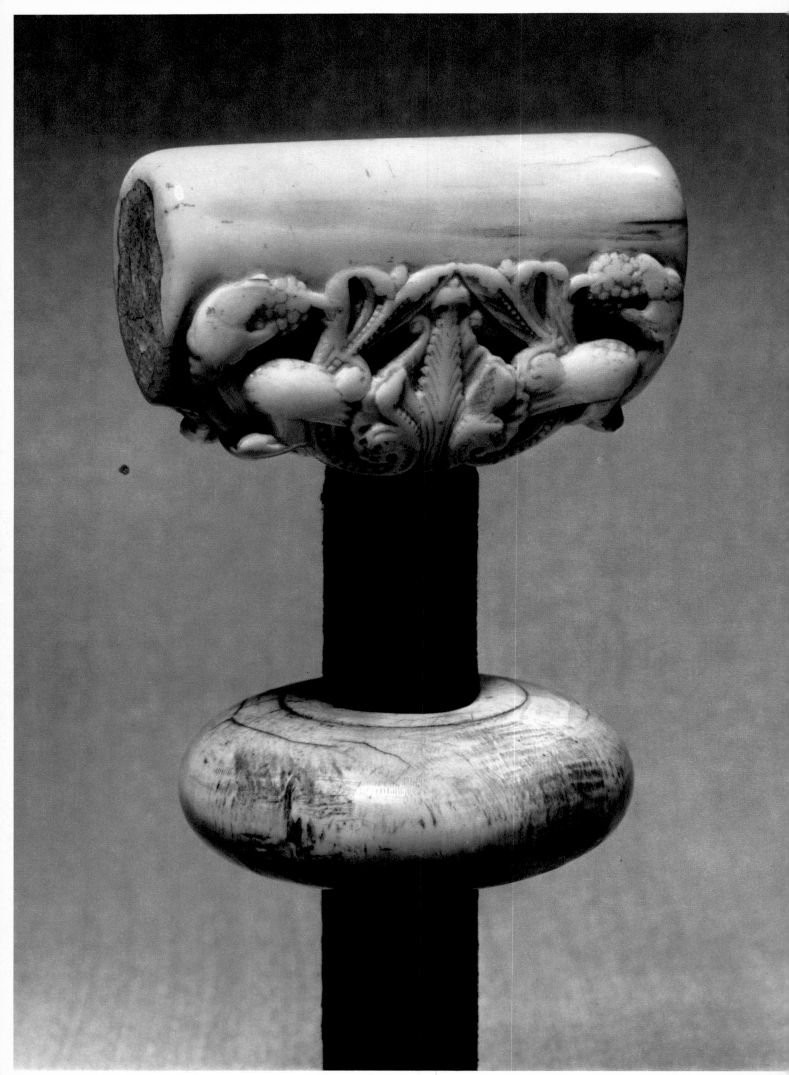

MOUTIERS Ivory statuette of Christ (detail)

SEEZ Monstrance, and det.

SALLANCHES Monstrance, and det.

SIXT Miter. Details on following pages

143

NORMANDY
ILE-DE-FRANCE

CHARTRES Casket of St. Anianus.   Detail on following pages   147

CHARTRES Reliquary of the Circumcision

152 CHARTRES Incense boat

EVREUX Casket of St. Taurinus. Detail above and on following pages

ROUEN Casket of St. Romanus

LOIRE VALLEY

EVRON Our Lady of the Thorn, and deta

EVRON Virgin and Child, and det.

EVRON Reliquary of Our Lady's Milk (detail)

Back view of angel reliquary on plate 168 ▶

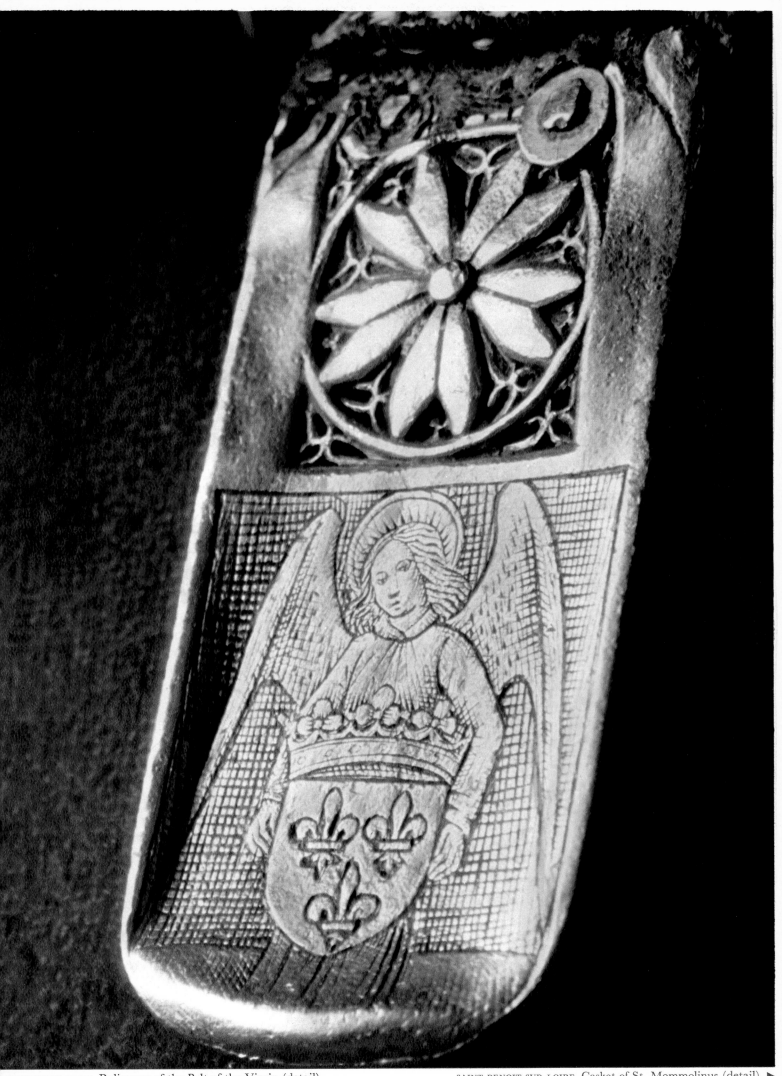

ORLEANS Cloisonné enamel disks (detail

174   SAINT-CALAIS Shroud of St. Carilefus of Calais (detail)

SAINT-MARS-SOUS-LA-FUTAYE Processional cross (detail)

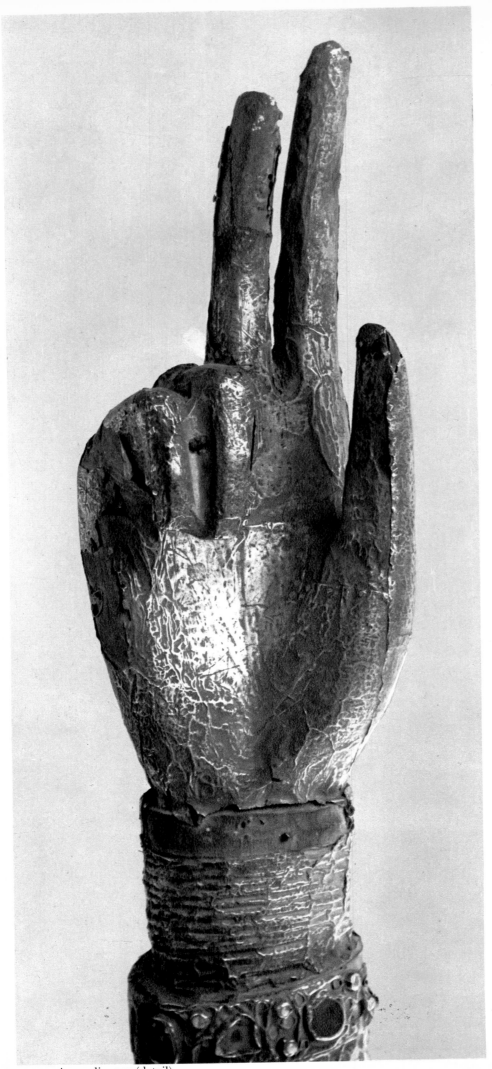

VARZY Arm reliquary (detail)

POITOU
LIMOUSIN

Detail of interior of plate 181

Small portable reliquary, interior of plate 182

184   Small gold reliquary, interior of plate 185

CHARROUX Reliquary   GIMEL Casket of St. Stephen (detail) ▶

AMBAZAC Casket of St. Stephen of Muret (detail)

SAINT-SULPICE-LES-FEUILLES Angel reliquary, and deta

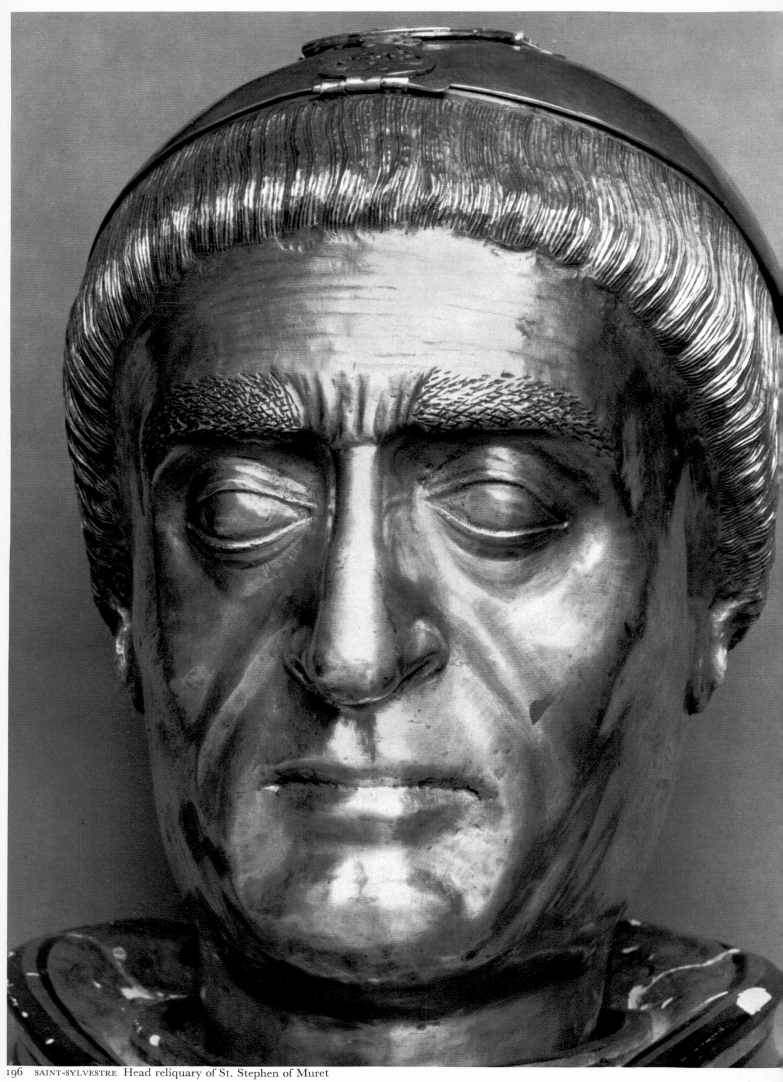

196 SAINT-SYLVESTRE Head reliquary of St. Stephen of Muret

SAINT-BONNET-AVALOUZE Casket

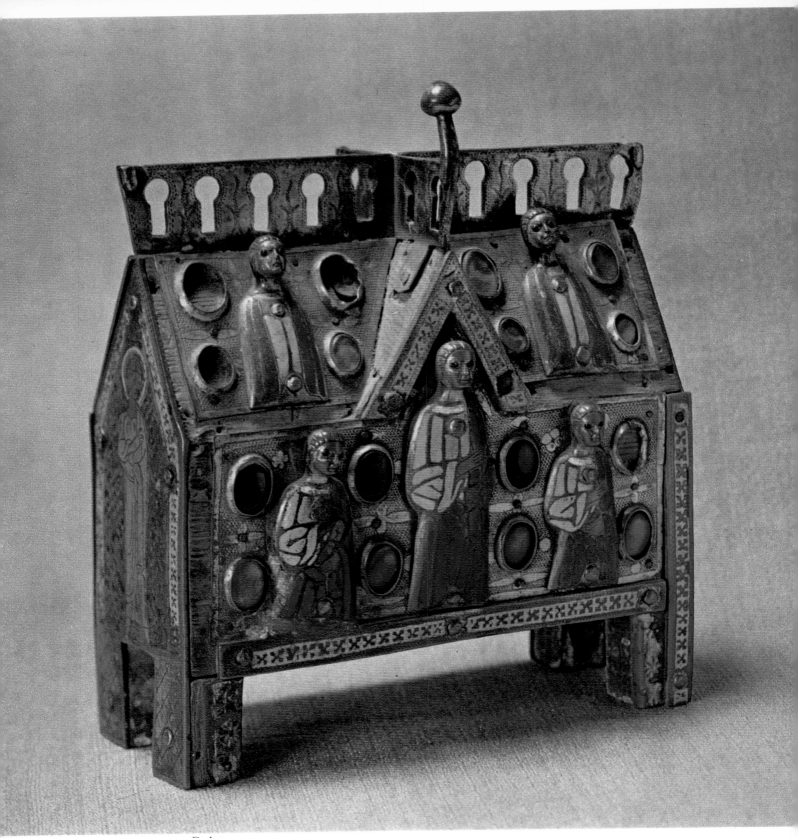

SAINT-PANTALEON-DE-LA-LAPLEAU Casket

ROUERGUE
AQUITAINE

Detail of plate 201

NQUES Fragment of an altar frontal

Detail of reliquary on plate 206 ▶

CONQUES Back and front of the Reliquary of Pep

208 Detail of plate 207

NQUES Gold repoussé plaque of the Crucifixion

210 CONQUES Pentagonal reliquary

ONQUES Hexagonal reliquary

CONQUES Lantern reliquary, and deta

CONQUES Reliquary of Pope Pascal, and deta

CONQUES Casket

220 CONQUES Virgin and Child reliquary (detail)

CONQUES Arm reliquary of St. George

CONQUES Triptych reliquary

t. Foy (detail of back of processional cross on plate 224)

CONQUES Processional cross, and deta

BOUILLAC Casket of the Crucifixion, and det

LAMOTHE-CAPDEVILLE Two views of a disk reliqua

ARRANCOLIN Casket of St. Ebbo (detail)

236 SEIX Monstrance reliquary of St. Stephen

SAINT-BERTRAND-DE-COMMINGES Cope of the Virgin (detail)

SAINT-BERTRAND-DE-COMMINGES Cope of the Passion (detail) ▶

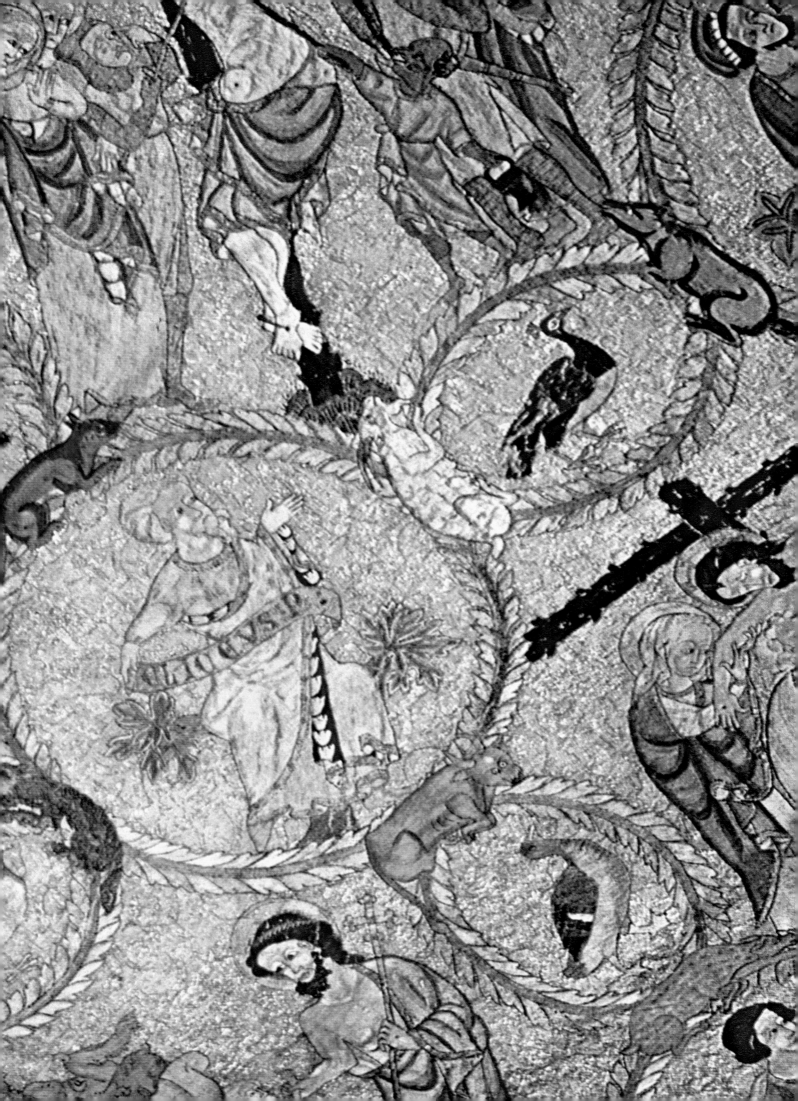

SATR
NIN
VS

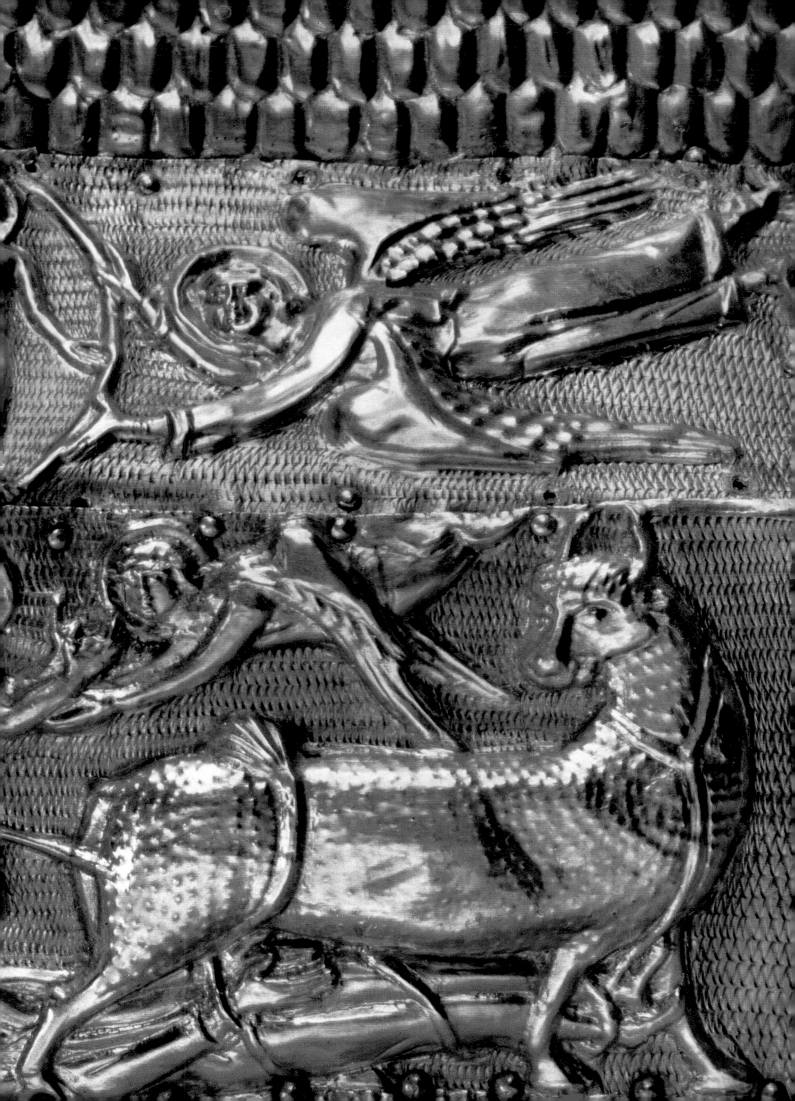

ROUSSILLON
LANGUEDOC

NARBONNE Ivory box

NARBONNE Reliquary of St. Prudentius

RIGARDA Monstrance reliquary, and deta

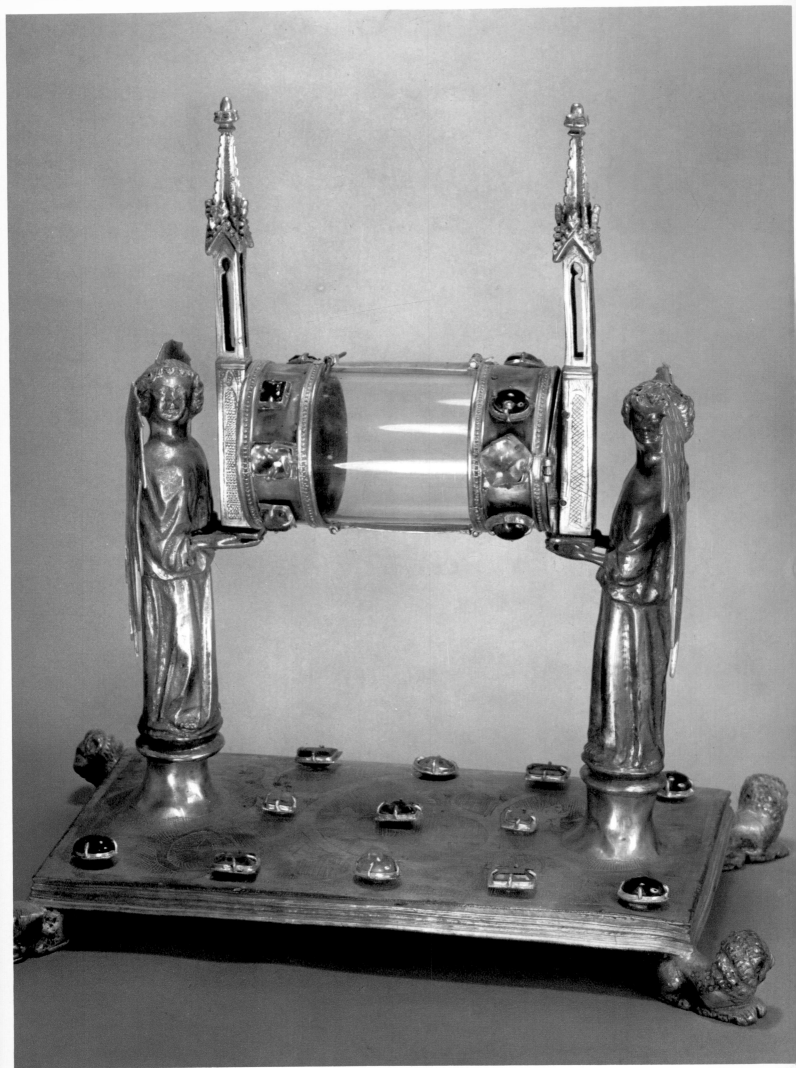

SAINT-POLYCARPE Head reliquary of St. Benedict (detail)   253

254 QUARANTE Head reliquary of John the Baptist

THUIR Virgin and Child

COMMENTARIES

Auvergne

GANNAT (Allier)

EVANGELIARY. 12th century. Front cover: silver gilt on wood; back cover: ivory plaque (9th–10th century) in vermeil border. H. 11⅞", w. 9". Presbytery, Sainte-Croix.

pl. 62   In the center of the front cover is a large Antique onyx cameo carved with the head of a Roman emperor. Above and below the cameo are plaques covered with a brown glaze decorated with a geometric design that includes the fleur-de-lis; down either side of the cover, medallions of champlevé enamel, two of which are now lost; various cabochon gems, one of which is an amethyst with an antique intaglio of a Victory supported by griffins. The plaques and medallions are Mosan work of the twelfth century.

pl. 61   On the ivory plaque of the back cover is a Crucifixion scene: Christ on the cross surrounded by angels, the Virgin and St. John, and figures representing the Church and the Synagogue; below, the soldier with the lance and Longinus with the sponge. A serpent is curled around the foot of the cross. In the lower register (not reproduced) is a scene of the Holy Women at the Sepulcher. This work has been atributed to the school of Metz of the ninth–tenth century, whose favorite theme was the Crucifixion.

LE MONASTIER (Haute-Loire)

TEXTILE WITH GRIFFINS. Byzantine? 10th century? Silk samite. W. 25⅝", l. 20¾". Church of Le Monastier.

The ancient abbey of Le Monastier, founded in the seventh century by St. Calminius in a wild and remote part of Le Velay, in the neighborhood of Le Puy, has preserved the bust reliquary of St. Chaffre (St. Theofredus), the second abbot, who died a martyr at the hands of the Saracens in 732. This twelfth-century bust, covered with thin sheets of silver, housed two magnificent silks. One of them, dating from the seventh century and supposedly of Spanish origin, is decorated with peacocks facing each other in beaded medallions.

pl. 63   The other, which is the more beautiful, portrays magnificent griffins face to face on either side of a hom (tree of life). Their green bodies outlined in yellow stand out against a dark red ground. They have red circles on their bodies and white claws. In their beaks they grasp small quadrupeds. In the area between their wings and tails are small, highly stylized eagles. The hom, in the form of a palmette tree, is also highly stylized, its upright simulating the trunk and the two horizontals, the branches, which support two pairs of small animals (birds and quadrupeds) face to face.

Mme Picard-Schmitter notes (*Monuments et Mémoires publiés par l'Acad. des Inscr. et Belles-lettres*, XLVII, 1953) that although the theme of the quadruped seized by a griffin is found in the art of the Orient and archaic Greece, it does not appear on any fabric before the twelfth century; however, she finds in this silk a stylization which, by comparison with other pieces of the tenth and eleventh centuries, in particular, the silk decorated with winged horses in the Vatican, leads her to attribute it to Byzantine workmanship of the tenth century.

MAURS (Cantal)

BUST RELIQUARY OF ST. CESARIUS. End of 12th century. Silver and copper gilt on a wood core. H. 35⅞". Church of Maurs.

pl. 65   The bust reliquary of St. Cesarius, bishop of Arles (died 542), contains a relic that is supposed to have been brought to this small city of the Auvergne after the destruction of the saint's tomb in the eighth century by the Saracens. The saint, represented in half length, is attired in liturgical vestments: the chasuble and stole are of copper gilt; the alb, of silver; the orphreys are decorated with cabochons arranged in rectangular patterns of groups of five. A small door of silver gilt, which opens on the relic enclosed in the breast, is framed by a rich border of filigree and precious stones. The other side of the door is engraved with an inscription in Gothic characters which indicates the nature of the relic: HIC EST CAPUT SANCTI CESARII ARELATENSIS EPISCOPI (Here is the head of St. Cesarius, bishop of Arles). There is another opening in the back, with a door of copper gilt decorated with scrolls and five small enamels. The head and the hands, with inordinately long fingers, are of polychromed wood.

The piece is not as sophisticated as the St. Baudimus of Saint-Nectaire (pl. 67), but is no less impressive in its primitive ingenuousness; the very awkwardness of the workmanship lends it a fierce grandeur which cannot fail to impress.

1

CROSIER. 13th century. Copper gilt and enamel. H. 12¼". Church of Maurs.

fig. 1   In addition to the bust reliquary of St. Cesarius, which constitutes the main part of its treasure, Maurs possesses a crosier of copper gilt and enamel of which only the volute, the socket, and the knob remain. Chased and gilded foliate scrolls stand out against a ground of blue-green enamel. Five of the eight precious stones that originally adorned it are still in place. The Annunciation is *pl. 64* depicted in the volute. The knob, decorated with interlaced chimeras, is supported by three lizards with coiled tails.

MOZAC (Puy-de-Dôme)

CASKET OF ST. CALMINIUS. End of 12th–beginning of 13th century. Enameled copper. H. 18⅞", w. 32¼". Saint-Pierre.

The large casket of St. Calminius was intended to house the saint's relics, which had been found in the church of Laguenne in 1172. It is one of a series of caskets "with enameled ground." The front consists of six large plaques: in the center, Christ in Majesty surrounded by symbols of the Evangelists; below, the Crucifixion; and distributed by threes on the remaining four plaques, the twelve Apostles, who stand out in relief under engraved arcades. The framing strips are decorated *fig. 2* with Kufic characters. The back also consists of six panels: reserved figures on an enameled ground of rosettes who

2

depict the story of St. Calminius and his wife, St. Namadia. On the sixth panel (upper right), is the figure of the abbot of Mozac, who commissioned the casket, with the inscription: PETRUS ABBAS MAUZIACUS FECIT CAPSAM PRECIO[SAM]. By reason of this inscription, the casket has been assigned a date earlier than 1181, when Abbot Peter III was at Mozac, but the date is in dispute.

ORCIVAL (Puy-de-Dôme)

VIRGIN IN MAJESTY. 12th century. Silver and silver gilt repoussé on a wood core. H. 29½". Church of Orcival.

pl. 66   The Virgin of Orcival is without doubt the most celebrated of the Romanesque Virgins of the Auvergne. It is the object of fervent devotion and still attracts a large number of pilgrims each year. The origin of this pilgrimage goes very far back and merges with legend. Tradition has it that the first image of the Virgin to be venerated had been sculptured by the Evangelist Luke. The Virgin of Orcival had been saved from destruction at the time of the Norman invasions and hidden by the inhabitants in a subterranean cavern known as the "Tomb of the Virgin." In the eleventh century, a small oratory was consecrated in honor of the statue; then, owing to the crowds of worshipers, a proper church was undertaken. At night, however, a mysterious hand would destroy whatever had been erected during the day. The discouraged workers were about to give up the job, believing that the Virgin was not satisfied with the site, but the master builder decided to throw his hammer into the air and to raise the new church wherever it fell. This was done. Nevertheless, once the building was completed, the Virgin continued to flee, returning "to her hiding place." It was therefore decided that, once a year, on Ascension Day, she should be solemnly escorted to the site of the "tomb." Thus the pilgrimage was born.

The Virgin is seated in majesty, holding the Child directly in front of her; the hieratic pose is consonant with the iconography defined by the Council of Ephesus which, in 431, had proclaimed Christ's divinity from the moment of his conception and termed the Virgin, Theotokos, or Mother of God. The statue, sheathed with sheets of silver and silver gilt in repoussé on a wood core, carries on the tradition of statue reliquaries originating in the pre-Romanesque period in southern France. According to Bréhier ("La Cathédrale de Clermont au Xᵉ siècle et la statue d'or de la Vierge," *Renaissance de l'Art français*, 1924, pp. 205ff)—whose opinion we do not follow here—the prototype of these statues was the gold Virgin that Stephen II, bishop of Clermont, commissioned the clerk, Alléaume, to make in 956, which we know from an illumination in a manuscript in the library of Clermont-Ferrand.

Unfortunately, the Virgin of Orcival suffered damage in the course of the centuries, and the repairs were often very clumsily done. Restoration work undertaken a few years ago created a veritable "technical dossier," and made it possible to remove certain deplorable alterations and to restore its original character to this magnificent work.

SAINT-NECTAIRE (Puy-de-Dôme)

BUST RELIQUARY OF ST. BAUDIMUS. End of 12th century. Copper gilt on a wood core. H. 28¾". Church of Saint-Nectaire.

pl. 67   The bust reliquary of St. Baudimus is one of the most impressive of the Middle Ages with its proud head ringed with short hair that begins at the tonsure and ends in little curls, the beard indicated by stippled engraving, the eyes, with an impenetrable expression, of black and white horn. The work illustrates what has already been said about the techniques employed in southwestern France in the Romanesque period: a torso formed of a tree trunk hollowed and shaped with a gouge by a joiner rather than a sculptor, on which sheets of repoussé metal were fitted, the art of the sculptor being confined to working on the metal of the head and hands. These observations stem from an analysis of the different parts composing the piece.

The wooden core is of walnut. It is made up of five parts held together by means of tenons, without gluing. *fig. 3* The torso consists of a hollowed-out tree trunk, its form barely indicated, open in the back. The base is oval. Because the excessively thin edges splintered, probably at a very early stage, the piece was braced by means of leather thongs to prevent further separation. To ensure stability, a piece, which created the socle, reinforced the oval of the base, to which it was attached with wooden

3

pins. The hollowed space inside the torso tapers toward the top, ending in a circular cavity into which the neck is fitted, held in place by pegs; the neck is a piece of hollowed branch, roughly gouged into cylindrical form. The head is set on this hollow cylinder (as in the case of St. Foy of Conques, pl. 201). The arms, held by square wooden pins, are conical stumps onto which the copper hands were fitted. The back is a board fastened with pins which could be removed to insert the relic.

On this wooden core, large copper-gilt plaques were fitted, embossed with sharp folds similar in style to the draperies of the Virgin of Beaulieu (pl. 179); these repre-

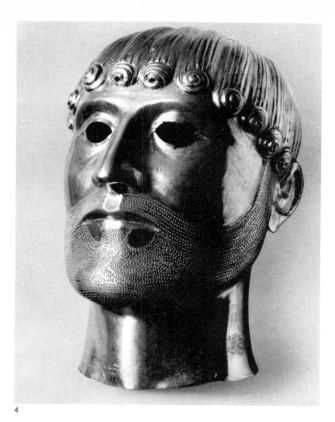

4

5

Burgundy

pl. 69
pl. 70

SAULIEU *(Côte d'Or)*

IVORY PLAQUES. 6th or 7th century. H. 7⅛″, w. 4¾″. Saint-Andoche.

The so-called Evangeliary of Charlemagne, which was at one time in the Treasury of the collegiate chapter of Saint-Andoche of Saulieu, dates from the twelfth century, and comes from Italy. The two ivory plaques of the binding, framed by silver strips of the Gothic period, are sixth- or seventh-century pieces. One shows the Virgin and Child between two angels. Each of the figures holds one hand open on the breast in token of reverence. On the other, a seated and bearded Christ is flanked by two Apostles, one of whom makes the same gesture.

These plaques may be compared with the diptych in five compartments of St. Lupicinus, in the Bibliothèque Nationale, which, being less highly stylized, seems to be the earlier work. For a long time it was accepted that ivory work had completely disappeared in Gaul during Merovingian times, and that these ivories had originated in either Antioch or Alexandria. The contrary view is now accepted, thanks to Volbach's studies (*Elfenbeinarbeiten der Spätantike und des frühen Mittelalters*, Mainz, 1952). Volbach has shown that the ivory work of Byzantium had penetrated Gaul in the sixth century, where the Byzantine style was interpreted in somewhat heavier form in the workshops established at Trier and in southern France. The crude aspect of the Saulieu ivories would seem to bear out the view that they are a late and decadent product of those workshops.

SENS *(Yonne)*

p. 16
p. 45
p. 22

Throughout the Middle Ages, Sens was the seat of the archdiocese to which the diocese of Paris belonged. Although it suffered as severely as the rest, its Cathedral Treasury still retains many objects which cause it to be ranked as one of the most important in France. It possesses valuable pieces of precious metalwork: a small portable casket of the eighth century, a thirteenth-century ciborium of silver gilt known as the Holy Cup, a fourteenth-century reliquary of St. Stephen, a number of crosses—one of which, decorated with filigree work, comes from the church of Nailly, while another, known as the Reliquary of the True Cross, is adorned with pearls and rubies—caskets, crosiers, enameled thirteenth-century pyxes, etc.; ivories: a small cylindrical box carved with hunting scenes, which had been a jewelry box in antiquity, a liturgical comb believed to have belonged to St. Lupus, a small thirteenth-century Byzantine casket known as the *Sainte Chasse*; magnificent tapestries, the most celebrated of which are those of the Coronation of the Virgin and the Adoration of the Magi, both dating from the end of the fifteenth century, and presented to the Cathedral about 1547 by Cardinal Louis de Bourbon; very interesting sacerdotal vestments, such as the chasuble of St. Ebbo (died 750), a Byzantine silk on a white ground strewn with rosettes and golden-yellow vine leaves, the chasuble of St. Thomas à Becket (died 1170), a vestment of St. Edme and, later in date, the chasuble of Queen Blanche of Navarre, an Italian silk of the fourteenth century.

But the most valuable part of the treasury is an extraordinary collection of ancient textiles—Byzantine, Persian, Coptic, Hispano-Moorish, Sicilian—which would have to be enumerated and described to convey some notion of the importance of what is a veritable "museum of textiles." The collection comprises some hundred odd pieces, ranging from the largest, such as the shroud of St. Siviard (length 53¼″, width 33½″), which is a seventh-century Byzantine textile decorated with griffins set in medallions, or that of St. Columba and St. Lupus (length 94½″ width 46½″), a tenth- or eleventh-century Byzantine stuff decorated with lions facing each other in

fig. 4
fig. 5

sent the chasuble worn by the saint over a tight-sleeved alb that grips the forearms in concentric folds and is decorated below in diamond point. Metal bands edged with torsades, which serve as butt straps, represent the orphreys, which are decorated with glass paste and cabochons, many of which are missing.

The rudimentary technique of these strips and plaques contrasts with that of the head and hands, which is extremely skillful. The head is of cast copper. The hair is engraved with remarkable vigor with a tracer. The beard is indicated by stippling. The treatment of the eyes remains in the Roman tradition: the outline of the upper lid covers the lower lid at its outer corner, while a depression inside the head holds the horn globes of the eyes, which are kept in place by the wax filling of the head (the present wax, which is a pure wax, seems to be original). The magnificent hands are of cast copper, as the head. Only the nails are reworked. The right hand is raised in a hortatory gesture; the left holds an object which has not yet been identified.

The treatment of the hair and beard is similar to that of a relief in the cloister of Moissac (c. 1110). The bust may be placed in the first half of the twelfth century.

Tradition has it that St. Baudimus was one of the priests who accompanied St. Nectarius, a disciple of St. Austremonius, first bishop of Clermont, who evangelized the province of Auvergne.

beaded medallions, to the smallest fragments, measuring no more than a few square inches but nevertheless most valuable for the study of ancient textiles. This wealth is to be explained by the history of the Treasury. As far back as the fourth century, Bishop Ursicinius, on his return from the exile into which he had been sent by the Emperor Constans for opposing Arianism, brought back from Jerusalem the relics of the Holy Innocents, and from Caesarea in Cappadocia those of St. Mammes. In the eighteenth century, numerous relics from the great abbeys of Saint-Pierre-le-Vif and Sainte-Colombe were added to the Treasury. At the time of the Revolution, these relics were removed from their precious metal caskets and placed in chests together with the materials in which they had been wrapped. During the nineteenth century they became the subject of study, and the materials were carefully collected and inventoried.

SHROUD OF ST. VICTOR. Second half of 8th century? Silk samite. W. 27⅛″, l. 63¾″. Treasury of the Cathedral.

pl. 74 One of the best known of the textiles is a large Byzantine samite known as the Shroud of St. Victor, believed to have been brought to Sens in 769 by St. Willicarius, who had been abbot of Saint-Maurice d'Agaune before becoming archbishop of Sens. He presented his new church with the remains of the martyred soldier of the Theban legion, which were wrapped in this silk. In an oval medallion outlined in torsades of pearls, a long-haired figure dressed in a short tunic repels two lions reared against him, while two others attack his feet. Some have interpreted the figure as the giant Gilgamesh; others, as Daniel in the lions' den; others again, on account of the long hair, as a female martyr. This silk, the theme of which also occurs on a piece at St. Walburga of Eichstätt in Bavaria, was fashioned in imitation of Sassanian models and probably originated in Constantinople in the second half of the eighth century. In technique, it is comparable to the elephant-tamer silk from Charlemagne's tomb at Aachen.

IVORY CASKET. Byzantine, 13th century. H. 13¾″, diameter 11⅞″. Treasury of the Cathedral.

pls. 71, 72 The small Byzantine ivory casket known as the *Sainte Chasse,* whose design of twelve sides culminating in a conical roof is reminiscent of the shape of Carolingian baptisteries, is carved with scenes from the lives of David and Joseph in superposed registers. The top registers of each side consist of semicircular arches that enclose animals face to face—peacocks, winged lions—like those frequently found on Oriental stuffs. The spandrels and the lower bands of these tympanums are decorated with foliate motifs similar to those found in the West during the Gothic period. For this reason, it does not seem possible to assign to the piece a date earlier than the thirteenth century, although it has thus far been regarded as belonging to the tenth. The base of the hinged lid is surrounded by an enameled band of thirteenth-century workmanship. The ivory was originally painted and gilded, and bore a Greek inscription. Because of similarities with certain ivories in the British Museum, a Venetian rather than a Byzantine origin has been ascribed to the piece.

CIBORIUM. 13th century. Silver gilt. H. 12¼″, diameter 6½″–7½″. Treasury of the Cathedral.

pl. 73 The silver-gilt ciborium known as the Holy Cup, very simple in design and shape, is one of the earliest to have survived to our day, since it is attributed to the very beginning of the thirteenth century. It belongs to the type of short-footed ciboria, such as that of Alpais in the Louvre, which it recalls, although it has greater elegance. Like the Alpais ciborium, it is composed of two symmetrical parts, the bowl with its foot, and the lid with its terminal knob, both of which are decorated with engraved foliate scrolls and engraved and embossed *fleurons.* Until 1824, it was suspended over the high altar under a canopy held by a bronze angel and housed the

6

reserved Sacrament. In 1541, it was stolen but was found a few days later under some debris. Every year, on August 4, a procession initiated by John Ferrand, archdeacon of Sens, commemorated this recovery. The ciborium escaped being melted down in 1792 thanks to the goldsmith responsible for opening caskets, who ransomed it by donating its equivalent in silver.

COMB OF ST. LUPUS. 7th or 8th century. Ivory, gold filigree, silver gilt, cabochons. H. 8⅞″, w. 4⅜″. Treasury of the Cathedral.

fig. 6 The liturgical comb of St. Lupus, archbishop of Sens (died 623), fashioned of a single piece of ivory dating from the seventh or eighth centuries, consists of a double row of teeth separated by a perforated semicircular arch, within which are shown two lions, face to face, on either side of a horn surmounted by a ram's head. The rim of the arch is outlined by a silver-gilt strip added in the thirteenth century, bearing the inscription PECTEN S. LUPI; the base rests on a gold band enriched with filigree work and cabochons.

A U T U N (Saone-et-Loire)

SHROUD OF ST. LAZARUS. 11th century. Fabric embroidered in silk and gold threads. L. 35½″, w. 66⅛″. Treasury of the Cathedral.

pl. 75 The fabric known as the Shroud of St. Lazarus in the Treasury of Autun is a silk- and gold-thread embroidery composed of six-lobed medallions representing alternately sphinxes and Assyrian-type horsemen with pointed beards and conical hats holding falcons. The field is decorated with stylized foliate scrolls. The ground is blue; the other colors, besides gold, are red, white, yellow, green, and black. This piece, which is believed to date from the eleventh century, is comparable with another material depicting horsemen preserved in Durham Cathedral, which also dates from the eleventh century and which Falke (*Kunstgeschichte des Seidenweberei,* I, Berlin, 1913, p. 113, fig. 175) classifies as Iraqi or Egyptian, but even more with the cope of St. Thomas à Becket in the Cathedral at Fermo, Italy, even though this is later in date, namely, 1116. A recent study has shown that both the Fermo cope and the Shroud of St. Lazarus came from the Almeria workshops in Andalusia. We are thus dealing with a Hispano-Arabic product derived from Sassanian art.

Britanny

PLOUGOURVEST *(Finistère)*

RELIQUARY. 14th century. Silver parcel-gilt. H. 9⅛″, w. 7½″, d. 4″. Saint-Pierre et Saint-Paul.

pl. 77 This "angel" reliquary of the fourteenth century has two peculiarities: the angels are not winged and the reliquary is a double one. It consists of a tablet held by the two angels, and a lower section pierced with semicircular arches which supports the angels. This pedestal is flanked by turrets and stands on feet decorated with seated lions. The sobriety of the entire piece has that suggestion of simplicity which characterizes Breton metalwork.

SAINT-GILDAS-DE-RHUYS *(Morbihan)*

KNEE AND THIGH RELIQUARY. 15th century. Silver gilt on a wood core, cabochons. H. 24¾″, diameter 7⅛″. Treasury of the Church.

According to tradition, the ancient abbey of Saint-Gildas-de-Rhuys was founded by St. Gildas, a celebrated British monk who evangelized Ireland in the sixth century. The Treasury contains important relics of the saint: the head, an arm, and a leg, all three of which are en-*pl. 78* shrined in reliquaries. The reliquary of the knee and thigh of St. Gildas is unique among French church treasures. It is decorated with sheets of silver applied to a wooden core, and owes its originality to the ingenuity of the goldsmith, who applied to a clumsy shape that is barely representational a decoration that is actually the tracery forms of flamboyant Gothic architecture.

SAINT-JEAN-DU-DOIGT *(Finistère)*

CHALICE. First half of 16th century. Silver gilt. H. 13⅝″, diameter of base 9⅛″, diameter of cup 6″. Saint-Jean-Baptiste.

This curious name (literally, St. John of the Finger) originated with the relic of the finger of the hand with which St. John baptized Christ; the relic still draws large numbers of pilgrims to this village in Finistère.

According to legend, the Emperor Julian the Apostate violated the Baptist's tomb and ordered the body to be burned, whereupon a miraculous rain extinguished the fire, and the index finger of the saint's right hand was preserved. The relic, brought back by St. Thecla, who had obtained it from the patriarch of Jerusalem, was venerated first near Saint-Lô, where St. Thecla had a church erected in its honor, and was then taken by an archer of the retinue of Duke John V to Traou-Mériadec, which was to become Saint-Jean-du-Doigt. A similar legend exists, incidentally, in connection with Saint-Jean-de-Maurienne, where a chapel in the cathedral is dedicated to St. Thecla. The crystal of the reliquary at Saint-Jean-du-Doigt is said to have been donated by Anne of Britanny in gratitude to the saint, whose help she had entreated in 1506 when afflicted with a malady of the eyes.

A veritable treasure was built up around the relic, which includes a number of important pieces, such as a sixteenth-century silver cross, typical of the Breton region with its little bells and its figures on brackets, a bust of St. Meriadec, and above all a chalice and paten that date from the first half of the sixteenth century, which may have been presented by Francis I or his wife, Claude.

pl. 79 The chalice, particularly well known by reason of its ornate decoration, is one of the earliest surviving examples of a piece of precious metalwork that uses purely Renaissance motifs. From an eight-lobed base decorated with cherubs' heads, palmettes, foliate scrolls, cornucopia, and interlaced dolphins, rises a very short stem with foliate scrolls, which leads to an octagonal knop, each of whose sides forms a niche, lined with blue enamel, surmounted by a shell arch, in which there is a figure of an Apostle. The splayed cup is set into an openwork "outer" cup decorated with facing cornucopia on either side of which is a thyrsus surmounted by a winged head.

VANNES *(Morbihan)*

MARRIAGE CASKET. About 1160–70. Wood covered with painted parchment. H. 8¼″, w. 20⅛″, d. 9½″. Treasury of the Cathedral.

This marriage chest, one of the principal pieces in the Vannes Treasury, is particularly interesting as an illustration of a secular object that was subsequently used for religious purposes. An ordinary wooden chest covered with parchment is painted in bright colors, in which green, red, and yellow predominate, with scenes of seignorial life in the Middle Ages, now romantic, now war-*pls. 80–81 above* like: a noble horseman holding a falcon advances toward a lady who seems to await him at the entrance to a tent; *pls. 80–81 below* a cleric invites a young woman whom he holds by the hand to mount a saddled horse; knights attired in coats of mail prepare to leave for the wars, while a lady hands one of them his shield; a musician playing the viol appears to be trying to console a lady grieving over the departure of the warriors; two men armed with lances and shields are prepared for the attack.

The origins of this little chest, which may be dated around 1160–70, have given rise to considerable controversy. In the first identification of relics in which it is mentioned, in 1637, it is described as a "small chest painted in the Flemish manner." In an inventory made in 1771, it is referred to as a "small box in Chinese style." More recently, it has been successively compared with the enamel plaque of Geoffrey Plantagenet (Musée des Beaux-Arts, Le Mans), with certain stained glass windows at Saint-Denis, with the illuminations of the *Hortus Deliciarum,* with the mural paintings of Maine-et-Loire or Charente. The most recent theory is that this work, which is clearly very much influenced by Limoges enamel work (typical border, white ring around the design), but also related as regards color and technique to the Catalonian antependia, might have originated in Catalonia.

Champagne

REIMS *(Marne)*

The Reims Treasury has had the good fortune to be the only royal treasury to have remained *in situ*, since those of Saint-Denis and the Sainte-Chapelle have been scattered, and most of the pieces which could be salvaged are now in the Louvre, the Cabinet des Médailles, or museums outside France. In the Cathedral at Reims we find the liturgical objects used at the coronation ceremonies of the kings of France, as well as the most rare and precious pieces of goldsmithery presented by the sovereigns on such occasions.

CHALICE OF ST. RÉMY. End of 12th century. Gold, enamel, precious stones. H. 6¾″, diameter of cup 5⅞″. Treasury of the Cathedral.

fig. 7 The gold chalice dating from the end of the twelfth century, known as the Chalice of St. Rémy as the result of an error in the inventories, was used, with a fourteenth-century paten that was destroyed during the Revolution, at the Communion of kings on the day of their coronation. The knop is adorned with filigree work, cabochons, pearls, and cloisonné enamels. The cup, which is similarly decorated, is the product of a nineteenth-century restoration, probably executed for the coronation of Charles X.

7

The base, which is also partially rebuilt, is engraved with an inscription calling down anathema on anyone who steals the chalice.

TALISMAN OF CHARLEMAGNE. 9th century. Gold repoussé, filigree, precious stones. H. 2⅞″, diameter 2½″. Treasury of the Cathedral.

pl. 83   The Talisman of Charlemagne is a circular jewel reliquary similar in form to the encolpia that were hung around the neck and credited with prophylactic powers. It is of gold, with a large, roughly cut sapphire on one side, and a blue glass insert, dating no earlier than the nineteenth century, on the other, both set in a foliated collet. All around, and on the rim, emeralds alternate with pearls and rubies set among filigree and scallops in repoussé, soldered onto the supporting base. The arrangement and design recall those of the cover of the ninth-century Gospel Book of Metz, now in the Bibliothèque Nationale. The reliquary originally enshrined some hair and "milk" of the Virgin.

The legendary tale of the talisman which Charlemagne is supposed to have worn during his life and to have been buried with appears in no record earlier than the sixteenth century. And the inventories made at the two exhumations of the emperor, under Otto III and then under Frederick Barbarossa, do not refer to it. But since the piece is Carolingian and remained in the Cathedral of Aachen where this tradition has persisted, there is no valid reason to question it.

In 1804, the Cathedral chapter presented the piece to Napoleon I for Josephine, the bishop of Aachen having first replaced the relics of the Virgin by a fragment of the True Cross. The talisman remained in the empress' possession after her divorce. Queen Hortense inherited it, then Napoleon III, whose devotion to it was properly superstitious; possession of the talisman, he would say, meant possession of the empire. Empress Eugénie took it with her into exile, and absolutely refused to part with it, despite the urgent entreaties of William II.

After the fire in the Cathedral during World War I the empress decided to present it to the archbishop of Reims. In 1927, Cardinal Luçon handed over the ownership of it to the diocesan association of the Cathedral, and it was agreed that the talisman should be exhibited in the Treasury, where it would be housed for the time being. A place of honor has been reserved in the new

presentation of the treasures for this marvelous piece, which thus far only a few, privileged people have been able to view.

RELIQUARY OF SAMSON. Beginning of 13th century. Enameled and gilt copper, silver gilt on a wood core. H. 22½″. Treasury of the Cathedral.

pl. 84   The filigreed and jeweled Samson reliquary is in the form of a gable supported by two clusters of colonettes, which culminates in an openwork foliated crest edged with studs of blue enamel; on the back, an engraved shutter with a plaque of enamel and perforated copper on which Samson and the lion are depicted. The circular

8

base is ornamented with a quatrefoil whose lobes are decorated with a foliate design and is surmounted by a barrel-shaped knop ornamented with four medallions on each of which, in relief on a blue ground, is the same subject of Samson and the lion.

This reliquary, which has been attributed to Archbishop Samson (1140–61), in fact dates from the beginning of the thirteenth century. It is in the tradition of the Mosan gable-shaped reliquaries, several examples of which have been preserved in the Musées Royaux d'Art et d'Histoire, Brussels, and which, like this one, have been mounted on bases. There was probably a statuette under the trefoil arch; if that is the case, then this might be the reliquary of the Virgin, referred to in the inventory of 1669.

RELIQUARY OF SS. SIXTUS AND SINICIUS. 13th century. Engraved and gilt copper. H. 13⅜″, diameter 6¾″. Treasury of the Cathedral.

pl. 85   The Reliquary of SS. Sixtus and Sinicius consists of a multifoil phylactery which belongs to the series of reliquaries in the form of brooches (such as that of the tooth of St. Nicholas of Arras, or that of St. Mary of Oignies, preserved in the Musées Royaux of Brussels) which have been mounted on a base (such as those of Bar-sur-Aube, Langres, or Saint-Menoux). The front, engraved with foliated and floral scrolls, is embellished with a large cabochon surrounded by six stones set in collets. On the back is a plaque engraved with the figure of Christ in Majesty. The circular base, ornamented with a foliate design and resting on three claws in the form of dragons, supports a thick knop from which rises an engraved stem that links two smaller knops each of which is set in foliate collars.

Various alterations made in the course of the eighteenth and nineteenth centuries successively changed the appearance of the reliquary, which is regarded as an early-thirteenth-century piece, and which is of Mosan origin. As can be seen from a lithograph of 1843, by J. -J. Macquart, the multifoil phylactery, the front of which had been pierced in the center, was placed obliquely on the stem, the height of which had been doubled by the addition of a second piece that copied it. It was subsequently put back in a vertical position, at which time green glass beads were substituted for the three emeralds and three amethysts that decorated the front. A recent restoration has given the whole piece its original aspect and proportions, by returning one of the missing intermediate knops to its place and eliminating a foliate flange that had been added in the nineteenth century, as well as the cylindrical piece that had raised the height of the stem. Finally, the green beads were replaced by six amethysts and a cabochon of rock crystal.

RELIQUARY OF THE HOLY THORN. About 1460–70. Rock crystal, enameled gold, pearls, and balas rubies. H. 9⅞″. Treasury of the Cathedral.

pl. 86 The Reliquary of the Holy Thorn consists of a Fatimid crystal of the eleventh century mounted in six strips of gold decorated with pearls and balas rubies in which is a little gold angel holding the relic. (At the time of the 1960 restoration, a facsimile was placed inside the *fig. 8* container and the original angel was mounted separately.) The lid is topped with a gold angel in a white enamel robe, holding the crown of thorns. The gold base is decorated with gadroons of alternating green and blue enamel, and edged with pearls and rubies. Under the base is the inscription: HANC SEQUIMUR SUMMIS HAEC PRAEMIA DIGNA TRIUMPHIS, as well as the mark (crowned fleur-de-lis and ink cruet) of Guillaume Lemaistre, a Parisian goldsmith who received the rank of master goldsmith on January 23, 1458.

The reliquary was part of the treasure of the French Crown, and is believed to have been given by Henry II, or perhaps Henry III, to Renée of Lorraine, abbess of Saint-Pierre-des-Dames at Reims. It is mentioned in an inventory of the abbey dated 1690, and has been in the Cathedral Treasury since 1822.

RELIQUARY OF THE RESURRECTION. Late 15th century. Silver parcel-gilt and enamel, copper gilt, sardonyx. H. 9⅞″, w. 12¼″. Treasury of the Cathedral.

pl. 88 The Reliquary of the Resurrection was a part of the treasure of the French Crown and was given by Henry II to Notre-Dame of Reims on the day of his coronation, as the inscription indicates: HENRICUS SECUNDUS CONSECRANDUS *pl. 87* HUC ME ASPORTAVIT 1547. The figure of Christ, of parcel-gilt silver and red enamel drapery, rises out of a sardonyx sepulcher decorated with blue enamel niches in which *pl. 89* stand silver angels carrying the instruments of the Passion. Around the tomb, four soldiers of copper gilt sleep on a ground that is still partially enameled, surrounded by a crenelated wall of silver gilt, the turrets of which are surmounted by angels, and on which are affixed the enameled monograms and emblems of Henry II and Catherine de' Medici. The hexagonal base, carried by four lions, does not seem to belong to the reliquary, for the signs of wear apparent on the turrets show that these originally supported the piece, and that there was no other base. The reliquary was restored in 1960. The statuette of Christ, which had been brushed with beige paint, was scraped, so that some of the original gilt detail reappeared. The type of armor worn by the soldiers shows that this reliquary is earlier than the date on the inscription, and that it must be regarded as of the late fifteenth century.

RELIQUARY OF ST. URSULA. 1574. Gold, silver, enameled copper, cornelian. H. 18⅛″, w. 11″. Treasury of the Cathedral.

pl. 90 The Reliquary of St. Ursula was one of the treasures of the French Crown and, according to the inventory of Francis II, had belonged to Queen Claude. It would even appear, according to a recent study based on a receipt dated 1505, that this piece, which had not orginally been designed for religious purposes, was a gift made to Queen Anne of Britanny upon the occasion of her entry into Tours in 1501. Henry III presented it to Notre-Dame of Reims for the pacification of the realm at his coronation.

pls. 92–93, The reliquary is in the form of a ship. The hull, of *91* cornelian, is set in a silver-gilt support; the stern and prow are adorned with silver turrets. On the deck stand ten enameled statuettes representing St. Ursula, with long golden hair, and her companions, as well as a sailor and a soldier of silver gilt. A furled sail of white enamel is affixed to the mast to which an oriflamme is attached. Waves and rocks are indicated in translucent enamel on silver, resting on a silver-gilt base with canted corners and a foliate gallery.

The reliquary was carefully restored in 1960. The openwork copper bulwark duplicating the original breastwork, which had been added in the nineteenth century, was eliminated. The deck, which had been reset upside down, was returned to its correct position, and the mast, of which the upper part had been cut off, was restored to its original height. A Victory perched on the top of a castle seems to have been added to the top of the mast during the reign of Henry II. It was mounted separately, so that it could be replaced by the detachable oriflamme and moved back into position whenever it was so desired. The plaque supporting it, which had been added in the nineteenth century, was removed, thereby making it possible to see the inside of the little castle, marked with the monogram of Henry II. The front of the reliquary bears the inscription: DE SAINCTE URSULE ET DE XI MIL VIERGES; on the back: HENRICUS III GALLIARUM POLONIA-RUMQUE REX HANC DEIPARAE VIRGINI NAVICULAM UT RES GALLICA DIUTURNIS IACTATA SEDITION FLUCTIBUS OPE DIVINA TANDEM CONFERRETUR IN TRANQUILLUM MORE MAIORUM INAUGURATUS POSUIT ANNO MDLXXIIII; on the sides, the heraldic arms of France and Poland. The mark—two crowned towers and the letter R—would appear, according to Charles Oman, to be that of Raymond Guyonnet, a goldsmith of Tours.

TROYES *(Aube)*

The Treasury of the Cathedral of Troyes suffered severely during the Revolution, and some of the pieces, such as the large casket reliquary of St. Bernard, dating from the thirteenth century, which, like the one in the Amiens Treasury, was of Mosan origin, were damaged.

IVORY CASKET. Byzantine, 11th century. H. 5½″, w. 10¼″, d. 5⅛″. Treasury of the Cathedral.

pl. 94 The small ivory casket is stained purple and carved on its long sides with hunting scenes: a lion hunt in front, a boar hunt in the back. Each of the short sides is decorated with a bird, perhaps a phoenix, amid foliage. On the center of the lid is a construction that symbolizes a fortified city; a door is open to allow a woman holding a crown to pass through; on either side, on a larger scale, a knight bearing a lance and a crown. These knights represent a victorious emperor, while the woman personifies the captured city. The theme is the same as that on a piece of silk found in the tomb of Bishop Gunther (died 1065), which is now in the Treasury of Bamberg Cathedral. The bird on the short side, which has certain Chinese features about it, also occurs on a Byzantine manuscript dating from the middle of the tenth century.

Thus the chest is interesting as constituting a point of convergence for influences from different sources. A. Grabar ("La Soie byzantine de l'évêque Gunther à Bamberg," *Münchner Jahrbuch*, VII, 1956, pp. 7ff) places it in the middle of the eleventh century; he sees in it a resemblance with the ivory plaque representing Romanus

II in the Cabinet des Médailles. According to tradition, it was brought back from Constantinople, after the sack of 1204, by John Langlois, chaplain to Garnier de Traisnel, Bishop of Troyes.

CLOISSONNE ENAMEL MEDALLIONS. 10th century. Translucent cloisonné on gold. Diameter 2″. Treasury of the Cathedral.

pl. 95 Two medallions of translucent cloisonné enamel on gold, each composed of two semicircles, represent the four Evangelists, with inscriptions citing the opening words of their Gospels: St. Matthew, *Liber*; St. John, *In principio*, St. Mark, *Sicut scriptum*, St. Luke, *Fuit in diebus*.

Swarzenski attributes them to workshops of Champagne of the end of the tenth century, by analogy with other works, such as the cloisonné enamels also representing the Evangelists on the cover of an Evangeliary from the Treasury of Saint-Denis which had been presented by Beatrice, wife of Count Frederick I de Bar (954–1011), and is now in the Louvre.

CHAMPLEVÉ ENAMEL PLAQUES. About 1160. Enamel on copper. Diameter 4″. Treasury of the Cathedral.

pl. 96 Nineteen semicircular plaques illustrate biblical scenes (here we have the Resurrection and the Last Judgment); while seventeen square or rectangular plaques represent prophets, Evangelists, etc. These enamels have long been attributed to the Rhineland. Their iconography, in particular, greatly resembles that of certain enamels in the Treasury of Cologne Cathedral. But it is now accepted that they originated in a workship of Troyes which was influenced by Mosan art, and that they may be dated around 1160.

THE PSYCHOMACHIA CASKET. 12th century. Champlevé enamel on copper. H 2″, l. 5⅛″, d. 2⅜″. Treasury of the Cathedral.

fig. 9 The lid of this small enameled casket is missing. The sides are decorated with scenes of the conflict between the Vices and the Virtues; the names of the Virtues are engraved on the upper band, those of the Vices on the *pl. 97* lower. The elongation of the figures, placed under arches and standing out against alternating green, red, and blue grounds, and their stylization have caused the piece to be attributed to an English workshop of the second half of the twelfth century.

9

PATEN AND BOX. 17th century. Repoussé and chased silver. Paten diameter 7⅝″; box h. 4¼″, diameter 5⅛″. Chapel of Edouard Colbert, Cathedral.

The chapel of Edouard Colbert, marquis de Villacerf, offers a very fine set of silverware of the period of Louis XIV; indeed, it is one of the most sumptuous of its kind. The set bears the stamp of the Parisian goldsmith, Nicolas *p. 33* Dolin (died 1695), and includes twelve pieces: a chalice *below* and paten, a ewer and its bowl, two cruets and their tray, *fig. 10* a box for hosts (the inside cover forms a Kiss of Peace), a small bell, an altar cross, and two candlesticks. Scenes from the Old and New Testaments, the symbolism of which is related to the liturgical function of each object, are represented in relief on the various pieces. The arms

10

are those of Bishop Edward Colbert of Troyes, marquis of Villacerf (a collateral branch of the family of the minister).

Dauphiné — Provence

LUCERAM *(Alpes-Maritimes)*

The church treasuries of the Alpes-Maritimes possess a number of interesting pieces: Saint-Sauveur, footed reliquary of St. Blaise of engraved copper, dating from the fifteenth century; Auribeau, Reliquary of the Jaw of St. Honoratus, decorated with translucent enamels, dating from the sixteenth century; Saint-Paul-de-Vence, statuettes of St. John the Baptist and the Virgin and Child, and a reliquary in the shape of a shoulder blade. The Treasury of Luceram possesses a work representing St. Margaret and the dragon which is remarkable in composition and style.

ST. MARGARET AND THE DRAGON. End of 15th century. Copper and silver gilt. H. 23⅝″, w. 19⅜″. Treasury of the Church.

pl. 99 The saint, erect, crowned, hands held in prayer, emerges from a monstrous beast with bristling spikes; his head is turned, with open jaw and menacing fangs, his tail is raised and coiled. The serenity of the saint and the fury of the animal are aesthetically reproduced through the contrast between the two axes, one vertical—the motionless, almost congealed posture of the Saint, the other horizontal—the animal's contortion rendered with astonishing sensitivity.

The group is of silver, with only occasional highlights of silver gilt on the dragon's wings and the saint's hair. It stands on an octagonal base of copper gilt that rests on four small lions. The statuette of St. Margaret, its wooden core sheathed with silver, fits inside the dragon, which is hollow and fashioned of extremely thin strips of metal; the metal of the wings is particularly thin, and is engraved and embossed with remarkable skill.

EMBRUN *(Hautes-Alpes)*

The Treasury of the former cathedral of Embrun has the richest collection of sacerdotal vestments in France, and the only one that can compare with the principal treasuries outside the country, such as that at Halberstadt. There are over one hundred of these vestments, recalling a time when this humble parish was one of the most important archdioceses, situated on the marches of France and Italy. Of this number, we show one of the earlier pieces, refashioned in the seventeenth century, so that its decoration no longer corresponds to sacerdotal vestments prior to that period.

CHASUBLE. 16th century. Velvet, embroidered with silk and gold threads. L. 42½″, w. 26⅜″. Treasury, Notre-Dame.

pl. 100 The chasuble appears to have originated in a French workshop of the middle of the sixteenth century, and was presented by Mgr. Hercules de Jarente, bishop of Embrun from 1548 to 1555, whose coat of arms was or, a saltier gules. The material is purple velvet, the thistles surrounded by delicate foliate scrolls, are embroidered in gold thread. The orphreys of the cross represent, on the front, St. Batholomew, St. Stephen, St. Andrew, and St. Catherine, and on the back, St. John and Mary Magdalen, SS. Peter and Catherine, St. James and an unidentified female saint: on the branches of the cross, the prophets Enoch and Elias holding scrolls inscribed with their names. All these figures, which are embroidered in bright colors on a gold ground, are treated with a vigor and robustness reminiscent of the somewhat crude techniques of wood sculpture and wood engraving.

ARLES *(Bouches-du-Rhône)*

IVORY BELT BUCKLE OF ST. CESARIUS. 6th century. H. 2″, w. 4⅛″. Notre-Dame-la-Major.

fig. 11 The ivory buckle of the belt of St. Cesarius treasured in the church of Notre-Dame-la-Major at Arles is supposed to have belonged to that holy bishop (died 542).
pl. 101 It consists of a rectangular plaque with a frame of an egg-and-dart motif which encloses a scene of the Holy Sepulcher guarded by two soldiers leaning on their lances and a catch decorated with an interlace of leaves and

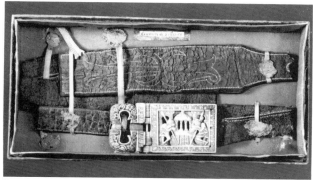

11

vine clusters. This ivory, in the classical tradition in which the familiar themes of Early Christian art are represented —themes which are also found in the sculptured Provencal sarcophagi—is attributed to Provençal workshops around the year 500. According to Volbach (*op. cit.*, No. 215), who adopts E. B. Smith's theory ("A Source of Mediaeval Style in France," *Art Studies*, 1924, pp. 85ff), this piece with its somewhat heavy style and its synthesized forms, should be regarded as a product of local workshops under Byzantine influence.

From the scalloped belt of coarse-grained leather, which bears a monogram cross, an alpha and omega are suspended by little chains.

SAINT-ANTOINE-EN-VIENNOIS *(Isère)*

The abbey of Saint-Antoine was originally a Benedictine priory, dependent after 1101 upon the abbey of Montmajour. In 1297, the church was given to the hospital of the Antonines, and raised to the dignity of mother house of the order. The relics of St. Anthony of La Mothe, or St. Anthony of the Desert, had been transported there in 1095. The role of the monks was always to care for the sick, which explains the presence of very ancient surgical instruments in the Treasury.

CRUCIFIX. 17th century. Ivory. H. 33⅛″. Treasury of the former Abbey Church.

pl. 102 In addition to the moving ivory Christ of the Antonines, one of the most celebrated seventeenth-century examples of this type of ivory work depicting Christ, the Treasury includes several series of very unusual objects: sixteenth-century halberds; antiphonaries whose leather bindings are decorated with the two-headed eagle stamped with the Antonine tau (the abbey's heraldic arms) and copper-gilt fleurs-de-lis; a large number of seventeenth- and eighteenth-century bust reliquaries; and especially an extraordinary series of seventeenth-century caskets of ebonized pearwood and embossed silver.

LARGE CASKET CONTAINING THE RELICS OF ST. ANTHONY. 17th century. Repoussé silver on a wood core. H. 41¾″, w. 47¼″, d. 21⅝″. Treasury of the former Abbey Church.
fig. 12 The largest of the caskets in this Treasury and also the finest as regards the quality of the silver work is the

12

casket containing the relics of St. Anthony situated under the high altar. The plaques with which it is covered, stamped with the mark of John Eynardon, a goldsmith of Grenoble, are devoted to episodes in the life of the holy hermit. Among these different scenes, the most astonishing
pl. 103 is that of St. Anthony repelling a temptation of the devil who appears to him in the guise of the Lord, whose hands the goldsmith has portrayed with long hooked clawlike fingers. On the short sides are represented the canting arms (argent, cow passant gules) of John du Vaché, knight, lord, and baron of Châteauneuf-de-l'Albenc, who donated the casket in 1648. The lid, with the Antonine tau on top, is decorated with four oval medallions in a field of embossed foliate scrolls.

Flanders—Artois—Picardy

AMIENS *(Somme)*

The Treasury of Amiens, whose first known inventory dates back to 1347, owed its wealth to the presence of a very precious relic which it still preserves today, that of the head of John the Baptist, brought back from Constantinople in 1206 by Walon de Barton, a canon of Picquigny, who presented it to Richard de Gerberoy, bishop of Amiens. The conclusions of expert paleontologists who have examined the skull, which bears the mark of a spear thrust, do not invalidate the relic's authenticity. It is in fact the head of a Bedouin of the first century of our era. The relic was the object of fervent devotion not only of the humble crowds of the faithful but also of princes and kings, who showered sumptuous gifts upon it. The inventory of 1419 states that the relic had been placed under a rock crystal on a silver dish decorated with precious stones. This dish was later replaced by a gold dish engraved with the arms of France which was presented by Isabella of Bavaria or Charles VII. The relic alone, with its crystal and its gold setting, was saved at the time of the Revolution; it is now set on a nineteenth-century enameled dish in the style of the previous one.

In addition to the head reliquary of John the Baptist, the Treasury possessed a reliquary of the True Cross; a silver-gilt bust of a queen, decorated with precious stones, in which was enshrined the head of St. Ulphe—a gift of Isabella, daughter of Philip the Fair and wife of Edward II of England; a chausible given by Queen Ingeborg, wife of Philip Augustus; vestments of cloth of gold presented by Isabella of Portugal, wife of Philip the Good, and others. All these are gone, and now there remain only some pieces of exceptional quality which the Cathedral received much later; among these are three pieces from the ancient abbey of Le Paraclet—a cross, a ciborium, and a votive crown—which were presented in 1858 by Mlle d'Ainval de Braches.

CROSS RELIQUARY FROM THE ABBEY OF LE PARACLET. 13th century. Silver parcel-gilt on a wood core, filigree, niello, intaglios. H. 24¾". Treasury of the Cathedral.

pl. 105
The cross is covered on one side with an engraved and nielloed plaque of silver gilt representing Christ on the cross, and at his feet, Adam rising from the tomb. On the other side, silver medallions, also engraved and nielloed, represent the Lamb of God in the center and, at the ends of the arms of the cross, which are in the form of quatrefoils, the four Evangelists. The relics are protected by five oblong crystals. On the periphery between the medallions, is an inscription in Gothic capitals.

The tradition according to which this cross was brought from the Holy Land at the beginning of the thirteenth century by Enguerrand de Boves, founder of the abbey of Le Paraclet, can apply only to the relics. The cross itself, which is perhaps one of the most exquisite of the known filigreed crosses, is indeed of that period, but is the product of one of the workshops of northern France.

CIBORIUM FROM THE ABBEY OF LE PARACLET. 14th century. Crystal, silver gilt, precious stones. H. 12⅝". Treasury of the Cathedral.

pl. 106
The ciborium is composed of a vase of cut crystal, mounted in the fourteenth century on a polygonal base of silver gilt which was formerly embellished with stones. The lid, enriched with garnets and pearls, is also of silver gilt; its upper part is of emerald-green enamel speckled with white and red dots, and recalls, though with somewhat less sophistication, the design of the Reliquary of the Precious Blood in Boulogne (pl. 111). The form of this object is found in secular goldsmithery, and was to exist up to the sixteenth century, as evidenced by the cup belonging to Philip the Good, which is now in the Imperial Treasury of Vienna.

CROWN RELIQUARY FROM THE ABBEY OF LE PARACLET. Late 13th century. Vermeil, cabochons, enamel. Diameter 7⅞". Treasury of the Cathedral.

pl. 108
The late-thirteenth-century crown reliquary is composed of six large and six small fleurs-de-lis decorated with cabochons, a number of which are missing. Circular crystal medallions which contain relics alternate on the face of the crown with translucent hexagonal enamels with a blue ground, representing secular subjects (small woodland pl. 107 animals, rabbits, young women in a landscape) treated with great charm; their presence on a religious object might be surprising were it not for the fact that all the art of this period within the Parisian sphere of influence is marked by a worldly elegance. The crown was suspended by three chains.

RELIQUARY OF THE TOOTH OF ST. NICHOLAS. Early 13th century. Copper and silver gilt, filigree, cabochons. H. 9⅞". Saint-Nicolas-en-Cité.

pl. 109
The phylactery reliquary of the tooth of St. Nicholas

belongs to the series of reliquaries which may be regarded as having been inspired by the art of costume. Like the Reliquary of St. Mary of Oignies, dating from about 1230, which is preserved in the Musées Royaux, Brussels, or the upper part of the Reliquary of SS. Sixtus and Sinicius at Reims (pl. 85), it is in the form of a brooch and has the character of jewelry. It is provided with a suspension ring. The main portion of the reliquary—almond-shaped and surrounded by a border of engraved leafwork—has trefoil *fleurons* at each of the cardinal points which, like the almond, are decorated with filigree and cabochons. The copper-gilt filigree is single-wired on the trefoils, and double-wired on the main part. A slightly convex medallion engraved with a floral design sets off the tooth, which is mounted like a precious stone; the words DENS S. NICHOLAI is inscribed beneath it. The back of the reliquary is covered with a silver plaque in repoussé representing the Agnus Dei in a stylized foliate design.

BOULOGNE-SUR-MER (Pas-de-Calais)

RELIQUARY OF THE PRECIOUS BLOOD. Beginning of 14th century. Gold, silver gilt, enamel. Diameter 3", depth ½". Saint-François-de-Sales.

According to tradition, the celebrated relic of the Precious Blood was sent by Godfrey de Bouillon to Boulogne, his native city, in 1101, but the reliquary— a circular, slightly convex box with a lid of enameled gold—in pl. 111 which it is enshrined is much later in date. It belonged to the Treasury of the church of Notre-Dame, and was saved during the Revolution by the Abbé Ballin whose heirs donated it, in 1856, to the church of Saint-Nicolas which subsequently turned it over to the church of Saint-François-de-Sales. Until 1792, the reliquary was supported by two angels of silver gilt resting on a base. In the center of the enameled gold lid was a crystal lens, through which the relic could be viewed.

On a field of translucent emerald-green enamel, gold foliate scrolls unfold, ending in trefoils and heart-shaped leaves, decorated with white, light-yellow, and brick-red opaque enamels. A wide gold band is inscribed in opaque red champlevé enamel with the words, DE SANGUINE IHU XPI. On the transparent, translucent enamel field of the remaining portion of the band are quatrefoils set into quatrefoils alternately translucent dark blue with opaque yellow centers and translucent purple with opaque green centers; on the outer band of emerald green, small trefoils, alternately white and red. The back, of silver gilt, is engraved with a rosette.

This magnificent piece is one of the finest surviving products of translucent enamel work, a medium which reappears in the Parisian workshops in the thirteenth century under the name *émail de plique*. There are samples of it on pieces now in the Cabinet des Médailles: a plaque of the Crucifixion on a floral ground, with corner pieces probably from the parament of the Sainte-Chapelle; and, especially, an enamel which is supposed to have adorned the orphrey of the bust reliquary of St. Louis, commissioned by Philip the Fair from Guillaume Jullien in 1306. The theory has been put forward that it was shortly after this date that Philip the Fair also commissioned from Guillaume Jullien, who was his official goldsmith, the Reliquary of the Precious Blood, and that he presented it to the church of Notre-Dame of Boulogne on the occasion of the marriage of his daughter, Isabella, to Edward II of England, which was celebrated in that church in 1308. The same enamel technique is also found on two medallions now in the Treasury of Tournai: one on a medallion from a Byzantine cross reliquary, the other on the Virgin's dress in the Adoration of the Magi on the casket by Nicholas of Verdun. These pieces, which closely resemble the Parisian enamels of Guillaume Jullien, may also have been given by Philip the Fair to the Cathedral of Tournai during one of his stays in that town, particularly in 1297 or 1301.

LONGPRÉ-LES-CORPS-SAINTS
(Somme)

This locality, which owes its name (literally, Long Meadow of the Holy Bodies) to relics sent from the Holy Land by Alléaume de Fontaine, who founded the local church, possesses several reliquaries, the most interesting of which is undoubtedly the statuette of St. Christopher bearing the Child on his shoulders.

STATUETTE RELIQUARY OF ST. CHRISTOPHER. End of 15th century. Silver and vermeil strips on a wood core. H. 20″. Treasury of the Church.

fig. 13   The statuette, fitted onto a hexagonal base of copper gilt resting on six small lions, is of wood sheathed with strips of silver that adhere to the detail of the sculpture with great fidelity, particularly in the case of the saint's legs, which are rendered with quite astonishing anatom-

pl. 110   ical verisimilitude. The saint is depicted as a bearded, turbaned giant. He leans on a tall, leafed staff; preparing to cross the stream, he hitches up his tunic, thus revealing a rectangular opening in his side, which contains the relics. The tunic is of silver gilt, and edged with a band ornamented with cabochons; only the hands and face are painted in natural tints. The style is very realistic, and, despite its small size, the statuette conveys a sense of monumental power that allies it to the large sculptures produced by the workshops in the eastern part of the country at the end of the fifteenth century.

13

CRESPIN (Nord)

The memory of Crespin abbey, founded around 640 by St. Landelinus and now destroyed, is preserved by certain remarkable pieces from its Treasury, the most important of which are a rock crystal monstrance reliquary and an arm reliquary.

ARM RELIQUARY OF ST. LANDELINUS. 13th century. Silver parcel-gilt. H. 23¼″. Church of Crespin.

fig. 14   The Arm Reliquary of St. Landelinus, the sleeve of which is of silver and the hand, raised in blessing, of silver gilt, is adorned with bands of filigree characteristic

of the first half of the thirteenth century. They are extremely ornate, set with precious stones and disks or lozenges of nielloed silver. On one side, between two bands of filigree, is the inscription in niello: PROTEGAT HEC DEXTRA NOS SEMPER ET INTUS ET DEXTRA QUE LANDELINI SACRA CONTINET OSSA BENIGNI.

MONTREUIL-SUR-MER (Pas-de-Calais)

CROSIER OF ST. AUSTREBERTA. 11th century. Silver gilt, copper gilt, filigree, and cabochons on a wood core. H. 48″. Treasury, Saint-Saulve.

14

pl. 112   The crosier at the church of Saint-Saulve is in the form of a very slightly curved wooden staff, the very archaic form of which recalls the shepherd's crook. There has been controversy as to the date of the silver-gilt plaques decorated with filigree and precious stones. Some authors attribute it to the time of St. Austreberta herself, that is, the seventh century; but the similarities in design and filigree technique with those of Rhenish or French objects executed around the year 1000 lead us to believe that this sumptuous decoration dates from the early years of the eleventh century. The only crosier similar in form is that at Quedlimburg, which dates from the end of the eleventh century; these are the two earliest surviving crosiers.

The Treasury includes other extremely interesting objects: the belt and a head reliquary of St. Austreberta, and a number of silver reliquaries of the seventeenth century (of SS. Lawrence, Paulinus, and Veronica, and of the head of St. Frameuse).

MAUBEUGE (Nord)

The church of Mauberge possesses pieces of exceptional interest, derived from the Benedictine abbey founded around 661 by Aldegundis, daughter of St. Valbertus and sister of St. Waldetrudis. All these pieces bear the saint's name and are connected with her legend.

CROSIER OF ST. ALDEGUNDIS. 14th century. Silver gilt. H. 13″. Church of Maubeuge.

pl. 113   The 53″ boxwood staff in three parts is carved with scenes from the life of Christ, somewhat crudely executed, and should probably be attributed to the thirteenth century. The crosier, of embossed silver gilt, ends in a volute of sumptuous foliage in the midst of which are tiny animals, dogs chasing boars, etc. The volute, which in style and technique is related to the art of Hugo of Oignies, may be placed around 1230. The knob, whose leafy decoration is very similar but is different in technique, as well as the socket into which it fits, may be said to date from the fourteenth century.

RELIQUARY OF THE VEIL OF ST. ALDEGUNDIS. 15th century. Silver gilt, enamel, rock crystal. H. 20¾", w. 15". Church of Maubeuge.

pl. 114   The Reliquary of the Veil of St. Aldegundis, one of the most elegant and skillfully composed pieces of French precious metalwork, takes up the favorite theme of two facing angels supporting an architectural form. The embossed silver-gilt angels, whose faces are painted in natural tints, are fashioned with extreme sophistication. They are regarded as among the most elegant figures of the early fifteenth century. The centrally oriented composition skillfully combines the horizontal line of a rock-crystal cylinder, mounted on a tall base, which contains the relic, and the vertical line of a small structure in flamboyant architectural style which surmounts it, and which *pl. 115*   shelters a minute and charming statuette of St. Aldegundis kneeling on her *prie-dieu* before a missal; the dove and the veil he brings her are of white enamel. The stamp on this piece—a lion rampant—has recently been identified as that of Valenciennes.

S A I N T - O M E R   *(Pas-de-Calais)*

CROSS RELIQUARY FROM THE ABBEY OF CLAIRMARAIS. 13th century. Silver filigree, intaglios, cabochons. H. 25¾", w. 13⅝". Treasury, Notre-Dame.

pl. 116   The cross from the abbey of Clairmarais, and the pyx, are the finest pieces in the Treasury at Saint-Omer. The two-armed cross is a reliquary of the True Cross, decorated on one side with bands of silver filigree, intaglios, and cabochons and, on the other, with an engraved and nielloed representation of Christ. Such use of niello, which occurs on the crosses of Blanchefosse and Le Paraclet, and of foliate filigree to cover the metal wires of the scrollwork (another feature of the Blanchefosse cross), has caused experts to compare this cross with Mosan works that have the same features and are derived from the art of the most famous goldsmith of the thirteenth century in the region between the Sambre and the Meuse, Hugo of Oignies.

PYX. End of 12th century. Copper gilt, filigree, cabochons. H. 7½". Treasury, Notre-Dame.

fig. 15   The pyx, which stands on a base engraved with stylized plant motifs, is composed of a vertical cylinder in two sections, each decorated with arcades and filigree bands with cabochons, surmounted by a little tower, also decorated with filigree arcades, which is topped with a conical filigree roof.

The curious reliquary, which, because of the stippled rush and buds filigree, should be placed at the end of the twelfth century, and whose arcade decoration is a survival from the previous century, may be compared in form with the monstrance in the Musée du Cinquantenaire in Brussels, although the latter is of later date and includes a central section—which seems to be missing here —in the form of a glass cylinder.

S A I N T - R I Q U I E R   *(Somme)*

The Benedictine abbey of Saint-Riquier (Centula), founded in the first quarter of the seventh century, was one of the largest in western Europe. The old abbey church, now the parish church, has preserved a number of pieces from its extremely rich Treasury: some seven-

15

teenth- and eighteenth-century altar canons, missal bindings, precentors' batons decorated with fleurs-de-lis, and sanctuary lamps; and, especially, three early-thirteenth-century reliquaries from the workshops of the Sambre-Meuse region. One is in the form of a tower flanked by two smaller towers, which, according to a recent study, was a model of the old Carolingian church; the other is made up of an engraved Fatimid crystal mounted horizontally on a base.

CRYSTAL RELIQUARY. 13th century. Copper gilt and nielloed silver. H. 9½". Treasury, Saint-Wulfran.

pl. 117   The third reliquary is formed of a crystal mounted vertically on a circular base ornamented with nielloed silver medallions, two of which are missing, surrounded by an engraved decoration. This base, which stands on three claws, is surmounted by a knop of silver gadroons set between two rows of stamped-out leafwork and held in place by copper-gilt filigree clasps. The crystal vessel, which is considered to be the oldest example of cut crystal in the west (c. 1230), rests on the knop and is set in a mount consisting of bands of stamped-out leafwork at the top and bottom which are connected by handles in the form of winged dragons; between them are upright bands engraved with lozenge designs; both handles and uprights are hinged. The conical roof, like the base, is ornamented with figures in nielloed silver, and is topped by a crystal ball surmounted by fir cones.

Alsace — Lorraine

M E T Z   *(Moselle)*

COPE OF CHARLEMAGNE. 12th century. Embroidered silk. H. 55", w. 119¾". Treasury of the Cathedral.

pl. 119   The Cope of Charlemagne is one of the most sumptuous treasures of France. The material is purple silk, on which are embroidered in gold and silver thread, and green, red, and blue silk thread, four colossal eagles in heraldic style, their tails and wings outspread and decorated with medallions of zoomorphic subjects—griffins and lions. Their heads are in profile, the feet of some are gripped by serpents. They stand out against a ground of crescents and foliate interlaces that terminate in palmettes and heads of monsters.

The purple silk and the theme of large eagles point to an Imperial Byzantine origin, for purple stuffs were reserved for the court, and the theme of the large, hieratic eagle, sometimes carrying a ring in its beak, adapted from the eagles of the throne of the Sassanid kings, was a symbol of Imperial power. It occurs (woven, rather than embroidered) on the Shroud of St. Germanus of Auxerre, on the Brixen Cope, and on the Pallium of St. Knut of Odense. However, certain stylistic details distinguish the Metz eagles from those of Brixen or Auxerre, particularly the medallions, which recur in the early twelfth century in the first products of western champlevé enameling (Conques, Bellac). The Metz piece has sometimes been attributed to the Imperial workshops at Palermo. But the most commonly accepted theory is that all these textiles, embroidered or woven, with their grandiose decoration of birds of prey, came from the Imperial workshops of Byzantium in the Macedonian period, at the time of the "second Golden Age," when the textile art had achieved its highest degree of perfection, that is, about the year 1000. This date thus makes a legend of the attribution to Charlemagne of this "royal mantle" which the master of ceremonies of Metz Cathedral wore each year at the procession of St. Mark. It is quite possible, however, that the piece was in fact conceived as an ample cloak, Imperial or royal, in the shape of a cope, which is borne out by the concentric arrangement of the design in a semicircular composition.

In the sixteenth century, the religious designation of the garment as a cope was confirmed by the addition of rich orphreys embroidered in gold and silk thread representing the Crucifixion, surrounded by six angels carrying the instruments of the Passion.

CROSIER. 14th century. Ivory. H. 58¼", volute h. 8¼". Treasury of the Cathedral.

In addition to the Charlemagne Cope, the Metz Treasury possesses many interesting pieces, including two ivory crosiers. One of these, very simple in form—coiled round on itself without any decorative motif—as were most of the Romanesque crosiers, dates from the twelfth century. The other is richly sculptured, and is a typical example of fourteenth-century ivory work. It is mentioned in an inventory of 1682, and is said to have been given to the Cathedral by Bishop Renaud de Bar (1301–16). A kneeling angel supports the volute, decorated with leaf work, which encloses two scenes: on one side, the crucified Christ between the Virgin and St. John; on the other, the Virgin and Child accompanied by two angels, each holding a torch. The stem is cut at the level of the angel's head. The shaft, too, is of ivory. With its somewhat formal artistry, this crosier closely resembles, in style and composition, those in the Musée de Cluny and the Victoria and Albert Museum, which Koechlin (Les Ivoires gothiques français, Paris, 1924) includes in his series of "crosiers with plant design, supported by a kneeling angel."

fig. 16

pl. 120

REININGUE (Haut-Rhin)

The number of pieces of Romanesque precious metalwork preserved in the churches of Alsace is fairly limited (a reliquary of 1049 at Aldorf, a twelfth-century casket of Molsheim). Hence the two casket reliquaries in the church at Reiningue are of particular importance for this region. One, which dates from the eleventh century, is of silver and silver gilt, and is decorated with figures under arches representing Christ on one side and, on the other, the Virgin surrounded by the wise and the foolish virgins. The other, which is larger, is known as the Casket of St. Romanus.

CASKET OF ST. ROMANUS. 12th century. Silver parcel-gilt on a wood core. H. 16⅛", w. 18⅞", d. 8⅝". Church of Reiningue.

fig. 17

This casket, too, is decorated with figures under arches: in front, Christ with six Apostles; in the back, the Virgin seated and also surrounded by six figures. Each of the short sides illustrates a scene from the life of St. Romanus:

16

17

pl. 121

his baptism by St. Lawrence, whose jailer he had been and who converted him to Christianity, and his decapitation. Each of the pediments is decorated with an angel with outspread wings. Inscriptions on the bands of each panel indicate the characters and the scenes. Another inscription was added on the base in the fifteenth century. The sloping sides of the roof are decorated with repoussé medallions in a border of foliate scrolls; in the medallions on one side, Christ surrounded by two angels and two symbols of the Evangelists, the lion and the angel, on the other, the Lamb, surrounded by two angels and the symbols of the other two Evangelists, the ox and the eagle.

According to one legend, Pope Leo IX, a native of Alsace, had given some relics to the church of Delenburq founded by his niece, Heilwig of Eguisheim-Dagsbourg, between the years 1049 and 1053, which were transferred in the following century to Reiningue. The style of the figures would indicate that this casket, on which reference is made to a certain priest named Aigodus, dates from the second quarter of the twelfth century. It was restored twice, once by Frederick Roth (1477–95), and again in 1510, by a goldsmith whose initials, G. W., are engraved on the piece.

In addition to these two caskets, the Reiningue church possesses a very fine bust reliquary of St. Romanus, dating from the sixteenth century.

NANCY (*Meurthe-et-Moselle*)

The Treasury at Nancy possesses three remarkable pieces from the abbey of Bouxières-aux-Dames, which are associated with the name of St. Gauzelin, bishop of Toul in the tenth century.

CHALICE AND PATEN OF ST. GAUZELIN. 10th century. Gold, filigree, enamel, precious stones. Chalice h. 5⅝″, paten diameter 5⅞″. Treasury of the Cathedral.

pls. 122, 123   The gold chalice and its paten may be placed at the beginning of the series of chalices preserved in the church treasuries. The chalice belongs to the very ancient type with handles, an example of which occurs as early as the fourth century in the little gold chalice found during the excavations at Gourdon. A rich filigree border ornamented with precious stones—pearls, amethysts, sapphires—decorates the rims of the cup and the base. The handles are also decorated with precious stones, and the cup itself has a large emerald cabochon on either side in a mount of pearls and precious stones; the fillets are beaded, or in the form of little chains or ribbons. During a recent restoration, the knop, which had been flattened, was returned to its original shape.

The rim of the paten is decorated with the same border as the chalice; in the center is a cinquefoil, at the intersections of each cusp are an antique intaglio on sardonyx representing a scarab, two garnets, and a ruby (the fifth mount is empty). The piece had been reinforced by a patina of silver gilt, which was removed at the time of the same restoration.

Both pieces, chalice and paten, seem to have come from tenth-century monastic workshops attached to the Imperial Ottonian court.

COVERS OF THE EVANGELIARY OF ST. GAUZELIN. 10th century (back cover later). Silver parcel-gilt, filigree, enamel, precious stones, on a wood core. H. 12¼″, w. 8⅝″. Treasury of the Cathedral.

pl. 125   The same place of origin may be allocated to the third piece, the binding of an Evangeliary, at least as regards the top cover, which presents all the features of the Lorrainese, Rhenish, and Mosan goldsmith's technique of that period—filigree design, setting of stones and cabochons, arcades to support the filigreed plaques. A large cross fits into a wide border, which it resembles in design, creating four compartments in which are engraved silver plaques representing the Evangelists.

p. 27   At the center of the cross, which is formed of three separate tiers supported by filigree arcades, is a cloisonné enamel on gold representing a haloed Virgin holding a lily. The branches of the cross, like the border, are made up of rectangular gold plaques decorated with filigree and precious stones (one was remodeled in the thirteenth century, another is missing).

This arrangement of a very ornate border and a central motif connected by bands meeting at right angles which form panels decorated with figures, occurs in other bindings of the same period, the ninth-century Codex Aureus of St. Emmeram of Lindau, now in Munich, and again in the twelfth-century Evangeliary attributed to St. Luibinus, in the Archiepiscopal Museum at Utrecht, where the Evangelists are of ivory instead of being engraved on silver as here or as on the portable altar of Emperor Henry II, in the Reiche Kapelle, Munich.

pl. 124   The back cover, although of a different technique and style, presents the same arrangement: a cross, this time with the Lamb in the center, creating four compartments in which are the symbols of the Evangelists. The technique is repoussé, and the work is crude enough to indicate that the two covers are neither of the same period, nor of the same artistic environment. However, the inferior quality of the execution may be due to a different develop-

ment of repoussé work in comparison with the technique of engraving and filigree.

Another object in the Nancy Treasury associated with St. Gauzelin is the famous ninth-century ivory comb.

SAINT-NICOLAS-DU-PORT (*Meurthe-et-Moselle*)

THE BOAT OF THE CARDINAL OF LORRAINE. 16th century. Mother-of-pearl and silver gilt. H. 20½″, w. 10⅝″. Treasury, Saint-Nicolas-du-Port.

pl. 126   The boat of Saint-Nicolas-du-Port is made of a mother-of-pearl shell set in a silver-gilt mount decorated with female heads and masks, the whole forming a ship that stands on four wheels. In the center rises the mast, surmounted by an oriflamme and a cross; its crow's-nest is in the shape of a foliate crown, its guys and sail are blown by the wind. Sailors and soldiers stand on the deck, while a cardinal sits in state in the stern, flanked by two halberdiers. Along the hull are engraved undulations representing waves. This piece, which bears the N of Nuremberg, is marked with the stamp of Hans Rappolt, a goldsmith active in 1579. According to tradition, it was presented to the church of Saint Nicolas-du-Port by Cardinal de Lorraine (1525–74), and had been made to replace the one that was supposed to have been given by Margaret of Provence, the wife of St. Louis, as fulfillment of a vow made during a storm off the coast of Cyprus. But it may also originally have been a piece of secular metalwork. It disappeared during the Revolution, but was redeemed in 1857 by the pastor of Saint-Nicolas, the Abbé Girmont, who gave it to his church. It was stolen in 1905, and "found" once more in about 1935.

A number of other small votive boats, more recent in date, gathered around this one, and together they form a veritable small flotilla, which lends the Treasury of Saint-Nicolas-du-Port a picturesque charm.

STRASBOURG (*Bas-Rhin*)

MONSTRANCE. 18th century. Copper gilt, silver parcel-gilt, cabochons. H. 34⅞″. Sainte-Madeleine.

pl. 127   The silver-gilt monstrance of the church of La Madeleine is one of the rare pieces of late Baroque art in the treasuries of France. It is composed of a sharply cambered copper-gilt base from which a thin stem rises, culminating in an asymmetrical knop that ends in a palmette that supports the "sun." The shape of the monstrance is essentially a modified lozenge, its corners rounded by swirling motifs. Surmounting the whole is a foliate cross on which the lance and sponge of the Crucifixion have been placed like diagonal rays. From around the lanula the body of the monstrance is formed of two superposed frameworks from which rays issue. Each section, embellished with rich naturalistic foliate decoration in which diamonds serve as flowers, is a complex of sinuous lines that undulate in curve and countercurve that echo and balance each other.

Vines, festooned and perforated volutes in S and C curves, fringes, lattice work, palmettes—the whole repertoire of the "picturesque genre" of the eighteenth-century decorators, from Meissonnier and Pineau, which we find on carved woodwork and the bronze decoration of furniture, is used here with an exuberance shown around the middle of the century in the *rocaille* cartouches of Babel or Civillies, whose influence made itself felt in Germany just as that style was tapering off in France. And the Strasbourg monstrance did in fact come from Germany. It is very similar to the monstrances of Wissemburg and Sallanches, and bears, as they do, the stamp of Augsburg (the letter Y, 1777–1779) and the stamp of master I.C.B. (John Carl Burger), who died in 1795.

The date when the monstrance came to the church of La Madeleine is unknown. One tradition is that it had belonged, before the Revolution, to the church of Saint-Etienne at Strasbourg.

Lyonnais — Savoy

LYONS (Rhône)

The Treasury of the primatial church of the Gauls, which was one of the richest in France, has retained almost nothing of its former possessions. The present treasures are on the whole pieces of fine quality, but of diverse and often uncertain origin. The presence of most of them in Lyons is due to the generosity of Cardinal Fesch, Napoleon's uncle, and especially to that of Cardinal de Bonald, who virtually rebuilt the entire Treasury of his cathedral in the nineteenth century. Among the pieces he assembled are several remarkable examples of Limoges enamel work, and, particularly, two plaques of a book cover (one representing the Crucifixion, the other, Christ surrounded by symbols of the Evangelists), a processional cross, a gemellione, an incense boat, some crosiers, etc. In addition, the Treasury owns a thirteenth-century nielloed silver crosier that is supposed to have belonged to St. Francis of Sales, and a small agate cross. Byzantine art is represented by a small ivory chest ornamented with rosettes and a portable altar.

PLAQUE OF A BOOK COVER SHOWING CHRIST IN MAJESTY. 13th century. Copper gilt, enamel. H. 9″, w. 4¾″. Treasury of the Cathedral.

pl. 132   The most beautiful of the book-cover plaques is a thirteenth-century copper-gilt piece representing Christ in Majesty against a dark-blue enameled ground. The figure, set in a mandorla between the alpha and the omega, sits on a cushion that rests on a rainbow. He blesses with his right hand and holds the Book in his left. Around His head is a cruciform halo of green and red enamel. The symbols of the Evangelists, with engraved bodies and cast heads, are at the four corners. This theme of Christ in Majesty, which is found in the manuscripts of the Carolingian period and which was often to occur in Romanesque tympanums, disappeared in Gothic times, but it was perpetuated in Limoges enamel work, which did not innovate, and indeed lagged in relation to other media in the matter of style and iconography.

GEMELLIONE. 14th century. Copper gilt, champlevé enamel. Diameter 9″. Treasury of the Cathedral.

fig. 18   The gemellione is decorated with scenes of secular subjects—a knight in combat with a monster, a woman walking on her hands, a juggler—and with one religious scene —St. Michael and the dragon. In the center of the composition an escutcheon (gules, lozenges or, a saltier or) in a circle of azure blue, is surrounded by the inscription: + S FULCONIS DE TUSSEIO. The spout is situated on the border, and ends in an animal head of copper gilt. This piece is a product of fourteenth-century Limoges workshops.

PORTABLE ALTAR. Byzantine, 13th century. Amethyst and silver gilt. H. 9½″, w. 11″. Treasury of the Cathedral.

fig. 19   The Byzantine portable altar consists of an amethyst plaque surrounded by a silver-gilt frame decorated with repoussé figures representing, on one side, St. Gregory the Theologian and, on the other, St. John Chrysostom: on the upper and lower borders are medallions: Christ between the Virgin and St. John above, St. Theodore and two archangels below. The medallions are set in a field of engraved foliate scrolls. On the back is an engraved inscription in Greek characters.

This portable altar, which has been compared with regard to the style of the figures to a triptych in the Victoria and Albert Museum and a silver reliquary in the Treasury of St. Mark's in Venice, is regarded as a product of thirteenth-century Byzantine art.

AGATE CROSS. 1528. Silver gilt, precious stones, H. 9½″, w. 4⅛″. Treasury of the Cathedral.

pl. 134   An agate cross enriched with precious stones, intaglios, and fine pearls, with a cornelian knob, is mounted in silver gilt on a rock crystal base. The extremities of the branches are decorated with cameos of cherubs' heads in trefoil settings. Below and on either side of Christ, two

18

19

silver-gilt statuettes represent the Virgin and St. John. This cross, which is extremely precious both in material and workmanship, is dated 1528.

SAVOY

The precious metalwork of Savoy is of a somewhat unusual character. Alongside the great treasuries of the diocesan cathedrals and abbeys, which were much depleted over the centuries, a large number of small treasuries were formed in the seventeenth century in parish churches. Most of the pieces contained in these treasuries had been made outside the region, and were the gifts of natives on their return to their villages after emigrating abroad as a part of the active movement of population which took place at this time. That is why we find in this province precious metalwork from Germany, Austria, France, Switzerland, Italy, and liturgical vestments of Genoese velvet or Lyons silk.

Virtually nothing remains of the treasuries of the diocesan cathedrals or monasteries. There is nothing at Saint-Jean-de-Maurienne, Hautecombe, Bellevaux, Bourget, or Reposoir; little, but of fine quality, at Chambéry, Abondance, Sixt, and Entremont. But parishes with a less important religious history—Saint-Nicolas-de-Véroce, Thonon, Sallanches, Séez, Sainte-Foy-en-Tarentaise, Tignes, Bellentre, and others—have treasuries which sometimes contain surprisingly good pieces. An examination of the goldsmith marks shows that, while some of these pieces were made by masters in Savoy, Paris, Lyons, Geneva, or Italy, others came from Germany or Austria, as for instance, the Bellentre monstrance, made by Georg Reischlid between 1661 and 1669, the Landry reliquary made by Hans Jacob Ernst between 1689 and 1703, the Montgirod cross, dated 1689, made by Gaspar Titz von Reissenfel, the Saint-Nicolas-de-Véroce monstrance from Vienna, dated 1733, and the Sallanches monstrance from Munich, dated about 1688.

BELLENTRE *(Savoy)*

SILVER CHEST.

fig. 20   This small silver chest is made by a method that is rare in France: stamped-out plaques are applied to a ground, the foliate scrolls joining in the center to form an eight-petaled daisy. The borders of the panels and the convex lid, in the form of a mansard roof, are similarly decorated. Between the two panels on the principal sides is a relief of fruit and an angel's head. The base is ornamented with a silver-gilt molding. This chest, which contains relics of St. Andrew and several other saints, may have originally been a jewel box. Although it bears no stamp, and no historical record exists of the circumstances in which it reached Bellentre in the seventeenth century, it may be assumed to be of Italian workmanship.

The same Treasury also contains two other interesting pieces: a monstrance—marked with the stamp of Georg Reischlid, donated in 1685 by J. F. Cléaz, who had emigrated to Augsburg, made his fortune in Austria, and wished to make a gift to his native country—and a cross.

PROCESSIONAL CROSS. 17th century.

fig. 21   On one side of the seventeenth-century processional cross is a figure of Christ, outlined against a rayonnant silver-gilt aureole; on the other, which was usually reserved for the Virgin, the patron saint of the church, St. Andrew.

pl. 129   The figure of the martyred Apostle is treated in very

21

20

vigorous style, conveying an impression of startling realism. The branches of the cross end in fleurs-de-lis. The crossing of the arms is decorated with a finely worked ornament of superposed quatrefoils.

CHAMBERY *(Savoy)*

IVORY DIPTYCH. Byzantine, 10th century. H. 11″, w. each   *pls. 130–*
panel 4¾″. Treasury of the Cathedral.   *131*

fig. 22   The Cathedral Treasury of Chambéry has the privilege of owning the most precious and ancient object of any Savoy church, an ivory Byzantine diptych of the tenth

22

century, which came into the Cathedral's possession relatively recently, since it was presented to the Treasury around the year 1846 by Mgr. Alexis Billiet, then archbishop of the city who had discovered it in a sacristy. The leaves, which are of exceptionally fine workmanship, are composed, like church portals, in superposed registers. In the lowest, figures of Apostles stand under arches over decorated medallions. In the central register, on one leaf, the Virgin in Majesty between SS. Peter and Paul and two angels, on the other, the Ascension—Christ in a mandorla seated on a rainbow surrounded by four angels above the Virgin who stands among the Apostles. In the compartments of the upper register are scenes from the life of Christ taken from the Gospels. In one tympanum is the Transfiguration, in the other, the Crucifixion, with two figures missing. The ivory was painted, and traces of polychrome are still visible, particularly on the rainbow. Inscriptions in Greek characters referring to the Triumph of the Virgin run along the borders of the leaves. The outside of the leaves is engraved with rosettes. The iconography of the Chambéry diptych, which is typically Byzantine, has been compared by Volbach with that of an ivory casket formerly in the Treasury of Saint-Denis, and now in the Louvre, who believes that the presence of such works in the west was consequent upon the particularly strong flow of imports from Byzantium in the tenth century, after the iconoclastic crisis had come to an end.

We might note, however, that Goldschmidt places the diptych in the twelfth century, and that J. G. Beckwith regards it not as a Byzantine but as a Venetian work, and places it in the thirteenth century.

MOUTIERS (Savoy)

The Treasury of the Cathedral of Moutiers, former capital of Tarentaise, is the only one of the three dioceses of Savoy, other than that of Chambéry, which has preserved important pieces from the medieval period.

IVORY TAU. 12th century. H. 35½″. Treasury of the Cathedral.

pl. 136   Tradition attributes the ivory tau to St. Peter II, founder of the Cistercian abbey of Tamié in 1132, archbishop of Tarentaise from 1138 to 1174. The head, in the form of a Romanesque capital of the Winchester school, is carved with dragons face to face among foliate scrolls devouring the vines. A flattened knob acts as a support below which is a ferrule into which the wooden shaft is fitted. The tau was recovered in 1818 in the ruins of the abbey of Tamié, and deposited in the monastery of La Novalaise; subsequently, it was placed in the Treasury of Moutiers Cathedral.

IVORY STATUETTE OF CHRIST. 17th century. H. 10¼″. Treasury of the Cathedral.

pl. 137   Another interesting piece at Moutiers is the seventeenth-century ivory statuette of Christ, whose contour follows the curve of the elephant's tusk out of which it was carved. The face, with its expressive eyes, is framed in dark hair and beard, which give it an Oriental cast marked by gentleness and resignation. The robe in which it is clothed is painted with a bold floral pattern of red and gold; the mantle is edged with gold and ornamented with rosettes and yellow and gold foliate scrolls. The feet and hands are missing. This piece, which was given to Moutiers in 1877 by the parish church of Albertville, is probably of Indo-Portuguese origin.

CASKET. Limoges, end of 12th century. Champlevé enamel on copper. H. 6¼″, w. 7⅞″, d. 3⅛″. Treasury of the Cathedral.

fig. 23   Moutiers also possesses a champlevé enamel casket that dates from the end of the twelfth century. On the front is Christ in a mandorla between the symbols of the Evangelists, and two Apostles standing under arches. The figures are enamel on a vermiculated ground, the heads, in relief, are attached. The back is decorated with circular medallions of a translucent red ground set in green enamel lozenges; on the medallions are scenes of struggle against monsters that symbolize the Vices. The short sides are

pl. 135   decorated with an angel and a haloed figure. On one side of the roof is the Lamb in a medallion supported by two angels; on the other, angels and human figures in medallions. The field between the lozenges is decorated with enamel foliage against a bright blue ground.

The Treasury at one time owned a very precious piece that is now in the Musée de Cluny: a casket formed of cut rock crystal, set in a silver-gilt mount richly decorated with filigree, pearls, and precious stones.

SALLANCHES (Haute-Savoie)

The Treasury of Sallanches, one of the most important of Savoy, includes, among other things, an ivory oliphant identified in a nineteenth-century inscription as a "hunt-

p. 33   ing horn of the priors of Chamonix before 1520," some
above   sixteenth-century silver cruets which are the oldest in France and recall in shape medical feeding cups, and two silver monstrances.

MONSTRANCE. 1688. Silver and silver parcel-gilt, embossed and engraved. H. 37⅞″. Treasury, Parish Church.

pl. 141   The larger of the two monstrances is very exuberantly ornamented with foliate scrolls, a host of figures in repoussé: God the Father surrounded by angels and saints;
pl. 140   the dove of the Holy Spirit; the pelican, symbolizing the Eucharist, with the crown of thorns for its nest; the Lamb carrying a banner marked with the cross and resting on

23

the Book with the seven pendant seals of the Apocalypse. In the back, the heart-shaped lanula is decorated with vines and sheaves of wheat. The very thin stem, with its unobtrusive knop, swells to a richly decorated base whose style is very typical of German precious metalwork of the seventeenth and eighteenth centuries. It bears the stamp of Munich as well as that of the goldsmith, J. G. Oxner, and the date 1688.

SEEZ (Savoy)

Of all the treasuries of Savoy, that of Séez possesses the most valuable collection of seventeenth-century precious metalwork, including pieces of exceptional quality which one is surprised to find in a small mountain village: embossed silver altar fittings dated 1683, a censer with its incense boat, cruets and their tray, donated in 1685 by three parishioners, a processional cross, and a very fine monstrance.

PROCESSIONAL CROSS. 1664. Silver sheets, embossed and engraved, on a wood core. H. (with shaft) 7′ 10½″, h. of cross 28″. Treasury, Parish Church.

fig. 24   The processional cross is sheathed—save at the extremities of the branches where parts have been lost—with delicately embossed and engraved sheets of silver representing the symbols of the Passion. The cross is attached to the knop by a flange that supports two statuettes, of SS. Peter and Paul. The knop itself is in the form of a miniature circular temple with arcades which shelter the twelve Apostles, whose figures are in repoussé; the top resembles a foliated cupola, and the whole rests on a

24

25

base of angels' heads. The staff, on which there are five beaded rings, is decorated with fleurs-de-lis. An inscription on the socket bears the name of the donor, François Michel, and the date, 1664.

MONSTRANCE. 1659–60. Silver, embossed and engraved. H. 17¾". Treasury, Parish Church.

pl. 138   The very graceful silver monstrance is composed of an oval base decorated with angels' heads from which rises a stem interrupted by two knops and three superposed flanges. Two brackets extend from the principal knop,
pl. 139 supporting graceful statuettes of angels whose raised arms seemed to support the rayed monstrance surmounted by a cross. The classical feeling is achieved here with a harmoniousness of proportions that is found in some other ostensories of the same kind; for example, that of Beaupréau, which was produced, as this one, by a Parisian workshop around the same years.

SIXT (Haute-Savoie)

CANDLESTICK. 12th century. Bronze. H. 11⅞". Treasury, Parish Church.

fig. 25   The Sixt Treasury possesses a very rare example of bronze Romanesque candlesticks. The base, which rests on three lions' paws, as well as the girandole, are decorated with winged monsters.

The Treasury also owns a twelfth-century ivory crosier, whose volute ends in the head of a dragon about to devour an ibex.

MITER. 14th century. Silk, embroidered with silk and gold threads. H. 11⅞", w. 11⅞". Treasury, Parish Church.

The very fine silk miter is embroidered in delicately tinted multicolored silk and gold thread. On one side is
pl. 143 the Coronation of the Virgin, on the other, the Annuncia-
pls. 144– tion. On the lappets, SS. Peter and Paul stand under
145 gables. This work, in the French manner, and influenced

by the art of miniature, is one of the most sophisticated examples of fourteenth-century workmanship in precious materials.

THONON (Haute-Savoie)

PROCESSIONAL CROSS. 16th century. Silver gilt, rock crystal. H. 23⅝". Church of Thonon.

fig. 26   The Thonon processional cross occupies a special place among the rock crystal crosses, of which there are examples from the fourteenth century onward. It is, with that of Joué-Etiau, in Maine-et-Loire, the finest sixteenth-century cross in the treasuries of France. The central portion, at the crossing, is in the *églomisé* technique, in which the back of a thin glass sheet is painted with black lacquer and a reflecting foil is put behind the picked-out drawing;
pl. 142 on one side, St. Claudius in bishop's attire with St. Mary the Egyptian, and on the other, the Deposition with St. Dominic. This technique and approach occur on a cross of the same period preserved in the Museu Machado de Castro at Coimbra. The cast silver-gilt knop is in the shape of a miniature temple with niches in which are statuettes of the Apostles; the staff is engraved with foliate scrolls. Below the knop is an engraved, dated inscription: PHYSSIO GALLSIUS REDEPTORE DICAVIT ET COVET VI SAE GYPTIACAE 1590. The donor, Gallois (GALLSIUS), was the younger brother of St. Francis of Sales; the stamp is that of Paris.

fig. 27 EAGLE LECTERN. 18th century. Sheet metal. Church of Thonon.

The eagle lectern of stamped-out and embossed sheet metal, dating from the eighteenth century, is of exceptionally skillful workmanship, particularly in the engraving of the eagle's feathers. The very elegantly designed base uses the ornamental device of daisies in a border of lozenged lattice work, which is characteristic of furniture and woodwork decoration of the early eighteenth century.

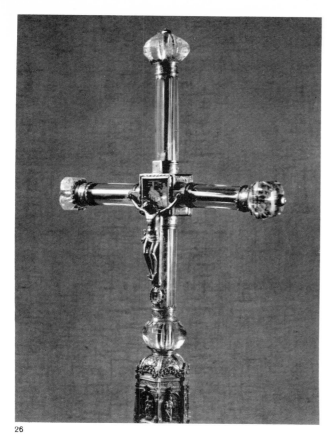

26

27

of great calamity. This relic, which still forms the chapter's arms, is no longer in the Treasury. It was enshrined in a casket known as the *Saint Châsse*, which was destroyed during the Revolution. This casket was covered with gold plaques and enriched with the most precious jewels, donated by illustrious visitors who came to pay homage to the Virgin: a gold belt set with 15 rubies, 10 sapphires, and 64 pearls, and finished with a buckle of gold and onyx, presented by Anne of Brittany; a large cross composed of 56 balas rubies and garnets, 18 sapphires, 22 pearls, 8 emeralds, 8 onyxes, and 4 jacinths, the whole arranged in three rows, set in large gold collets; "a piece of jewel work in the form of a rose surrounded by pearls, the heart of which was a circle of white and green enamel enriched with small stones with a large ruby in a gold setting in the center"; or again, "a big M, enameled and enriched with three diamonds, two emeralds, and a jacinth," etc. All these valuables were seized and dispersed during the Revolution. Only a few precious stones, including a cameo representing Jupiter, and the eagle donated by Charles V, were salvaged and deposited in the Cabinet des Médailles, where they remain to this day.

fig. 28

CHALICE OF HENRY III. 16th century. Copper gilt and translucent enamels. H. 8¼″. Treasury of the Cathedral.

In addition to the *Sainte Châsse*, the Chartres Treasury possessed many exceedingly rare pieces of goldsmithery, of which only three remain: a fourteenth-century portable altar of porphyry, said to have been donated by the English; a chalice decorated with flamelike motifs and fleurs-de-lis, and with translucent enamels—the Crucifixion on the base, and various busts on the knop. This chalice,

28

Normandy — Ile-de-France

CHARTRES *(Eure-et-Loir)*

A glance at the inventory of the Chartres Treasury as it existed in 1682 reveals an astonishing richness of precious pieces. The most celebrated piece, whose reputation extended throughout the length and breadth of Christendom in medieval times, was the skirt of the Virgin, a gift, according to legend, of Charles the Bald, who had inherited it from his ancestor, Charlemagne, and which was exhibited for the veneration of the people in times

bestowed by Henry III, makes us wish that the "very considerable" gift made by the same king in 1582 was still in the Treasury, namely, a cross of emeralds, pearls, and turquoises.

INCENSE BOAT. 16th century. Mother-of-pearl, silver gilt. H. 10⅝″. Treasury of the Cathedral.

pl. 152

The third piece is the large incense boat of mother-of-pearl which stands on a silver-gilt base. The upper part of the silver-gilt mount consists of Gothic pinnacles, while the base is exquisitely engraved with dolphins and arabesques in Renaissance style. Two angels stand on the base and display an escutcheon with the arms of the donor: or, six annulets gules, three, two, and one. Below, a scroll bears the following inscription: DES BIENS DE MONSEIGNEUR MILE D'ILLIERS EVESQUE DE LUCON DOYEN DE CHARTRES ET NEPVEU DE MESSYEURS MILE ET RENE D'ILLIERS EVESQUES DE CHARTRES (among the possessions of Mgr. Mile d'Illiers, bishop of Luçon and dean of Chartres, and nephew of Messrs Mile and René d'Illiers, bishops of Chartres).

The differences in style between the setting and the base have caused some authorities to believe that this incense boat, which was given to the Treasury in 1540, was not a homogeneous work. Nevertheless, the same mingling of Gothic and Renaissance styles occurs in much of the building of the same period, the closest example being the cloisters and choir of the Cathedral itself.

Two other very valuable pieces, which, however, did not belong to the original treasury, are also preserved in the Cathedral: the Casket of St. Anianus and the Reliquary of the Circumcision.

CASKET OF ST. ANIANUS. Limoges, 13th century. Copper gilt, champlevé enamel, cabochons, wood. H. 31⅛", w. closed 27⅛", open 31⅛", d. 11½". Treasury of the Cathedral.

pl. 147

The piece known as the Casket of St. Anianus, in the form of a gabled building with two doors, resembles a triptych when open, a tabernacle when closed. Copper figures with enamel eyes have been applied to a blue enamel ground decorated with copper foliate scrolls and enamel *fleurons*. On the outer leaves the twelve Apostles, under trefoil arches, receive the Holy Spirit, while red enamel flames descend upon them from two hands above.

pls. 148–149

On the inner leaves a female saint in a mandorla is on the left, an Apostle in a mandorla, on the right. These two applied figures have replaced the figures that were originally there: the Virgin surrounded by angels, and Christ in Majesty surrounded by the symbols of the Evangelists. The central part of the triptych depicts the Crucifixion, from which the figure of Christ is missing. On one side of the Cross stands the Virgin and a figure symbolizing the Church, on the other, St. John and a figure symbolizing the Synagogue. Above the cross is a half-length angel with outstretched arms; on either side, two angels, one carrying the sun, the other the moon. The roof and sides are decorated with a lattice-work design and busts of angels in medallions. The gable is edged with a stamped-out crest decorated with cabochons.

The piece, one of the finest products of thirteenth-century Limoges enamel work, was believed to have come from the church of Saint-Aignan. It is supposed to have been acquired in 1793 by Garnier-Sayer, a goldsmith, who sold it to the Cathedral in 1806. The suggestion that this was the casket made at the request of Pierre de Maincy after the fire of 1262 would appear to lack foundation. The recently advanced theory that the piece was a tabernacle seems to be borne out by the fact that it is comparable, as M. Jean Feray has pointed out, with two tabernacles, one discovered at Plumejeau near Cognac (Charente), now in the Metropolitan Museum of Art, New York, the other in the Valencia de Don Juan museum in Madrid. In that case, it is the earliest tabernacle preserved in France.

RELIQUARY OF THE CIRCUMCISION. 12th century and c. 1520. Silver gilt, rock crystal, ivory, gold. H. 7⅞". Treasury of the Cathedral.

pls. 150, 151

The Reliquary of the Circumcision comes from the abbey of Coulombs. It is gable-shaped, decorated with finials, and has two leaves which open. The outer leaves have an engraved scene of the Annunciation. On the back is a cross with the titulus and three nails between two escutcheons representing, on the right, the arms of the abbey of Coulombs: azure, three martlets sable, two and one; on the left, the arms of Mile d'Illiers, dean of Chartres, abbot of Coulombs from 1518 to 1526, then bishop of Luçon: or, a crosier surmounted by six annulets gules,

29

three, two, and one. There is no trace of any stamp or inscription. The reliquary may have been fashioned by J. Levasseur, goldsmith, who worked for the chapter of which Mile d'Illiers was dean.

The reliquary can be carried on a shaft in processions. Inside, protected by a rock-crystal plaque, is an ivory crucifix with a divine hand at the top, the whole set in a mount of gold filigree work decorated with pearls and precious stones. According to J. G. Beckwith, the ivory and filigree work may be credited to the early eleventh century, and may be of Anglo-Saxon origin. According to local tradition, the relic itself, of which no trace remains, and which was originally enshrined behind this cross, was brought back from the East by two knights of the Morbier family who had taken part in the first crusade. It was regarded as effective in soothing the pain of women in labor, a belief which gained it immense fame and thus made of it a source of considerable revenue for the abbey. In 1422, the relic of the Circumcision was sent to England at the request of Catherine of France, wife of Henry V. On its return, it was deposited in the Sainte-Chapelle in Paris, then in 1427, in the abbey of Saint-Magloire. It did not return to Coulombs until 1445. In 1790, after the destruction of the abbey, the reliquary was placed in the parish church, then, in 1906, in the town hall. In 1947, it was deposited in the Cathedral Treasury.

fig. 29

EVREUX (Eure)

CASKET OF ST. TAURINUS. 13th century. Copper and silver gilt, enamel plaques. H. 27⅝", base 41 x 17¾". Saint-Taurin.

St. Taurinus, the first bishop of Evreux, evangelized the area in the fourth century. A Benedictine abbey was founded by St. Landulphus in the seventh century on the site of St. Taurinus' tomb, and the holy bishop's relics were enshrined in a casket, around the middle of the thirteenth century during the abbacy of Gilbert (1240–55), as evidenced by an enameled inscription on the base: ABBAS GIBERTUS FECIT ME FIERI.

fig. 30

This celebrated casket is the finest example of the period, with its skillfully combined architectural and

30

sculptured decoration, it takes its place in the tradition of the great Mosan and Rhenish caskets in the shape of churches. Its only equivalent was the one at Nivelles in Belgium, which was in large part destroyed during the last war. And it has the advantage over another large Norman Gothic casket, in the Cathedral of Rouen, in that it has preserved its original appearance.

It is in the form of a church with a transept, the four gables enclose serried arches supported by colonnettes which terminate in a trefoil archway decorated with a foliate motif. On the long sides, two matching arches flank the principal one. Four pilasters that end in a complex of niches housing statuettes, fenestration, gables, pinnacles, and bell turrets are on either side of the gables that are crowned with a finial decorated with a knop consisting of six enameled faces on which lilies of France and Castilian castles alternate, and ends with a cone set in a foliate cluster. The octagonal tower that rises at the crossing is topped with the same motif. The base is supported by claws.

Every technique was used to create this masterpiece of goldsmithery: cast metal for the claws, the cones of the summits, the capitals of the colonnettes, the foliate scrolls that form the crests of the gables and the ridge of the roof, the leafy crockets of the extrados of the arches; bent metal for the architectural parts; engraving for the plaques decorated with lozenges stamped with fleurs-de-lis which fill the four major archways, and for the masonry of the pilasters; filigree for the trefoiled archways, composed of cusped volutes for the two at the ends of the nave and of foliate scrolls at those of the transept and their lateral arches. The figures and a band on the base decorated with foliate scrolls are in repoussé, as are the knops of the finials. The inscription is enameled. Plaques alternately filigreed and enameled with geometrical patterns simulate the voussoirs of the arches at the gables; similar plaques are along the ridge of the roof, and on the base, where the enameled motifs are of zoomorphic subjects.

The figures appear in the arcades and on the roof. Each of the short sides is occupied by a separate figure: at one end of the nave, Christ seated, at the other, an angel standing; at either end of the transept, St. Taurinus, and another saint, probably St. Landulphus. The four lateral arches of the long sides are devoted to the miracles

pl. 153

pls. 154– 155

of St. Taurinus, among them the Raising of Euphrosia, daughter of the provost of the city. The scenes depicted on the roof relate to the saint's life: prophecy of his birth by an angel, and presentation of the newborn infant by his mother, Euticia, to Pope Clement I; his baptism by St. Denis in the presence of St. Clement, who blesses him; presentation of the youthful Taurinus to the pope, and his consecration as a bishop; St. Taurinus raising a young man named Marinus; death of St. Taurinus seated in prayer in his coffin beneath a divine hand.

The casket had been stolen in 1564 by four thieves, who were condemned to death. It was plundered at the time; in particular, it was noted that some of the precious stones had disappeared. And a copper plate indicates that it was "repaired and regilded" in 1830, which led to the general conclusion that considerable remodeling had been done. However, a careful examination of the piece in 1959, in connection with cleaning and preservation, made it possible to determine the extent of such restoration, which had not been as considerable as expected, and had been confined to the following: the wooden core had been rebuilt and the casket regilded, but with mercury, according to the ancient practice, rather than by electrolysis, and only on the rebuilt surfaces; the angel of the nave end, the forearms of Christ, the body (with the exception of the head) of the purported St. Landulphus, all the small, paired figures in the niches date from the 1830 restoration; of the finials over the gables, only the one over the arch occupied by St. Taurinus is old; the foliated stems of the crockets on the extrados of the lateral arches of the long sides, some of the filigreed or enameled plaques of the base, gables, and arches were also remade, as was a part of the band at the base.

The Casket of St. Taurinus, which dates from the same period as the Sainte-Chapelle in Paris, was included in the 1960 exhibition devoted to St. Louis in the Sainte-Chapelle. The catalogue of the exhibition recalled that the saintly king had had the opportunity to examine the casket on the occasion of the enthronement in the Abbey of Saint-Taurin of one of his guardians of the Seal, Raoul de Grosparmin, subsequently cardinal-bishop of Albano, who took part as a legate in the eighth crusade, and died of the plague a few days before the king in 1270.

ROUEN *(Seine-Maritime)*

The description we possess of the former treasures of Rouen indicate that they were worthy of the primatial church of Normandy. But they suffered many vicissitudes over the centuries. As far back as the years between 1151 and 1153, the chapter gave Henry II certain pieces to help him in his struggle against Stephen of Blois for the throne of England. Then, in succession, came famines, fires, plunderings—in 1562, in the course of a single day, the Treasury was despoiled of over 50 pounds of gold and 300 pounds of silver—and finally the Revolution. This series of tribulations explains why nothing remains that is of very early date, or of very precious metal. The oldest pieces, with the exception of a thirteenth-century pyx of Limoges enamel, do not go farther back than the fourteenth century—for instance, the reliquary and the casket associated with St. Romanus. The best piece of fifteenth-century goldsmithery is a fine monstrance of copper gilt. The sixteenth century is represented by only a few objects, such as crosses, and osculatories (kisses-of-peace). The rest, which is more valuable, dates from the seventeenth and eighteenth centuries. Of all the objects in the Treasury, the most extraordinary is the Reliquary of St. Romanus; the most celebrated, the Casket of St. Romanus.

p. 38 above

RELIQUARY OF ST. ROMANUS. 14th and 17th centuries. Copper and silver gilt, rock crystal, ivory. H. 15⅛", h. of angels 9⅞". Treasury of the Cathedral.

fig. 31

The Reliquary of St. Romanus came to Rouen rela-

31

tively late. Before 1793, it belonged to the Treasury of Saint-Denis, and was known as the Reliquary of St. Placidus. In 1793, to protect it from destruction during the Revolution, the committee responsible for monuments placed it in the central museum of the arts (the future Louvre); then, at the order of the Ministry of the Interior, it was handed over to Cambacérès for his brother, the archbishop of Rouen.

The reliquary is first mentioned in 1655; it is described as follows in an inventory drawn up in 1726: a silver-gilt pedestal, two superposed rock crystals, one of them enshrining the relics of St. Placidus and his sister, Flavia, two ivory angels holding laurel branches, a silver-gilt cross surmounting the whole, and finally a copper-gilt base bearing an inscription with the names of Pierre de Plailly, prior, and Gautier de Pontoise, chamberlain of the monastery, and dated 1340. Two of these parts no longer exist, namely, the silver-gilt cross, which was replaced by a small ball of contemporary crystal, and the laurel branches held by the angels.

The reliquary is not homogeneous, but formed of pieces of varying dates and origins. The 1340 base has no connection, as far as origin is concerned, with the pedestal or the reliquary proper, which are of seventeenth-century workmanship; the rock crystals came from the ancient tomb of the saints which was destroyed in 1627; and the ivory angels, which comprise the most precious and rare element in the reliquary, may be dated somewhere around 1300 (the original wings were replaced by copper-gilt wings in the seventeenth century, then refashioned of ivory in the nineteenth century, and the head of the
pl. 157 angel on the right was restored in the seventeenth century). These two statuettes were not intended to decorate a reliquary; together with an ivory Virgin, now in the Taft Museum in Cincinnati, they formed a group which was dismantled in the seventeenth century.

CASKET OF ST. ROMANUS. 14th century. Copper gilt, champlevé enamel. H. 28¾″, l. 33½″, d. 16½″. Treasury of the Cathedral.
pl. 156 The Casket of St. Romanus is traditionally known as the *fierte.* The origin of the particular veneration it enjoyed lies in a miracle that legend attributes to St. Ro-

manus, bishop of Rouen in the seventh century. The population was being terrorized by a dragon, and the holy bishop, accompanied by a man who had been condemned to death, approached the monster and chained him up. Since then, the cathedral chapter had enjoyed the privilege each year of setting at liberty a man condemned to death. On this occasion, the *fierte* was carried in procession to the prison on Ascension Day. From there, the procession would make its way to a part of the city also known as the *fierte,* where the prisoner would raise the casket three times, and then leave, a free man.

This casket was known as the "casket of all saints" until 1776, when it replaced the *fierte* that had been given to the Cathedral in 1119 by Archbishop Rotrou; the latter piece had been damaged during the Protestant sack of 1562, and was in ruins. The present casket is of copper gilt. Its oldest portions date back to the fourteenth cen-
p. 25 tury. It represents a church decorated on each side with arches beneath which are repoussé figures. In 1776, those that were missing were replaced by others cast on those that existed. In addition, to underline the new purpose of the casket, two statuettes were placed on the roof: St. Romanus with the dragon at his feet, and before him, the kneeling prisoner. This bizarre and ill-proportioned arrangement was further aggravated in 1869 by a clumsy restoration. The statuettes on the roof were replaced by others, still more ill-proportioned, and neo-Gothic elements were introduced in order to render the work "harmonious." At the same time, the number of statuettes around Christ and the Virgin was increased from eight to twelve, obviously in order to transform the saints of this former "casket of all saints" into Apostles. Six new figures, created by means of electroplating from ancient models, appeared on the casket, while some of the originals disappeared. Two of them were recently identified, one in the David Weill collection, the other in the Wallace Collection in London.

The casket, which was carefully restored in 1956, has been left as it appeared in 1869, except that certain figures which were altogether too shocking were removed, in particular those perched on the roof, whose presence deprived the work of all traces of authenticity.

The Loire Valley

ANGERS (Maine-et-Loire)

The history of the Angers Treasury resembles that of most of the great treasuries of France which, after possessing great riches that testify to the generosity of kings, ecclesiastics, and even the humble faithful, were depleted as a result of wars, the needs of the State, and especially the Revolution, which scattered all these marvels. Of the caskets, reliquaries, sacred vessels, precious ivories, tapestries, etc., enumerated in the various inventories drawn up since 1255, there remain only two pieces: an antique vase of red prophyry which King René of Anjou sent to the chapter of Angers on September 13, 1450, and which was believed to have contained the water changed into wine by Christ at the marriage feast of Cana, and an ivory oliphant which, according to legend, had enshrined the relics of Abraham, Isaac, and Jacob, and had been bestowed by William of Beaumont, bishop of Angers from 1202 to 1240, on his return from the fifth crusade. Nevertheless, the new Treasury that was gradually built up now contains a number of valuable pieces, such as the very fine seventeenth-century rock-crystal cross enshrining a sacred thorn presented by King René, and especially some very interesting objects recovered in the course of excavations. Such objects include the furnishings found in 1923 in the tomb of Bishop Ulger, who was
p. 34 buried in 1148 in the Cathedral, among which are a
left number of fabrics, a pewter chalice, and:

IVORY CROSIER. 12th century. H. of staff 35″, h. of volute
4½″. Treasury of the Cathedral.

fig. 32   The volute is decorated with buds, curves over in twigs
and pearled branches, and ends in a human head with a
long mustache. The crosier is probably of English origin,
since its style is similar to that of the Winchester school.

LEAD SEAL. 12th century. Diameter 2¼″, thickness ⅛″.
Treasury of the Cathedral.

fig. 33   A seal of cast lead, which was hung about the bishop's
neck by a silk cord. The bishop is represented on the
seal as robed in a chasuble, bareheaded, his right hand
blessing, his left holding a crosier.

33

32

BRONZE PLAQUE WITH THE IMAGE OF A MONK. 14th century.
Treasury of the Cathedral.

pl. 159   A fourteenth-century bronze plaque, bearing the effigy
of a monk, was discovered during the excavations at the
ancient abbey of Ronceray, and is provisionally deposited
in the Treasury of Angers.

E V R O N *(Mayenne)*

The Treasury of the Benedictine abbey of Evron, founded
in the seventh century, was built up around a devotion
linked to the legendary origins of the abbey, that of the
Holy Thorn and Our Lady's Milk, which has been perpetuated by pilgrimages that continue to this day, and
the theme of which was repeated in the sculpture, mural
painting, stained glass, and furnishings of the old abbey
church, which became the basilica of Notre-Dame de
l'Epine (Our Lady of the Thorn).

The miracle which determined the foundation of the
abbey is related in the *Acta* of the bishops of Le Mans,
an apocryphal ninth-century text. A pilgrim had brought
from the Holy Land a relic of the "milk of the Virgin."
One night before he lay down to sleep, he hung his
precious burden on the branches of a hawthorn. When
he awakened, he could not recover it, because the bush
had grown so high. St. Haduinus began to pray. The

branches bowed down, and the venerable bishop of Le
Mans was able to reach the Sacred Milk. Having thus
recognized the intentions of the Mother of God, he built
a monastery dedicated to her on the site of the miraculous
hawthorn. Here we have an illustration of the devotion
to the relics of the Virgin's Milk, which pilgrims brought
back with them from Palestine, and to which we referred
in the introductory text.

We have little information about the contents of the
Treasury before the fifteenth century. We know from the
chartulary that it possessed three remarkable pieces: "a
crucifix covered with strips of gold weighing 2 pounds,
6 ounces, a statue of the Holy Virgin covered with strips
of silver, and 4 feet, 4 inches high, and a silver-gilt reliquary," which was that of the Sacred Milk. The only one
of these three pieces now remaining is the Virgin known
as Our Lady of the Thorn. The crucifix disappeared, and
the reliquary of the Sacred Milk, stolen in 1508, was
replaced by the one we have now. This reliquary, together with Our Lady of the Thorn and three other pieces
also connected with the legendary miracle constitute the
present Treasury.

VIRGIN AND CHILD. 15th century. Silver parcel-gilt. H.
13¾″. Notre-Dame de l'Epine.

The three pieces mentioned above are: two large busts,
one of St. Haduinus, bishop of Le Mans, and one of
pls. 162, Pope St. Leo; and a small and graceful silver Virgin, very
163   feminine with its long silver-gilt hair framing a little
curved forehead under a crown of high leafy *fleurons.*

OUR LADY OF THE THORN. 13th century. Silver parcel-gilt,
translucent enamels, rock crystal, precious stones over a
wood core. H. 56⅜″. Notre-Dame de l'Epine.

pls. 160,   Thus the oldest piece, since the Calvinist devastations
161   in the sixteenth century and then those of the Revolution,
is the statue of Our Lady of The Thorn. It is both sculpture and precious metalwork, and is comparable in style
to the productions of the workshops of the Ile-de-France
in the early part of the thirteenth century. It represents
a Virgin seated in the manner of the *Sedes Sapientiae,*
those sovereign and impassive Majesties of a type that
originated in Carolingian times and, like this one, continued into the Gothic period, when, after the second half

of the thirteenth century, the representation of a more recognizable humanity developed.

The figure and the throne are sculptured of a single block of oak; the piece is life-size and is the largest surviving statue reliquary in France. The Virgin sits enthroned on a backless seat, wearing a crown, her left hand holding the Child, who blesses and holds the cruciform orb. In her right hand, a wild rose unfolds—the Thorn. Wild roses also decorate the translucent blue and green enamels, surrounded by rock crystals, of the crown, which is of silver gilt, and the veil on which it rests. The clothes of both Virgin and Child are fashioned of sheets of silver nailed to the wooden statue. Under her cloak, the Virgin wears a garment held at the waist by a belt and edged at the neck and wrist with inserted strips of embossed silver gilt; the same edging, on a smaller scale, occurs at the neck and wrists of the Child. On the belt, which is closed by a buckle embellished with a turquoise and four garnets, pieces of rock crystal and glass paste, mounted in pairs, separate the translucent enamels with alternating green and blue grounds, in the middle of each of which a letter stands out in silver gilt. Together all the letters form the words, "Maria Virgo."

By their size and by the preciousness of the materials of which they are made, the crown and belt resemble the real crown and belt of a thirteenth-century queen. However, since the statue was intended to be seen only from the front, neither crown nor belt go around the figure; they are semicircular. The metal is confined to the clothing. The faces, feet and hands are painted an ivory tint. The seat is red and green. The flower that the Virgin holds is scarlet.

The piece was so clumsily repaired in 1858 that its authenticity could be doubted; it was extremely hard to distinguish the original portions under the parts that had been painted over or added. A meticulous restoration in 1961, however, brought back all its original qualities, thereby revealing a work whose extraordinary beauty had gone unsuspected.

RELIQUARY OF OUR LADY'S MILK. 16th century. Silver gilt, enamel, cabochon, crystal. H. 9⅞″. Notre-Dame de l'Epine.

fig. 34   The Reliquary of Our Lady's Milk contained the relic whose miraculous origin was hallowed by tradition. For the monks, therefore, it was the most precious piece in the Treasury. This was the piece that was concealed during public calamities; thus, when the abbey was pillaged in 1577 by the militia of the Calvinist regiment of Sieur de Bussy, the reliquary escaped destruction because the monks had taken it with them when they fled. The original reliquary was stolen in 1508; the present one, which is still in the Evron church, was fashioned after the earlier one at the request of François de Chateaubriand, second commendatory abbot, for the new relic that he had brought back from Rome in 1515. It is of silver gilt, cast, and exquisitely engraved, and bears the stamp of Angers; it is ascribed to Hayeneufve, a goldsmith of that city. It is shaped like a centrally planned miniature temple surmounted by a ribbed dome that rests on four pillars that culminate in Corinthian capitals and are topped with pinnacles. The enameled arms of the donor (gules, semée of fleur-de-lis or) are on the frontals, save on one side, which is embellished pl. 164 with a marvelous jewel consisting of a thick molded glass cabochon, of a very deep, dark blue—perhaps a piece of antique glass—set in gold enameled white, green, and red. Under the vault formed by the intersecting arches, a pyramid of crystal and silver gilt shelters the relic, which is enclosed in a pewter cylinder.

LE MANS (Sarthe)

Among the vicissitudes suffered by the Treasury of Le Mans, the most recent was the theft of reliquaries and chalices committed one night in 1903. The Treasury still

34

contains liturgical vestments embroidered with fleurs-de-lis and silver which, according to tradition, were the gifts of Louis XIV; seventeenth-century chalices; a small sixteenth-century reliquary with translucent enamels; two osculatories (pax, kiss-of-peace), one of which is dated 1550; a vertical rock-crystal and silver-gilt fifteenth-century reliquary containing the relic of the finger of St. Julian, first bishop of Le Mans, with the inscription LE DOY DE MONS. S. JULIEN and engraved with the scene of the holy bishop of Le Mans, in full episcopal regalia, miraculously causing the spring of Centonomius to flow; also:

ALTAR CROSS. 17th century. Silver gilt and rock crystal. H. 35½″. Treasury of the Cathedral.
pl. 165   The large rock-crystal altar cross was donated in 1626 by Etienne Gueffier, a diplomat born in Le Maine, whose arms are engraved on the base.

RELIQUARY. 15th century. Silver gilt and rock crystal. H. 7½″. Treasury of the Cathedral.
fig. 35   This reliquary is of the same period as the Reliquary of the Finger of St. Julian. Its horizontal cylinder, which terminates in six-petaled daisies, is supported by a hexagonal stem that rises from a six-sided base delicately engraved with leaves.

In addition, two pieces that belong to two small churches of the area have been deposited in the Cathedral Treasury within the last few years:

RELIQUARY OF THE TRUE CROSS. 17th century. Silver gilt and rock crystal. H. 15¾″. From the church of Meurcé.
fig. 36   The Reliquary of the True Cross is in the form of a crystal cross mounted on a silver-gilt base. It is mentioned in the 1628 inventories as follows: "Cross of rock crystal, supported by silver gilt, at the intersection are four pieces of the True Cross of Our Lord, Jesus Christ, given by the late Madame Jeanne de Poyet, lady of Bourdelan and lady of Meurcé." We know that the donor was living as late as 1591. The crystal base, which had probably been broken, was replaced by cut glass, and the metal part regilded in 1858, as evidenced by the stamp.

ANGEL RELIQUARY. 16th century. Silver parcel-gilt and copper gilt. H. 7½″. From the church of Saint-Pavace.

pls. 166–168 This reliquary, discovered in 1957 in a cupboard in the sacristy of the church of Saint-Pavace, is a charming statuette of an angel of repoussé silver partially gilded, resting on a copper base which is also in repoussé. This angel, dating from the sixteenth century, recalls by its attitude the stone or marble cherubs that accompany recumbent tomb figures and carry on cushions the arms or crowns of the deceased. Like them, this angel kneels and holds in his hands a medallion closed with a rock crystal which contains the relic. The inscription that circles the medallion says: DU CHIEF DE SAINT PAVACE (of the head of St. Pavace).

36

35

LE PUY-NOTRE-DAME (Maine-et-Loire)

RELIQUARY OF THE BELT OF THE VIRGIN. 16th century. Gold, silver gilt, crystal. Church of Le-Puy-Notre-Dame.

The relic of the Belt of the Virgin (length 64″, width 2″) is wrapped in an ancient piece of red, green, and white material, which is itself concealed under a multicolored modern textile. On the material are two crystal lenses set in silver-gilt denticulated mounts and at either end of the belt is a gold clasp (2″ x 1″) decorated on either side with pierced rosettes and engraved figures representing, on one of the clasps, an angel holding pl. 169 an escutcheon with three fleurs-de-lis, and on the back a Virgin of the Annunciation, and on the other, a Virgin and Child and an angel of the Annunciation. The records make it possible to establish that they were fashioned around the year 1537 by Matthew Dupont, a goldsmith of Saumur.

The relic, which is mentioned as far back as 1391, was reputed to be particularly effective in pregnancy. It was therefore borrowed in 1495 by Queen Anne, wife of Charles VIII; then, years later, by Queen Anne of Austria, who ordered the "holy belt" to be brought to her at Saint-Germain several times in the course of the year 1638. On September 5 of that year, the future Louis XIV was born. The two lenses bought by the queen from Roberdot, the goldsmith, for 35 livres, are evidence of her gratitude. The belt was long preserved in a magnificent silver gilt casket donated by Louis XIII; it dis-

appeared at the time of the Revolution, but was returned to the vestry in 1802 by a man named Guillon.

SAINT-BENOIT-SUR-LOIRE (Loiret)

CASKET OF ST. MOMMOLINUS. 7th century. Repoussé copper plaques over a wood core. H. 4⅜″, w. 5⅛″, d. 1⅞″. Abbey Church.

fig. 37 The celebrated abbey of Saint-Benoît-sur-Loire, formerly the abbey of Fleury, possesses a piece of exceptional interest which is known as the Casket of St. Mommolinus, which was discovered in 1642 under the altar of the Abbey Church. It is shaped like a tomb or ossuary, covered with copper plaques worked in a repoussé decoration of interlaced circles enclosing crosses and stars, motifs derived from the East; on each side of the sloping roof, six busts of angels with wings lowered; on one of the short pls. 170–sides, beneath an interlace, a figure with raised arms, in 171 very archaic style. This representation of an orant, which goes back to Early Christian times, occurs also on Frankish and Burgundian buckles of bronze or ivory, on an eighth-century piece of linen in the Treasury of Sens, on which is the oldest illustration of the theme of the Assumption, on the sarcophagus of Lurs, etc. The casket can be dated from the inscription on the back: MUMMA FIERI JUSSIT IN AMORE SCE. MARIE ET SCI. PETRI. The abbey had been dedicated to the Virgin and St. Peter before the translation of the relics of St. Benedict, which took place in 655, and the deed of gift to the original patron saints could only have been previous to that date. The rudimentary workmanship and the crudeness of the representation of human figures are very characteristic of the Merovingian period to which this casket belongs; with that of Saint-Bonnet-Avalouze (fig. 46, pl. 197), it is the oldest of French treasures.

ORLEANS (Loiret)

ENAMEL DISKS. About 1075. Cloisonné enamel on gold. Diameter 1⅞″. Treasury of the Cathedral.

The excavations of 1937 in the area of Orléans Cathedral undertaken by Canon Chenesseau led to important

285

37

38

discoveries of funerary furnishings (chalice) and liturgical objects (crosiers). The most important discovery was made in the tomb of Raoul Grosparmin, bishop of Orléans from *fig. 38* 1306 to 1311, of two disks of Byzantine origin; they were found on the skeletal remains of the hands, and had thus served as plaques of episcopal gloves. One represents the *pl. 172* Pantocrator, between the sigla IC and XC, the other, whose workmanship seems less skilled, represents the *pl. 173* Virgin, between the sigla MP and OV, extending both hands forward in a gesture of prayer. By comparison with the disk of St. Demetrius in the Louvre, which appears to be slightly later in date, these disks have been dated by Marquet de Vasselot to the last quarter of the eleventh century. It has been pointed out that the bishop was a friend of Philip the Fair, who might have bestowed the plaques. A. Frolow takes a different view and suggests a later date on the basis of certain paleographic details.

SAINT-CALAIS *(Sarthe)*

SHROUD OF ST. CARILEFUS OF CALAIS. 7th century? Multi-colored silk. H. 25¼″, l. 30⅜″. Parish Church.
pl. 174 The fabric known as the Shroud of St. Calais, in which the head of the saint was wrapped, was discovered in a reliquary of the parish church in 1947. The subject in the repeated medallions is one of the most common themes in Sassanian art: horsemen facing one another on either side of a hom (tree of life), which is derived from the classical story of the hunt of the fifth-century Persian king, Bahram V, called Gor, who with a single arrow killed a lion that was devouring a wild ass. Two horsemen in conical hats turn in their saddles to shoot arrows at two lions attacking some wild asses. Dogs, stags, and birds also take part in the scene. The tree is in the form of a palm. The border design of the roundels is made up of cruciform motifs and a garland of heart-shaped palmettes. The design is yellow, green, and pink on a pale-blue ground.

This fabric may be compared with the textiles from the Reliquary of St. Cunibert, in the Diözesan Museum, Cologne; of St. Gervase of Maastricht, in the Victoria and Albert Museum; of Sant'Ambrogio in Milan; and of Mozat, in the Musée Historique des Tissus in Lyons. Some authorities (Volbach, D. Shepherd) regard it as a work in the Sassanian tradition executed in Constantinople in the seventh century. This opinion, however, is disputed by J. G. Beckwith and D. Schlumberger, who agree on the place of origin but put the date at the end of the eighth or the beginning of the ninth century. An interesting technical point should be noted in connection with this material, which has been studied by G. Vial, a professor at the International Center for the Study of Ancient Textiles *(Bulletin de liaison du Centre international d'étude des textiles anciens,* July 1964, pp. 27–38): although the material is woven silk, the threads of certain colors (pink and green) are not included in the weft, but are brocaded.

SAINT-MARS-SOUS-LA-FUTAYE *(Mayenne)*

The church of this village in Mayenne possesses objects of exceptional quality, of whose origin we have no information: liturgical vestments (a chasuble and two dalmatics of crimson velvet with appliqué bands decorated with a plant design embroidered in gold thread, dating from the early seventeenth century), which an unauthenticated tradition associates with the name of Mazarin, and especially a bronze processional cross.

PROCESSIONAL CROSS. End of 11th century, beginning of 12th. Bronze, rock crystal cabochons. H. 24¾″, w. of arms 12⅝″. Parish Church.
This is one of the most ancient processional crosses preserved in the treasuries of France. Like most of the Romanesque crosses, it is quite small, and is supported by a metal shaft whose knop is a slightly flattened sphere decorated with rock crystals. It is a cross patté edged with a raised border of a beaded design; olive-shaped ovals project from each angle. Rock crystal cabochons decorate the branches, the intersection of which *pl. 175* expands to a square. The figure of Christ is clothed in a short *perizonium,* fastened at the right hip, which discloses the knees. The feet, attached by two nails, rest side by side on the suppedaneum. The head, on which there is no crown, leans to the right. The face is bearded, and the shoulder-length hair is arranged in parallel symmetrical strands on either side of a central parting. The ribs are very prominent.
All these features place the Christ of Saint-Mars-sous-la-Futaye in the tradition of the eleventh-century Ottonian Christs (of Bernard of Hildesheim, of Werden, etc.), but with a less sophisticated engraving. Comparable pieces in France are in Saint-Julien-aux-Bois and in the museum of Saint-Jean d'Angers, but in these there is greater concern with anatomic detail. The Saint-Mars piece seems to be of an earlier date. If this is so, it might be placed at the end of the eleventh or the beginning of the twelfth century. The shape of the cross would confirm this date; it is a very ancient one (similar, for instance, to that of the cross of St. Eligius at Saint-Denis), but the central square rarely occurs before the twelfth century (the Fulda cross).

VARZY *(Nièvre)*

The Varzy Treasury houses the relics of St. Eugenia, brought back in 923 by Bishop Gaudry of Auxerre, as well as parts of the body of St. Regnobert, bishop of Bayeux (whose chasuble, of twelfth-century workmanship, is in the Treasury of Bayeux Cathedral).

RELIQUARY OF THE SKULL OF ST. REGNOBERTUS. Mid 13th century with parts of the 15th century. Silver, copper gilt on a wood core. H. 13¾″, diameter 13¾″. Treasury, Saint-Pierre.

fig. 39   The reliquary of the saint's skull is octagonal in form, and rests on a filigreed base supported by claw-shaped feet. It is covered by a hexagonal copper-gilt dome which is decorated with an engraved design and whose "ribs" are emphasized by stamped-out crests. The octagonal portion is ornamented with seated figures of *pl. 177* repoussé silver—probably Apostles—separated by columns. The very classical treatment of these figures is an interesting example of the classicizing tendency that is apparent in a whole series of pieces of precious metalwork made around the year 1200 principally in the workshops of the banks of the Meuse, and evident particularly in the art of Nicholas of Verdun, whose sculpture workshops, such as the one at Reims, are the apogee.

ARM RELIQUARY. Beginning of 11th century. Gold on a wood core. H. 22″. Treasury, Saint-Pierre.

fig. 40   The Treasury also owns an arm reliquary which is *pl. 176* exceptional not only by reason of its execution and style, but also because of its age and of the preciousness of the material of which it is made; it is the only surviving example of an arm reliquary sheathed not with silver nor silver gilt, but with gold. On the basis of the style of the fiiligree decoration, it may be placed at the beginning of the eleventh century. This means that this reliquary and the one in Braunschweig are the oldest surviving arm reliquaries.

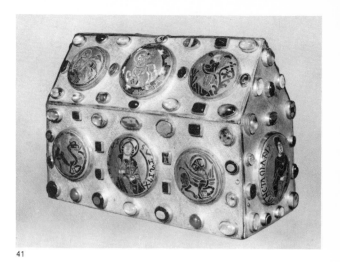

41

touches of white or pink, stand out against the copper and gilt ground. These medallions are very similar to those which decorate the small casket reliquary in Conques (pl. 219), which an inscription places in the abbacy of Boniface (1107–8); they are greatly influenced by the forms and style of Byzantine enamels, which early champlevé enameling sought to imitate, and by Oriental textiles, whose zoomorphic themes occur inside the medallions. The Bellac casket may thus be placed in the first quarter of the twelfth century, and would thus take its place, as Mme M. M. Gauthier has pointed out (*Emaux limousins champlevés,* Paris, 1950, p. 151) at the beginning of the series of enameled caskets produced in the Limoges region.

BEAULIEU *(Corrèze)*

Beaulieu was originally a Benedictine abbey, founded in 840, in a little valley of the Seye, by Raoul of Turenne, archbishop of Bourges. In 1141 or 1144, it received the Cistercian rule from St. Bernard, who came in person to visit the house, and sent twelve monks there from Clairvaux. The new monastery grew so fast that, by the end of the twelfth century, it had become necessary to rebuild it on a larger scale. Conventual buildings from that period are still extant around the church, which was rebuilt in the thirteenth century. The monastery lasted until the Revolution. Several remarkable pieces in its Treasury have been preserved: an early-twelfth-century reliquary of Byzantine origin, in the form of a lantern (p. 51, top left), two thirteenth-century arm reliquaries, and a very celebrated Virgin which probably dates from the time of the reform of the monastery.

VIRGIN AND CHILD. Beginning of 13th century. Repoussé silver, silver gilt, intaglios, fiiligree on a wood core. H. 24″. Church of Beaulieu.

pl. 179   Seated in majesty, the figure of the Virgin is entirely sheathed with silver plaques, as is that of the Child, who holds the Book in his left hand and blesses with his right. The Virgin is dressed in a long robe and a cloak secured at the right shoulder; on her breast is an antique sardonyx cameo representing the head of a woman, perhaps an empress. Her hair is covered with a veil on top of which is a crown in the form of a diadem, ornamented with stones and antique intaglios set in smooth-wired filigree work. The Child wears a similar crown. The seat has no back. It, too, is sheathed with silver plaques, and its uprights are decorated with a repoussé egg-and-dart motif. The veil, cloak, hair, and orphreys are of silver gilt.

The Virgin of Beaulieu, like that of Orcival (pl. 66)— the two most celebrated of the *Sedes Sapientiae* of the Auvergne region—belongs to the series of skillfully fashioned figures of the Virgin in Majesty with which popular devotion lined the medieval pilgrimage routes.

39   40

Poitou — Limousin

BELLAC *(Haute-Vienne)*

CASKET. 12th century. Copper gilt, cabochons, enamels. H. 7¾″, w. 10⅝″, d. 5⅛″. Church of Bellac.

fig. 41   The Bellac casket, in the shape of a house, is sheathed with crosshatched copper-gilt plaques onto which cabochons and intaglios mounted in bezels have been applied, some oval, some rectangular, alternating with enamel medallions. The figures represented are: on the front, Christ surrounded by symbols of the Evangelists; on one short side, the Virgin, on the other, the Lamb; on the roof of the back, stylized animals (the three medallions of this side are missing). The enamels, which are predominantly blue, turquoise, and green with occasional

CHAMBON-SUR-VOUEZE (Creuse)

BUST RELIQUARY OF ST. VALERIA. Beginning of 15th century. Repoussé silver, parcel-gilt, cabochons, enamels, semiprecious stones. H. 12″, diameter of base 10⅝″, diameter of crown 5⅛″. Church of Chambon-sur-Voueze.

pl. 180
The bust reliquary of St. Valeria is of repoussé silver. The hair and bodice are gilded, the lips painted pink. The top of the head is hinged, and can be opened to insert the skull in the reliquary. The neck is cut, in memory of the martyrdom of the saint, who was decapitated. On her curled hair is a crown formed of a narrow engraved band edged with torsades and decorated with an intaglio of sardonyx and four-petaled flowers whose centers consist alternately of two small silver balls, an emerald, and an enameled plaque. The saint wears a collar which opens by means of a hinge and, like the crown, consists of a narrow band, but with a plain ground, edged with torsades; it is decorated with escutcheons enameled with the arms of France and the counts of the Marches, and with cabochons set in claw mounts. One of the escutcheons represents the Virgin and Child in translucent enamel. Only three of the eight pendants originally attached to the collar remain. The central jewel consists of a silver-gilt circle in which is a trefoil ornamented with a ruby, rose diamonds, pearls, and green glass beads. According to tradition, the collar was presented in 1440 by King Charles VII, in memory of the victory of the dauphin, Louis, at Chambon. Another theory is that it was donated by James II, count of the Marches, in 1412, on the occasion of his liberation from the tower of Bourges.

CHARROUX (Vienne)

The abbey of Charroux, founded in Charlemagne's reign by Roger, count of Limoges, and Euphrasia, was renowned

42

throughout the Middle Ages. Successive churches were built in 1028, 1095, and 1136. The last of these was set on fire by the Protestants during the wars of religion, and nothing remains of it save the circular lantern at the crossing of the transept. The abbey was very wealthy and possessed valuable treasures, of which there remain two very fine reliquaries found accidentally in 1856 under an arcade in the cloisters, in a hiding place which may have been made there during the wars of religion.

PANEL RELIQUARY. 13th century. Silver parcel-gilt and niello, filigree, cabochons. H. 10¼″. Former Abbey Church.

pl. 181
The first is a panel reliquary that dates from the middle of the thirteenth century. It is of partially gilded and nielloed silver and is supported on a circular base whose stem is decorated with a knop. When the reliquary is closed, it forms a square composed of three triangular hinged leaves; when these leaves are open, they form an equilateral triangle. These three leaves are decorated on the outside with filigree work and enamels bearing the arms of France and Castile; on the inside are engraved figures of Christ blessing and two monks kneeling.
pl. 182
In the center of the triangle, in a rectangular niche, two silver-gilt repoussé statuettes of angels hold a receptacle that has been pierced with a quatrefoil that frames an oval silver box that is engraved on either side with a figure of Christ and on the periphery with the inscription: HIC CARO SANGUINIS CRISTI CONTINETUR.

This little box, which may be placed at the end of the twelfth century, in turn contains a Byzantine encolpion (a small portable reliquary that was hung around the neck) of gold with silver and green-gold niello. On one
pl. 183
side is the Virgin with a Greek inscription that says, "Behold thy Son." On the other side are two saints with their names, Demetrius and Pantaleon. Finally, around the outer edge, there is an invocation to the Virgin, which reads, according to Jacques Coupry, "All holy Mother of God, during my life, abandon not the human being that I am. Protectress, do not deliver me to hunger, but come to my aid and have pity on me. Amen." Inside are enshrined some fragments of a cross and of bones.

RELIQUARY. Venetian, 14th century. Silver gilt. H. 15″, diameter of box 4¾″. Former Abbey Church.

pl. 185
The second reliquary, which dates from the fourteenth century, is altogether different in style from the first. It appears to be the work of a Venetian goldsmith. From a polylobe base richly decorated with stones set in bezels, monsters, and interlaced scrolls, rises a long stem interrupted by a knop decorated with flamboyant architecture. Four statuettes of the Evangelists rise obliquely from this knop, mounted on hinges that are attached to the reliquary proper. The latter is a round horn box, decorated with four rectangular enamel plaques and covered by a lid with gables and pinnacles surmounting trefoiled arches under which are miniatures done on parchment. Above the gables rise seven round turrets. This lid opens on a crystal cylinder containing a little gold reliquary in the form of the earthenware phials that pilgrims often brought home from Palestine. On
pl. 184
one face, surrounding a rosette, is the inscription: AZO COMES IUSI. The other face is convex and smooth. The outer edge is decorated with a band of interlace.

HEAD OF A TAU. About 1020. Ivory. H. 3⅝″. Former Abbey Church.
fig. 42
We should also mention an ivory tau in the Treasury, which forms a triangle that ends in animal heads. It was found in 1935, together with a gold pastoral ring, in the tomb of Girard, bishop of Limoges, who had gone to Poitiers for the feast of All Saints in the year 1020, and died at Charroux, where he was buried.

GIMEL (Corrèze)

CASKET OF ST. STEPHEN. End of 12th century–beginning of 13th. Copper gilt, enamels. H. 8¼″, w. 11″, d. 4⅜″. Church of Gimel.

pls. 186–188
The Gimel casket is decorated with enamel figures, some with reserved and engraved heads, some with heads in relief and enameled eyes, on a vermiculated copper ground. The principal side is devoted to scenes from
fig. 43
the life of St. Stephen—his preaching, arrest, and stoning. On the back, four Apostles stand under arches, while on the roof are three half-length angels in medallions separated by an enamel foliage design on a blue ground. This casket, which is one of the finest products of Limoges enamel work of the end of the twelfth century or the

43

beginning of the thirteenth, is remarkable for its skilled composition in which unsymmetrical groups of figures are distributed in perfectly harmonious relation to the buildings and arcs that symbolize earth or heaven. The casket belonged to the Treasury of Saint-Etienne-de-Braguse (Corrèze) up to the eighteenth century.

The Grandmont Treasury

The order of Grandmont was founded by Stephen of Thiers, who established himself at Muret in 1076 where he proposed to live according to extremely severe rules inspired by those which he had experienced in certain Calabrian monasteries. Almost immediately, several monks were drawn by his spirit of humility and austerity to join him and to form a community, which rapidly expanded. The abbey moved to Grandmont after 1124, the year of the founder's death, and became increasingly important. In 1189, the founder was canonized. The abbey enjoyed immense prestige in the twelfth and thirteenth centuries; it was protected by princes and kings, including Henry I of England and his daughter, the Empress Mathilda of Germany, who showered it with sumptuous gifts. It possessed a magnificent Treasury, whose wealth we can gauge from the inventories drawn up between 1495 and 1790. Notwithstanding the losses it sustained, some very important pieces have survived thanks to their dispersal in various churches of Haute-Vienne (Ambazac, Arnac-la-Poste, Les Billanges, Châteauponsac, Eymoutiers, Gorres, Limoges, Mailhac, Milhaguet, Saint-Sulpice-les-Feuilles, Saint-Sylvestre) and in certain museums (Limoges, Musée de Cluny in Paris).

AMBAZAC (Haute-Vienne)

Casket of St. Stephen of Muret. End of 12th century or beginning of 13th. Copper gilt and enamel. H. 24⅞″, w. 28¾″, d. 10¼″. Church of Ambazac.

fig. 44   The church of Ambazac received the piece known as the Casket of St. Stephen of Muret, and a dalmatic which, according to tradition, had belonged to the saint. Of the seven caskets on the high altar of the abbey church, this one—the only one still extant—is said to have been made to house the relics presented by the abbot of Siegburg, archbishop of Cologne, and brought to Grandmont by two monks at the end of the twelfth century. We know from the inventory of 1666 that it was placed on the right-hand (south side) of the altar and contained the relics of St. Macarius, a martyr of the Theban legion, donated in 1269 by Thibaut, king of Navarre and count of Champagne. Rupin noted in the nineteenth century (*L'Oeuvre de Limoges*, Paris, 1890, I, pp. 137-44) that

the casket contained a fragment of bone of St. Stephen of Muret and the dalmatic.

This casket, "conceived in the image of the heavenly Jerusalem," was designed to enshrine the remains of a saint. It stands out from most of the products of Limoges goldsmithery by the proliferation of motifs and techniques peculiar to enamel work, treated, save in a few instances, in a purely decorative manner. In the form of a church with three transepts, the casket is covered with sheets of copper gilt embossed with diamond point, rosettes, imbrications, foliated scrolls, and palmettes. Its *pl. 189* principal side is richly decorated with filigree work, enameled medallions, intaglios, stones set in bezels, among them large aquamarines and a considerable number of turquoises; the other side, with arabesques ending in palmettes or enamel foliate designs, among which are four square enamel plaques with a large cabochon in the cen-

44

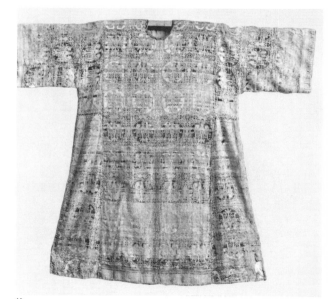

45

ter. Two enamel plaques on which are two half-length angels, with the heads in relief, constitute the only figure representations in this work. The date of the piece may be set at the end of the twelfth century, or the beginning of the thirteenth. The pierced crest of the roof is decorated with enamels and cabochons, and surmounted by a dove.

Dalmatic. 13th century. Linen and silk samite. H. 51⅝″, w. 62⅝″. Church of Ambazac.

fig. 45   The dalmatic, described in the inventories of the abbey of 1575 and 1666, traditionally is held to have been given to St. Stephen of Muret in 1121 by the Empress Mathilda of Germany, wife of Henry V. The decorative motif of this garment, which is composed of juxtaposed fragments of a single fabric, is that of eagles in roundels. The eagles' heads are turned alternately to the left and to the right. The field between the roundels is filled with stylized leafwork. This motif, repeated in parallel rows, is in golden yellow on a dull-red ground. The fabric is interrupted at the bottom of the panels and the edge of the sleeves by an ornamental band which utilizes—and distorts—Kufic characters; this band is itself bordered by three solid bands. A braid woven of gold thread and yellow and purple silk surrounds the opening at the neck.

In a recent study, Miss Dorothy Shepherd has clarified the matter of the origin and date of this material. Comparing it with certain stuffs found in the royal tombs of Las Huelgas in Burgos, she classifies it among the linen and silk samites belonging to the group known as "half-silks" attributed to Moslem workshops in northern Spain in the thirteenth century.

ARNAC-LA-POSTE (Haute-Vienne)

RELIQUARY. About 1200. Copper gilt, rock crystal. H. 11½", diameter of base 5⅞". Church of Arnac-la-Poste.

pl. 191 This reliquary, described in the inventory of the Treasury of Grandmont of 1666 and dated around the year 1200, is of special interest owing to the originality of its shape. The principle of a crystal phial containing relics and enclosed in metal bands, which frequently occurs in the thirteenth century and of which we have an example at Saint-Riquier, is here multiplied in an architectural structure which rises from a platform. This platform, supported by a polylobe base of copper gilt richly decorated with filigree work, stones, and intaglios which continue onto a knop and a very short stem, supports a crystal phial surrounded by six smaller ones, held in place by bands of engraved copper and closed by lids furnished with rings, which originally made it possible to connect them by means of small chains. The central phial consists of two superposed crystals. One of the six small phials is a crystal engraved with a palmette, probably of Fatimid origin. All around the platform, small rings indicate that, as on the Châteauponsac reliquary, there must have been pendants which have now disappeared. The reliquary was placed in the church of Arnac-la-Poste in 1790, and is still there. The same workshop produced the phylactery of Châteauponsac, the original of which has unfortunately been replaced by a copy.

LES BILLANGES (Haute-Vienne)

STATUETTE RELIQUARY OF ST. STEPHEN OF MURET. End of 12th century. Engraved and repoussé copper. H. 19¼", h. of statuette 12⅝". Church of Les Billanges.

pl. 192 The appliqué figure of repoussé and engraved copper represents a person in deacon's clothing who is believed to be St. Stephen of Muret, founder of the abbey of Grandmont. It is known that, out of humility and devotion to his patron saint, Stephen of Muret remained a deacon all his life, and did not wish to be ordained a priest. The dalmatic in which he is attired is decorated with crescents set in a network of lozenges which stand out against a crosshatched ground; the bottom of the garment, the neck, and the sleeves are bordered with orphreys decorated with cabochons mounted in bezels on an engraved ground. The same border occurs around the rectangular reliquary containing a patriarchal cross which the saint holds on a cushion before him with both hands. According to Abbé Texier (*Dictionnaire d'orfèvrerie,* Paris, 1857, col. 891), this reliquary is a replica of the Byzantine reliquary containing a fragment of the True Cross presented to the abbey by King Amaury of Jerusalem. The alb bunches about the neck and falls on the

feet which are shod in sandals and rest on a pedestal decorated with foliate scrolls. Fixed on a base decorated with dragons surmounted by a fluted knop, this figure, whose back is hollow, was probably applied on a casket. According to a recent study by Mme Souchal, it probably comes from the large casket that held the body of St. Stephen of Muret which has now disappeared, which was placed on the high altar of the abbey church in 1189, the year of his canonization. If this is so, then the date of the statuette, which was previously placed in the third quarter of the thirteenth century, should be set at the end of the twelfth.

MILHAGUET (Haute-Vienne)

RELIQUARY. 13th century. Copper gilt, nielloed silver, rock crystal. H. 11", h. of cruet 7⅛". Church of Milhaguet.

pl. 193 The church of Milhaguet possesses a very precious piece, the only one of its kind among the many reliquaries preserved in the church treasuries: a cruet of a Fatimid rock crystal engraved with an eagle, which was set in the thirteenth century in an engraved, nielloed silver mount made up of a round base decorated with lobes and quatrefoils, two bands with hinges, and a collar decorated with foliate scrolls. The lid is also decorated with lobes and foliate scrolls. The handle is in the shape of a snake. The cruet is mentioned in the 1666 inventory of Grandmont, and was probably used as a phial for holy oils. The copper-gilt base with its crystal knop, on which the cruet was placed after it had been transformed into a reliquary, is engraved with scenes set in roundels relating to Christ, the Virgin, St. Martial, St. Valeria, and St. Stephen of Muret.

SAINT-SULPICE-LES-FEUILLES (Haute-Vienne)

ANGEL RELIQUARY. End of 12th century. Copper gilt, enamel, rock crystal. H. 9⅜". Church of Saint-Sulpice-les-Feuilles.

pls. 194, 195 The angel of repoussé and enameled copper is mentioned in the inventory of the abbey of Grandmont in 1575 as having belonged to the chapel of Balesis. Draped in a tunic edged with orphreys and pearls, he raises his right hand and holds a book on his breast with his left. As in Romanesque sculpture, the folds of the garment emphasize the verticality and elongation of the body. The wings are of turquoise blue, red, and green champlevé enamel. The horizontal band is decorated with small disks of cloisonné enamel. The hair is in stylized curls and fits like a cap over the forehead; the pupils of the eyes are formed of two small pieces of black enamel. This figure, which may be placed at the end of the twelfth century, probably originally decorated the corner of a tabernacle or casket. In order to turn it into a reliquary, a little crystal vase was placed on the angel's head, and at the same time the figure was placed on a four-legged base.

SAINT-SYLVESTRE (Haute-Vienne)

HEAD RELIQUARY OF ST. STEPHEN OF MURET. End of 15th century. Silver parcel-gilt. H. 11⅞". Church of Saint-Sylvestre.

pl. 196 The church of Saint-Sylvestre possesses two very important pieces from the Grandmont Treasury: a reliquary of Mosan origin dating from the early thirteenth century, formed of a crystal cylinder mounted on a base, which contained the relics of St. Junian; and the head reliquary of St. Stephen of Muret, founder of the order. This magnificent piece, which was given to the abbey by Cardinal Brissonnet, formerly bishop of Saint-Malo, archbishop of Reims, then prior of Grandmont from 1494, is described in the inventory of the Treasury made in

1666 as it appeared at the time. The head rested on a silver corselet whose base was decorated with twelve enamel figures representing scenes from the life of St. Stephen of Muret and the arms of the donor. The corselet disappeared during the Revolution, so that only the head of repoussé silver, containing the saint's head, was saved. Above the crown of silver-gilt hair the tonsure, which resembles a skull cap, is mounted on a hinge (a seventeenth-century addition) and opens on a little grating through which the precious relic could be viewed. The magnificent expression of these features of an ascetic monk, reproduced with extraordinary realism by the technique of repoussé and engraving, marks this piece as one of the finest productions of late-fifteenth-century goldsmithery.

SAINT-BONNET-AVALOUZE *(Corrèze)*

CASKET. 7th century. Repoussé copper, enamel, cabochons. H. 4¾″, w. 5⅛″, d. 2⅝″. Church of Saint-Bonnet-Avalouze.

pl. 197   In contrast to the casket of Saint-Benoît-sur-Loire, which also dates from the Merovingian period but which is in the form of a tomb, the casket of Saint-Bonnet-Avalouze is in the form of a purse that could be hung around the neck, as evidenced by two rings—also found on the chrismal at Mortain (p. 21 bottom) and the small casket at Sens (p. 16). The portable character of the object is emphasized on the casket of Saint-Bonnet-Avalouze by the composition of the design of one of its sides, which remains in the tradition of Barbarian fibula. This side is composed of a cloisonné cross whose cells are filled with a green mastic imitating enamel or glass, while the center and ends are decorated with cabochons. The space between the arms is filled with an interlace surrounded by repoussé beading. These interlaces are also on the short sides and along the border, of which considerable

46

fig. 46   portions are missing. One of the short sides opens to allow the insertion of the relic. The rear side is divided by two diagonal fillets into four sections, filled horizontally with two crosses potent and vertically with two haloed half-length figures, their hands raised in a gesture of prayer. The style is crude and is carried out in a rudimentary technique in which an engraving needle is used on the copper, so that the repoussé is in very shallow relief.

Rupin relates (*op. cit.,* II, pp. 325–26) that as late as the nineteenth century the casket of Saint-Bonnet-Avalouze was locally known by the name of *discle,* a dialect expression for "disk." As the same word also means "tears," or

"cries," the reliquary, by a strange association, was credited with having the power to make small children stop crying.

SAINT-PANTALEON-DE-LAPLEAU *(Corrèze)*

CASKET. 13th century. Enameled copper. H. 7½″, w. 5⅞″, d. 2⅜″. Church of Saint-Pantaléon-de-Lapleau.

pl. 198   The little thirteenth-century casket of enameled copper is in the form of a church with a transept. It is decorated with simple half-length figures in relief, which have been nicknamed "dolls," just as this type of casket, belonging to a popular line of Limoges productions, is known as "gimcrack caskets." St. Pantaleon, a doctor who suffered martyrdom under Diocletian at the beginning of the fourth century, was invoked during epidemics of plague.

SAINTE-FORTUNADE *(Corrèze)*

HEAD RELIQUARY OF ST. FORTUNATA. About 1490 and 1801. Plated bronze and copper. H. 12″. Church of Sainte-Fortunade.

pl. 199   The head reliquary of St. Fortunata owes it fame to the charm of this exquisite face of a young girl with a rounded forehead, turned-up nose, and half-closed eyes, bent forward in a deliciously mannered pose. And we recall the young saint, martyred at Agen, of whom the legend tells that when an attempt was made to carry her body back to her native Burgundy, it became so heavy upon arrival at Saint-Martial-le-Noir, near Tulle, that it had to be left in that village, which thereupon assumed the name of Sainte-Fortunade.

The head, which is more sculpture than precious metalwork, is of plated bronze and consists of two parts, the face and the back of the neck. The face is framed in delicately engraved wavy hair; the rear portion, which is less skillfully engraved and does not reproduce the same movement of the hair, was undoubtedly added later, probably in 1801—the date inscribed on the plinth—to form a bust of what was originally designed to be an appliqué figure. Thus only the face would appear to be authentic; on the other hand, a recent spectrographic analysis would seem to indicate that it was a cast made from an original that was melted down in 1801.

It is unlikely, therefore, that the lovely St. Fortunata was originally intended to be a reliquary. This, as well as its delicately wordly character, distinguishes it from most of the pieces in church treasuries.

Rouergue — Aquitaine

CONQUES *(Aveyron)*

Treasury of Conques

When we think of the Conques Treasury, we think of the gold St. Foy. But around the "Majesty" of the earliest statue of the Christian West to have come down to us, there are a number of pieces whose origins are shrouded in the mystery of a very remote past: the A of Charlemagne, the Reliquary of Pepin, the Reliquary of Pope Pascal. Even when they are only fragmentary, like the portions reset on the phylacteries, they contribute to the exceptional importance of this Treasury. This importance is still further enhanced by the large number of objects preserved from the Gothic period. As a result, the Conques Treasury has the remarkable feature that it has enjoyed a continuity that spans a thousand years, from the eighth to the eighteenth centuries.

ST. FOY IN MAJESTY. 5th–16th centuries. Gold, silver gilt repoussé, filigree, precious stones, cameos, intaglios, cloisonné enamel, rock crystal, on a wood core. H. 33½″,

h. of throne 9½″, w. of throne 14¼″. Treasury of the former Abbey Church.

The martyr, wearing a closed crown and a robe in the form of a dalmatic, is seated very erect on a throne with a rounded back, the four uprights of which end in balls of rock crystal. The head, disproportionately large for the body, is thrown back. It is a strictly frontal pose: the two forearms extend parallel to one another, the two legs descend vertically. The robe ends at the feet, which are shod in long shoes. The neck, sleeves, and bottom of the dress (p. 23) are edged with bands of filigree set with jewels; the same design and technique occurs on the butt straps of the shoes, on the two vertical bands between the front uprights of the throne, as well as on the ornamental bands of the throne and on the crown.

The piece dates from a number of different periods: the gold head (p. 13), from the latter part of the Roman empire, perhaps the fifth century; the statue and its first gold sheath, from the last quarter of the ninth century; new gold elements were introduced in the last quarter of the tenth century (the crown; filigree pendant earrings decorated with pearls, rock crystals, and garnets; filigree bands; the throne). By comparison with other, similar, ones found in tombs, the crystal balls of the uprights may be credited to the Merovingian period. The forearms and hands of cast and gilded silver date from the sixteenth century. The bronze plaques of the shoes and the silver-gilt fillet in which they are set antedate the seventeenth century. At an indeterminate time a quatrefoil monstrance in a structure with a fourteenth-century type of gable was placed at her belt and the wood of the statue was cut out to match the quatrefoil pattern to render visible the relic contained in an opening in the back.

Over the years jewelry was added to the robe and the back of the throne, either as gifts of pilgrims to enrich the Majesty, or, at a later date, perhaps in the sixteenth century, to conceal spots where portions of the gold plaques had previously been removed. Belonging to the first category: the circular silver-gilt jewel of the fifteenth century which closes the filigree collar, composed of three emeralds and red and green enamel studs around a rock crystal set in a claw mount decorated with leaves and beading in repoussé; three silver-gilt belts of the fourteenth century attached in separate parts, which are mounted on hinges set with stones; one of these is decorated with pearls and a foliate design of leaves and buds surrounding enamels on a pierced quatrefoil support. Finally, an enamel escutcheon of the thirteenth century in a filigree frame.

In the second category, made up of existing pieces broken up to fill the gaps, we may place the stones set in bezels (intaglios, cameos), for the most part removed from the filigree bands on the back of the throne; a late thirteenth-century plaque of repoussé and gilded silver representing a female saint under a trefoil arch set on the martyr's lap; two silver-gilt filigree plaques which frame the monstrance of the belt, reminiscent of the axial bands of the Cross of Theophano in the Essen Treasury which, like the latter, may be placed around the year 1000; the thick plaques of embossed and gilded silver loaded with rock crystals attached to the knees, dating probably from the eighteenth century; a small fifteenth-century foliate cross (whose arms have been cut down) of cast and gilded silver, decorated with the symbols of the Evangelists; some twelfth-century filigree bands from outworn reliquaries; two fourteenth-century medallions of repoussé silver gilt, on one, the Pascal Lamb, on the other, the Crucifixion; etc. There were other fragments before the restoration of 1954, which were assembled to form, from one set, a part of a tenth-century antependium (pl. 203), from another, a twelfth-century evangeliary cover (fig. 47).

As we know, the statue was made to enshrine the relic of the head of St. Foy, a young Christian girl martyred at Agen in 303 during the Dacian persecution. The relic still exists, reinforced with a plaque of pure silver. If we discount the additions, mutilations, and modifications just referred to, the Majesty in its present state corresponds to Bernard of Angers' description of it in his *Liber Miraculorum Sanctae Fidis*, written between 1007 and 1029. It is the sole surviving example of the pre-Romanesque Majesties that had become widespread in the areas mentioned by Bernard. He writes: "According to ancient usage and antique custom especially vigorous in the region of the Auvergne, Rouergue, and Toulouse, and in other neighboring regions, each church has a statue made of gold, or silver, or some other metal, according to its means, and enshrines in it, with due honor, either the head or some other important relic of the saint." The custom was thus already time-honored in those parts.

Bréhier believed (*Renaissance de l'Art français*, 1924, pp. 205–10) that the prototype of such statues was the gold Virgin of Clermont Cathedral which Stephen II, whose episcopate was somewhere between 942 and 984, commissioned prior to 959 (date of an inventory mentioning the statue). However, it seems unlikely that the official grammarian of Angers would have used expressions such as "ancient usage" and "antique custom" to refer to a period of little more than a half a century. And the proliferation of such Majesties around the year 1000, to which he refers, is another argument in favor of a much older prototype. On the other hand, because Stephen II was abbot of Conques as well as bishop of Clermont, Bréhier argues that the gold St. Foy should also be credited to him. But we know, again from Bernard of Angers, that even before the miracle of Vuitbert the enlightened, "the principal wealth of the treasury was the statue of ancient fashioning (*ab antiquo fabricata*)." He says, further, that after the miracle, this statue was "de integro reformata," which can be interpreted as "entirely transformed" or "entirely remodeled." According to the first interpretation, the ancient statue would simply have been covered with more sumptuous ornaments, which would have transformed it; according to the second, it would have been replaced by another. In either case, it seems difficult to accept Bréhier's theory. Stephen II could not have been responsible either for the statue "of ancient fashioning," or for that "de integro reformata." As regards the latter, the miracle took place around the year 985, under his successor, Aldarus. And as regards the former, as J. Hubert has pointed out, Bernard of Angers would not have used the expression "of ancient fashioning" for a work that was so recent.

This statue "of ancient fashioning," which was already sheathed with gold (Gimon, the custodian, who lived before the miracle, used to hear "the gold of the statue ring in the night"), probably dates from the end of the ninth century. All that can be stated about it is that it was later than the "furtive translation" of the body of St. Foy, which may be placed, according to the liturgical date of the feast of the translation, on January 14, between 864 (according to Lot) and 875 (according to Levillain, *Revue Mabillon*, III, 1917, pp. 95–115).

As for the two possible interpretations of the term *reformata*—transformed or remodeled—an analysis made in 1954, during the restoration of the Conques reliquaries prior to their installation in the new Treasury, leads us to accept the first; the original statue is still in existence. It was embellished at the end of the tenth century, after the Vuitbert miracle. At that point, it was given its character of triumphant Majesty; a crown was placed on its head (p. 20), and it was robed in a dalmatic with sumptuous orphreys of filigree and intaglios, very similar in style to the precious metalwork executed around the year 1000, principally in the Ottonian workshops. And the seat, originally hewn out of the same piece of wood as the statue, was transformed into a throne, sheathed with strips of gold filigree of a design similar to that of the orphreys, and decorated in the back with a large intaglio of rock crystal on which the Crucifixion is represented; it was the throne of triumphant martyrs to which we referred earlier. From these observations, we may infer that the periods of the statue represent two different iconographic intentions. In its original state, the St. Foy represented only the "figurative expression of the relic." In the second, it is the glorious Majesty with which we are familiar.

Of the original statue there remains, nailed to the wood core, the gold leaf of the bodice and robe to which, in the course of the "transformation," orphreys were added, fashioned in imitation of the crown but with a different quality of gold and different tools. And this statue, which was carved out of a yew root, had been carved without a head. The neck, conceived merely as a cylindrical strut, fits into the neck of a repoussé gold head taken from a bust made during the latter years of the Roman empire (p. 13). The discovery that the head dated from antiquity might explain Bernard of Angers' expression, "ab antiquo fabricata." This is a hypothesis that cannot be ignored.

Among the problems raised by the gold St. Foy is that of the presence at Conques, around the year 1000, at the time of the transformation of the statue, of elements that may well have originated in an Imperial or royal treasury. The closed crown (p. 20), of the type of Imperial crowns from the Carolingian period on, had originally been larger. It was made smaller in order to fit the head. Thus it was not made for the statue, and had originally been the crown of an Imperial child. The relic of the martyr's head was wrapped in a purple cloth that probably came from the Imperial workshops of Constantinople. Such fabrics were not sold, but were reserved for the courts. The Carolingian intaglio on the throne, other examples of which existed only in Imperial or royal treasuries and the profusion of antique intaglios on cornelians, amethysts, or emeralds of enormous size—everything points to the conclusion that the gifts made for the embellishment of the Majesty were of an altogether exceptional nature.

FRAGMENT OF AN ALTAR FRONTAL. 10th century. Repoussé silver parcel-gilt. H. 8⅝", w. 10⅝". Treasury of the former Abbey Church.

pl. 203

We turn next to the fragment of an antependium (altar frontal) that dates from the end of the tenth century. Describing "a silver plaque representing the head of Christ applied to the back of the statue of St. Foy," Darcel wrote in 1861 (Annales archéologiques), "Because of its crudeness, it seemed to us interesting to publish this fragment, for it reminds us of the appalling miniatures that one finds from time to time in eighth- or ninth-century manuscripts." This plaque was removed from the back of the statue at the time of the 1954 restoration, and replaced by a plain sheet of silver gilt. Four additional fragments that had belonged to the same piece were discovered—another on the St. Foy statue, one on the base of the A of Charlemagne, two more at the top of the hexagonal reliquary (pl. 211) — and reassembled.

Christ, beardless and surrounded by a cruciform halo, is seated in glory in a mandorla, holding the Book with his left hand, the right hand raised. He is acclaimed by two figures who also have haloes; whether they are angels or Apostles is impossible to determine, since they are incomplete.

Despite the archaizing treatment resulting from the clumsiness of the design and from the technique used, namely, repoussé with a punch, which traces parallel lines without suggesting volume (p. 21 top), and is reminiscent of some seventh- or eighth-century goldsmithery, or sculptured stone imitating goldsmithery (San Pedro de Nave, Santa Maria de Quintanilla de las Viñas, in Spain, altar frontal of Ratchis at Cividale in Frioul, angel of San Lorenzo del Pasenatico, whose hands are treated in the same way as here), it is difficult to date this fragment any earlier than the tenth century, owing to the almost Romanesque aspect of the figures, which seems to presage certain stone reliefs in Roussillon in the first third of the eleventh century (lintels of Saint-Denis-des-Fontaines and Saint-André-de-Sorède). The arrangement of the scene,

which marked the center of a large composition, would indicate that it was a fragment of an antependium. Not, however, of that of the high altar of the Abbey Church to which Bernard of Angers refers in Book I, chapter XVII, of his *Livre des Miracles de Sainte Foy,* for that was of gold ("How St. Foy collected gold everywhere for the fashioning of an altar").

PLAQUE OF AN EVANGELIARY COVER. 12th century. Repoussé silver gilt. H. 7⅞", w. 4¾". Treasury of the former Abbey Church.

fig. 47

Seven fragments placed on various parts of the statue of St. Foy (arm, shoulder, bottom of the dress, etc.) were reassembled during the restoration work of 1954 to form the plaque of an evangeliary cover which dates from the early twelfth century. It is complete, and shows the Pantocrator with a cruciform halo holding the Book, and blessing with one finger raised, surrounded by symbols of the Evangelists.

RELIQUARY OF PEPIN. About 1000, with some parts earlier. Repoussé gold sheets, filigree, precious stones, intaglios, pearls, mother-of-pearl, translucent enamels, on a wood core. H. 7¼", w. 7⅜", d. 3½". Treasury of the former Abbey Church.

The piece known as the Reliquary of Pepin dates from about the year 1000, but parts of it are from the Carolingian period. It is shaped like a house or tomb,

47

pl. 207

with a pyramidal roof. On the principal side, Christ is shown on a cross edged with a row of pearls set between beaded fillets. The repoussé halo is cruciform, with four pearls mounted in bezels placed between the arms of the cross. The letters of the titulus are in filigree. On either side of the Christ figure, and on the same level, are the figures of the Virgin and St. John. On the sloping roof, the sun and the moon, in repoussé, are surrounded by a filigree collar that emerges from a filigree ground of trefoils set under overlapping arches. The area below the arms of the cross is occupied by two rectangular blind windows, each cut into a plaque whose lower part is similarly decorated with overlapping filigree work. These windows are edged with a repoussé beaded border. The ledges and reveals are decorated with diamond point.

On the reverse side, between two vertical filigree bands surmounted by two translucent enamels on a red ground, are three blind windows with round arches supported by repoussé twisted colonettes; the ledges are decorated in diamond point. The archivolts are set in a plaque that occupies the whole of the upper part of the side and are formed by a double row of beaded fillets between which are pearls mounted in bezels. In contrast to the windows of the other side, which were always blind, these windows once had transparent plaques, for the grooves into which they fitted are still present.

On the sloping roof are two eagles with wings of deep blue, red, and white translucent cloisonné enamel on a diamond-pointed ground divided in the center by a filigree band edged with beaded fillets, which is crowned by a large intaglio on cornelion mounted in an inserted filigree bezel. The slopes of the gables are also decorated with diamond point.

Each side and the four slopes of the roof are edged with filigreed and jeweled bands. The two vertical ones on the reverse side include square-shaped bezels which project onto the face proper. They are on arcades, as are all the other bands on this side, except those on the roof. On this same face, at the lower edge of the roof, a horizontal band of filigree work, dating from the fourteenth century, has been added, and at the ridge, a repoussé band of sixteenth-century workmanship. Two enamels on a red ground similar to those between the windows of the reverse side and, like them, decorated, with gold foliate scrolls issuing symmetrically from a central stem, adorn the inside of the windows of the front side. They are *repercés* enamels, made up of two soldered plaques, the foliate scrolls having been stamped out of the upper plaque. The rear walls of the windows of the reverse side are ornamented with three segmented enamels on a green ground, of the same style as those of the red ground. A fourth has been nailed to the center of a filigreed band at the ridge of the roof on the front side.

This design is not homogeneous, even discounting the inserted elements, such as the mysterious translucent enamels on gold with C. de Linas (*Gazette archéologique*, 1887) compares with those of the *paliotto* of Sant'Ambrogio in Milan, or the fragments of repoussé gold, some of which (twenty-four fragments removed in 1954) made possible the reconstruction of a Crucifixion (pl. 209), while eight other fragments, decorated with a design of tapered leaves, have been left where they were inside the two windows of the front face.

Many other examples of such mixtures could be cited. The filigree work is of different periods, the oldest seeming to be the bands at the ridge of the roof on the front side and on the slopes of the gables, which are in the Merovingian tradition. The other is of a kind common around the year 1000, particularly in the Ottonian workshops. The filigree bands are for the most part incomplete, or too short, or made up of juxtaposed elements (the band at the bottom of the reverse face was created by combining three different bands). Along the edges, the only complete ones are the two vertical bands between the windows on the reverse face (which, however, seem to be mounted upside down and may at one time have bordered one of the short sides).

The Crucifixion scene, in particular, seems to have been made for something other than this reliquary. The figures are too large for it, and their arrangement does not appear to be the original one. The suppedaneum of the Christ figure was flattened and cut even with the bottom edge. The plaques in which the figures of the Virgin and St. John are embossed were cut out and nailed on the casket so clumsily that their upper portions are partially covered by the ends of the arms of the cross. The sun and the moon are not embossed in the filigree plaque, but are inserted and mounted, which would indicate that they were not of the same origin as the plaque. This group seems, therefore, to have come from elsewhere. This was confirmed by the evidence

assembled during the restoration of 1954: the outlines of the plaques of the Virgin and St. John match those of the cross when the plaques are placed below the arms. The group thus belonged to a single plaque, which also included the sun and the moon. The composition was vertical, and not, as now, horizontal. It may have been a panel reliquary, and it is not unreasonable to imagine that the plaque with the eagles belonged to it too, since its upper edge is of exactly the same width as that of the plaque of the Crucifixion when the figures of the Virgin and St. John are replaced in their original positions.

The overlapping filigree pattern on the roof and under the windows cannot be later than the eleventh century (it may be compared with the Cross of Lothair, in the Cathedral Treasury at Aachen, the gem of the Empress Gisela in the Schlossmuseum in Berlin, the plaques of the crown of St. Oswald, etc.). But this design was executed especially in order to enclose the elements of the Crucifixion when it was transformed, as is shown by the titulus, which was remodeled at this time with the same kind of beaded wire that is used for the filigree, for the wires around the four pearls inserted between the arms of the cross on the halo, and on the beaded border of the cross itself, which were then soldered to the original plaque. In order to connect the cross to the slope of the roof and the vertical of the cross, two small triangular plaques and one rectangular plaque, all decorated with filigree rings, were soldered between the top of the upright of the cross and the roof. The halo was also stamped out and straightened.

Taking these remarks into account, it must be conceded that, whatever similarities may be found between the Christ of the reliquary and the Ottonian Christ figures of the Rhenish region (that of Archbishop Aribert of Milan, those of the crosses in the Cathedral Treasury at Essen, etc.), this Crucifixion dates before the year 1000; otherwise it is difficult to understand how a gold piece of such importance should have been altered almost as soon as it was completed. We thus return, by a detour, to the view of de Linas, who recalls that the piece was traditionally known as the Reliquary of Pepin, and attributes it to Pepin I of Aquitaine (817–838). For stylistic reasons, J. Borchgrave d'Altena (*Revue belge d'Archéologie et d'Histoire de l'Art*, 1954, pp. 21–52) and J. Hubert have assigned the piece to the same period. But this dating refers only to the Crucifixion in its original aspect, that is, before it was arranged on the reliquary. As for the reliquary itself, the discovery in 1954 of a "first Crucifixion" (pl. 209) leaves open the question of its original date and of the identity, among the many great figures named Pepin, of the one who may have been the donor.

CRUCIFIXION. 8th century. Repoussé silver parcel-gilt. H. 3″, w. 6″. Treasury of the former Abbey Church.

The Crucifixion is represented in shallow repoussé on a gold plaque that is slightly trapezoidal in shape, with a beaded border. This piece was created by the juxtaposition of twenty-four fragments found on the Pepin reliquary at the time of its restoration in 1954. The upper part of the composition—from the middle of the arms of the cross—is missing, save at the right, where the whole arm is visible beneath a design of tapered leaves. The cross patté, which is wide and short, is simply indicated by a molding. The figure of Christ is in a frontal position. The feet do not rest on a suppedaneum. Christ is flanked by the figures of Longinus and Stefatonus who kneel on one knee; their names are inscribed on scrolls. Birds face the cross; under them are fantastic animals (the one on the left turns round) placed on either side of the figures carrying the spear and the sponge.

The surface is virtually the same as that occupied by the Crucifixion on the front side of the Pepin reliquary. Since the fragments were found on the reliquary—and we know with what respect outworn parts of reliquaries were preserved at Conques up to the sixteenth century—it may be assumed that the group now on the reliquary replaced what would have been the "first Crucifixion" on the reliquary.

The point is to determine the date of this "first Crucifixion." From the awkwardness of technique and design, the presence of pre-Carolingian ornamental themes, such as the helix, or spiral (which indicates Longinus' knee), the absence of a suppedaneum, the theme of paradisial birds and maleficent animals symbolizing the powers of evil, the treatment of the hair of the figures by geometric hatchings, as for instance in the Merovingian coins of the southwest, are we justified in placing the plaque in the Merovingian period, or are these so many instances of an archaizing tendency? These awkwardnesses make it inconceivable that the work should have been bestowed by royal gift—as its material, gold, would indicate—in the Carolingian period. It must therefore be of either earlier or later date. If later, then it must be credited to the tenth century. If earlier, as is probable, then it must belong to the eighth century. In any case, if the idea of a "first Crucifixion" on the Pepin reliquary were to be accepted, then its connection with one of the two Pepins of Aquitaine would have to be reconsidered.

The so-called phylacteries at Conques are two pieces which are also known as a "hexagonal reliquary" and a "pentagonal reliquary," whose heterogeneity has impressed all archeologists since Darcel *(op. cit.)*. Each consists of a fairly crude wooden form to which many small relics were transferred, probably in the sixteenth century, from out-worn reliquaries—the multiplicity of these relics would explain the designation of these pieces as phylacteries—and decorated in arbitrary fashion with fragments of precious metalwork from these same reliquaries, ranging from the Merovingian to the Gothic periods.

HEXAGONAL RELIQUARY. Assembled in 16th century. Nielloed silver gilt, filigree, repoussé copper, glass beads, cabochons on a wood core. H. 13⅜″, w. 12″. Treasury of the former Abbey Church.

pl. 211
Among the fragments of various origins (bands or filigreed panels, etc.), the most interesting part is made up of elements dating from a very early period. In the center, a large hemispherical cabochon of dark-gray-blue glass is mounted in a large bezel decorated with pearls which is surrounded by a cloisonné ring on copper filled with red glass, which in its turn is surrounded by a nielloed ring bordered by two knurled rings. These concentric circles are contained in a nielloed square engraved with heartshaped and trefoiled leafwork and interlaces, on which mounted stones have been set in massive bezels derived from other pieces.

This group, as well as two rectangular cloisonné plaques of red glass above the windows, may be of eighth-century origin. The lower band, decorated with small crosses joined at their intersections by studs and serving as brackets between cabochons set in thick stepped bezels, is one of the rare examples in France—another is the binding of the Psalter of Charles the Bald (Reiche Kapelle, Munich)—of a ninth-century decorative motif that occurs, but in more highly developed form, on the Portable Altar of Arnulf at Munich (Reiche Kapelle) and on the *paliotto* of Sant'Ambrogio in Milan.

PENTAGONAL RELIQUARY. Assembled in 16th century. Silver gilt, copper, filigree, cabochons on a wood core. H. 15¾″, w. 10⅝″. Treasury of the former Abbey Church.

pl. 210
The pentagonal reliquary has a similar composition, but includes in the center a thirteenth-century filigree quatrefoil. Also belonging to very early periods, as on the hexagonal reliquary, is a plaque of red glass cloisonné on copper placed on the lower part between two bands of repoussé silver with foliate scrolls which apparently date from the tenth century. The reliquary is bordered with wide filigreed and jeweled bands that date from the eleventh century, one of which, set horizontally, is in the same style as those on the A of Charlemagne (pl. 212).

THE "A" OF CHARLEMAGNE. End of the 11th century. Silver gilt repoussé, filigree, intaglios, precious stones, pearls, cabochons, enamels on a wood core. H. 17″, w. 15¾″. Treasury of the former Abbey Church.

pl. 212

pl. 213
The "A" of Charlemagne is in the form of a triangle with a disk at the top. On the inside of each arm is some sort of spur. On the base are two stelae on which are two incense-bearing angels in repoussé; the backs of the stelae are simply decorated with vertical bands of foliate scrolls which seem to have come from some other object. Each face of the arms is covered with bands of filigree and jewels. This design continues on the front face of the terminal disk, around a large piece of rock crystal placed in the center. The reverse side of this disk, which was originally decorated with a geometric design in repoussé, was subsequently embellished with a circular jewel of silver gilt with an intaglio in the center, consisting of two circles of filigree surmounted by a trefoil translucent enamel on copper marked with a cross, surrounded by thirteen disks ending in buds, composed alternately of translucent cloisonné enamels on copper and silver-gilt daisies. The plaques covering the inner sides of the arms are decorated with diamond point. On the outer edges, two incomplete inscriptions are embossed on plaques of silver gilt. Their script is identical with that of the inscription relating to Abbot Bego on the Bego lantern (pl. 214), and makes it possible to date the reliquary to the same abbacy. They consist of two Leonine verses, which C. Perrat has reconstructed as follows: ABBAS FORMAVIT BEGO RELIQUIAS QUE LO[CAVIT]. [OMNI]S SUM DOMINI QUE CRUX O[BTINUIT]. The base is covered with heterogeneous fragments in repoussé from outworn reliquaries, among them a titulus with large characters, which must have come from a very big cross. One of the fragments used to reconstruct the tenth-century antependium (pl. 203) was found on this base.

There has been considerable, but inconclusive, discussion concerning the unusual form of the reliquary. The legendary attribution to Charlemagne is based on the story of the twenty-four abbeys among which the emperor was purported to have distributed twenty-four letters of the alphabet in precious metalwork, Conques having received the letter A. It has also been suggested that this A might have been the alpha of a giant crucifix. More simply, it may be supposed that this elementary form, achieved with the rudimentary means available at the time, originated in the idea of presenting a relic censed by two angels, since these two figures are original, as is evidenced by the technique of the repoussé and the gilding, which is similar to that of other parts of the reliquary.

LANTERN RELIQUARY. End of 11th century. Silver plaques on a wood core, all ornamental repoussé and parcel gilt. H. 16½″, base 5⅛″ square. Treasury of the former Abbey Church.

pl. 214
The reliquary known as the Lantern of Bego, and also as the Lantern of St. Vincent, is in the form of a central plan building topped with a conical dome. The dome rests on a hoop that is supported by six posts which are in their turn supported by a cube-shaped pedestal whose upper corners are chamfered. Originally, each of the chamfered surfaces was covered with a small triangular plaque ornamented with a foliate motif (two have disappeared), and each of the sides was decorated with a beaded border, medallions enclosing figures above Latin inscriptions in Leonine verse, and a three-petaled flower in each of the corners. An opening was made in one of the sides so that a relic could be inserted. This opening is closed by a lid formed by an inserted medallion on which

p. 21 center
is a representation of Samson and the lion. On the original plaque, cut out in circular shape, on which the medallion was applied, are the words: SIC, NOSTER DAVID S

[eight or nine letters missing] TANAM SUPERAVIT.

On the next side the medallion was cut out and applied on a ground that is not the original one, so that the inscription is missing. The scene is God trampling under foot the adder and the dragon (Ps. 91:13). The figure is seated on a throne, surrounded by the rainbow that is his symbol, holding the book in his left hand and the orb in his right. There is no halo, but the head is surmounted by a cross patté (this head was altered at an undetermined date).

On the third side we have a reverse situation: the medallion was cut out of the plaque that serves as the ground, and is missing. On the plaque is inscribed the beginning of the verse: AUCTOREM MORTIS . . . (some twenty-two to twenty-five letters are missing).

Finally, on the fourth side, God is again enthroned beneath the rainbow, holding on his lap the Lamb surrounded with a cruciform halo, which represents, according to Canon Tonnellier, Christ the Lamb of God, the Lamb of the Shepherd. Only the end of the last verse remains, with some eighteen to twenty-one letters missing: . . . STET PASTOR ET AGNUS.

The intermediary register consists of a single tubular plaque held in place by rods set at the right of the pilasters embossed in it. In the lower part, the area between these pilasters is occupied by six half-length figures of angels represented front face, holding a scroll in the left hand and making a gesture of preaching or teaching with the right, each with a different movement of the hand. They appear on a ground of clouds divided by a band of three rows of diamond point. The halos consist of striped rays.

The area above the angels has been cut out between the pilasters, the spaces forming windows provided with (modern) glass, so that the relics may be viewed. The pilasters, so far as one can determine in view of the fact that so much is missing, rise from a simple base. They are decorated with overlapping foliate scrolls or oblique parallel lines, and culminate in thick capitals with palmette motifs.

All around the band that supports the dome runs an inscription edged with beading which has almost entirely disappeared: ABBAS SANCTORUM BEGO PARTES HIC HAB [some seven to nine letters missing] ET HORUM DANIELIS TRI . . . (sixteen to eighteen letters missing). The dome was originally edged with a festoon above a beaded border which must have belonged to the frame around the inscription. Thus, the inscription itself was originally embossed in the same plaque as the roof and was not, as now, separate from it. The dome is divided into concentric alternating rows of silver and silver gilt, which resembles tiles. It is surmounted by a small hollow cylinder decorated with filigree, pearls, and turquoises.

Bego III was abbot of Conques from 1087 to 1106. It is generally accepted that the inscription refers to him, and this view is confirmed by the paleographic evidence. Nevertheless, the archaizing style of the figures, in some points reminiscent of Carolingian design, as much as the very primitive technique (repoussé executed with a punch), have made Rupin (op. cit., pp. 56–58) and Molinier hesitate. And F. de Lasteyrie (Mémoires des Antiquaires de France, XXVIII, pp. 6–9) argues from the tradition identifying this reliquary with St. Vincent, whose relics had been brought to Conques before those of St. Foy (c. 855), that it should be attributed to Bego I, abbot of Conques in the ninth century.

The style, reminiscent of Romanesque monumental sculpture of the southwest, and the extremely skillful treatment of the scene of Samson and the lion which comes from another reliquary of the mid-twelfth century which had been destroyed, are unlike anything else to be found at Conques.

RELIQUARY OF POPE PASCAL. End of 11th century. Silver gilt repoussé, inserted bands of filigree on a rebuilt wood core. H. 14⅝″, w. 7½″, d. 4⅜″. Treasury of the former Abbey Church.

The Reliquary of Pope Pascal is a panel reliquary whose central rectangle, on which is a Crucifixion, rests on a sloping base covered with an inscription, and is crowned with a graceful pediment edged with beading. The front face of the pediment is decorated with repoussé palmettes beneath a medallion that contains a relic of the True Cross, which is reproduced on the roundel in the center; the back is decorated with vines and clusters of grapes in repoussé. The sides of the panel are covered with repoussé bands of oval medallions containing cabochons. The central plaque, bordered at the sides with bands of repoussé flowers in a Gothic lozenge pattern and at the top by an inserted band of filigree work, shows Christ on the Cross between the Virgin and St. John mounted on high pedestals, like figures in certain Byzantine ivories. On either side of a long titulus are the sun and the moon. At the bottom is an engraved inscription: ME FIERI IVSSIT BEGO CLEMENS CVI DOMINVS SIT. Another inscription is engraved on the base: ANNO AB INCARNATIONE DOMINI MILLESIMO C DOMINVS PASCALIS II PAPA II A ROMA HAS MISIT RELIQVAS DE + X P ET SEPVLCRO EJVS ATQ PLVRIMORVM SANCTORVM.

It seems that, at least in its upper portion, the reliquary remains in its original form. The wood was replaced, but at quite an early date, for it has shrunk, and the beaded border of the pediment has been bent back slightly to fit it. The plaque of the Crucifixion appears to be from an Evangeliary cover. The inscription at the bottom does not seem to have been originally connected with this reliquary, for it begins on a short side and the letters are truncated at the corners where the base has been beveled. It was partially restored with the help of a plaque taken from another reliquary, on which an angel is represented, on the back of which new letters were embossed. A fragment of the original inscription was found on the base of the silver Virgin and Child reliquary (pl. 220).

PORTABLE ALTAR OF BEGO. 1100. Porphyry, engraved and nielloed silver. H. 1⅞″, l. 10⅛″, w. 6⅜″. Treasury of the former Abbey Church.

The porphyry table is set in a frame of inserted bands that are stamped on the long sides, filigreed on the others. At the short sides are two silver plaques with three-lined nielloed inscriptions indicating the consecration of the altar by Pons, bishop of Barbastre, and the date (1100); at the top: ANNO AB INCARNATIONE DOMINI MILLESIMO C SEXTO K L IVLII DOMINVS PONCIVS BARBASTRENSIS EPISCOPVS ET SANCTE FIDIS VIRGINIS MONACHVS, and at the bottom: HOC ALTARE BEGONIS ABBATIS DEDICAVIT ET DE + XPI ET SEPVLCRO EIVS MVLTASQVE ALIAS SANCTAS RELIQVIAS HIC REPOSVIT.

The four edges are decorated in nielloed silver with arcades in which are half-length figures above a band bearing their names. Each of the long sides has seven; each of the short sides, four. One edge shows Christ, with the Virgin on his right and St. Foy on his left, flanked on one side by St. Cecilia and St. Peter, and on the other by St. Vincent of Agen and St. Paul. The other edges show: Matthew, Luke, Mark, Caprasius, Stephen, Thaddeus, Simon; Andrew, James, John the Evangelist, Thomas; Matthew, Bartholomew, Philip, James.

PORTABLE ALTAR OF ST. FOY. 11th century. Alabaster, silver gilt, filigree, cloisonné enamels on gold and copper. L. 11½″, w. 8⅛″. Treasury of the former Abbey Church.

The alabaster plaque, which is cracked, is surrounded by a silver-gilt border stamped with an egg-and-dart motif between a beaded edging (one section is missing and was completed at an unknown date by Gothic bands in repoussé). The outer frame is made up of four wide bands of silver-gilt filigree, enamels, and cabochons. The cloisonné enamels on copper gilt with half-length figures are

pl. 215

pl. 216

pl. 217

fig. 48

fig. 49

pl. 218

circular on the short sides, rectangular on the long sides. On the top band is Christ between the symbols of Matthew and John; on the lower one, the Lamb between the symbols of Luke and Mark. On the sides are, above, St. Foy and the Virgin, identified by inscriptions, wearing triangular crowns; below them are two haloed women saints. On the same long sides are four small disks of translucent cloisonné enamel on gold.

The arrangement resembles that of Byzantine Evangeliary covers (e.g., that of the Emperor Henry II in the Munich library), or cross reliquaries (as at Limburg-an-der-Lahn, at Cologne, or in St. Mark's, Venice). The enamels themselves are executed in imitation of Byzantine enamels, but in a technique peculiar to the West to which

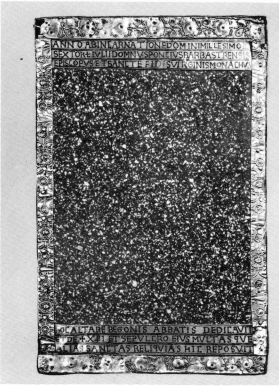

48

49

Molinier drew attention, and of which we have other examples (enamel at the center of the cover of the Evangeliary of St. Gauzelin, pl. 62): the enamels on copper are composed of two superposed plaques that are soldered together; the lower plaque is solid but the upper one is cut out according to a design, and the cloisonné wires are soldered onto the ground of the resulting cavity.

CASKET. Beginning of 12th century. Studded leather, champlevé enamel medallions on copper on a wood core. H. 10¼", w. 20½", d. 22⅞". Treasury of the former Abbey Church.

pl. 219   The lock is old, as is the wood of the lid and of the main side. The leather, studded with nails forming a design of foliate scrolls, is also original on the lid, the main side, and the front half of the short sides. Thirty-one medallions, circular or almond-shaped, only twelve of which are old, are distributed over the four sides and the lid. They are decorated with animal (fantastic birds, winged monsters) or plant motifs. The old medallions are the eight on the lid and the four lateral ones on the main side, which once served as sconces and are therefore pierced with holes. Two inscriptions engraved on the edges of two of these medallions enable us to date the set to the time of Abbot Boniface (1107–19) : + SCHRINIA CONCHARUM MONSTRANT OPUS UNDIQUE CLARUM (upper left medallion of the main side), and + HOC ORNAMENTUM BONE SIT FACII MONIMENTUM (medallion on the lid above the lock). The medallions may be compared with those of the Bellac casket (fig. 41). They are generally regarded as dating from the beginning of champlevé enamel production in the southwest.

Five similar medallions are in the Metropolitan Museum in New York (former Carrand, Boy, Bardoc, Hoentschel, Morgan collections), and three in the Louvre (former V. Gay collection). All have representations of fantastic animals such as those of the Conques casket, but with an enameled Greek border, whereas on the casket the border is beaded.

The casket, which contained relics and many fragments of outworn reliquaries, was discovered in 1875 when a wall that had reinforced the columns of the ambulatory of the abbey church was demolished. It had been concealed there at the time of the wars of religion, as is evidenced by a double *tournois* of 1590 that was found inside.

VIRGIN AND CHILD RELIQUARY. 13th century. Silver parcel-gilt on a wood core. H. 15", w. 7⅞", d. 7⅛". Treasury of the former Abbey Church.

pl. 220   The Virgin wears a robe that is gilded at the border and belt and a generous mantle decorated on the shoulders with two circular medallions set in cabochons and bearing an escutcheon on a green ground: azure, a tower, a portcullis, three crosslets saltier. The Virgin's hair is gilded and she wears a veil held in place by a crown adorned with cabochons. The right hand, which rests on the knee, must have held an attribute. The left hand rests on the shoulder of the Child who is similarly dressed in a long robe and mantle with gilded edging. The child blesses with the right hand, and holds the Book on his left knee.

The Virgin is seated on a cushion placed on a very ornate chair whose arms are pierced with trefoils and terminate in three ribbed and gilded balls. The sides of the chair are covered with repoussé silver parcel-gilt plaques decorated with lozenges that contain fleurs-de-lis and foliate motifs. The back is covered with a silver plaque decorated with a checkered pattern in repoussé; a rectangular door in the plaque closes the cavity containing the relics. The base is edged with plaques decorated with stamped foliate scrolls; at the rear there is a fragment of a band that still shows part of an inscription: DE + XP, from the Reliquary of Pope Pascal (see above, pl. 216).

The face of the Child and the hand raised in benediction were remodeled at an undetermined date, prior, in any case, to the nineteenth century. An unidentified mark, FL, appears in a rectangle; it would seem to be the earliest known French mark to date.

ARM RELIQUARY OF ST. GEORGE. 13th century. Silver parcel-gilt on a wood core. H. 22⅞". Treasury of the former Abbey Church.

pl. 221   The hand is shown in a gesture of blessing. The cuff encircling the wrist is decorated with a lozenge pattern in repoussé; the lozenges along the edges contain six-lobed rosettes, the rest contain stamped and gilded griffins. The sleeve, which is wider, is covered with repoussé silver plaques and has as its only decoration a filigreed, gilded, and jeweled door that covers the cavity which houses the relics, and below, in repoussé, a crucified Christ surmounted by a haloed eagle holding a scroll in its claws.

TRIPTYCH RELIQUARY. 13th century. Silver parcel-gilt and repoussé on a wood core. H. 16½″, w. when open 15½″. Treasury of the former Abbey Church.

pl. 222

The top of the central panel of the triptych is formed by a trefoil of modified pointed arches. Each wing is equal to half the width of this panel. They are sheathed with silver-gilt plaques with beaded borders in which ovals, trefoils, and quatrefoils have been cut out and surrounded by filigree and jewels, and are intended to allow the viewer to see the relics, which are indicated by inscriptions in repoussé Gothic script. The central panel has fifteen apertures, with the following inscriptions (from bottom to top):

H[IC] S[UN]T RELIQVI[A]E AP[OSTO]LORV[M]
S[AN]C[T]I PET[R]I
MART[IN]I STEPH[AN]I
S[AN]C[T]I PAVLI
[BENE]D[I]CTI INNOC[EN]CIV[M]
S[AN]C[T]I ANDRE[A]E
[SIL]VEST[R]I
SIMO[N]IS [E]T IVD[A]E
GERALDI LAV[R]E[N]CII
IOH[ANN]IS B[A]B[TISTA]E
IACOBI ET PHILIPPI

The right wing has six apertures accompanied by inscriptions:

D[E] SEPVLC[R]O D[OMI]NI
D[E] TVNICA B[EATA]E M[ARIA]E
D[E] SEPVLC[R]O B[EATA]E M[ARIA]E
D[E]PA[N]E C[O]EN[A]E
M[ARIA]E MA[G]DALEN[A]E
AGATH[A]E

The left wing also has six openings accompanied by inscriptions:

ANTO[N]INI
MAVRICII
PRIECTI
LVCI[A]E
C[A]ECILI[AE]
ANASTASI[A]E

RELIQUARY STATUETTE OF ST. FOY. End of 15th century. Silver parcel-gilt repoussé on a wood base. H. 18½″. Treasury of the former Abbey Church.

fig. 50

St. Foy is shown standing and crowned. She is clothed in a robe that is fitted at the waist and covered with a mantle with wide folds which is drawn back over the left arm. The right hand holds a sword and gridiron, the instruments of her martyrdom; the left hand holds the martyr's palm. The statuette is in repoussé. The crown, the hair, the neckline, and belt of the robe, the facings of the mantle, the gridiron, and the palm are gilded. The piece was ordered on the basis of work in lieu of rent on August 17, 1493, for the abbot and monastery of Sainte-Foy of Conques from the goldsmiths Huc Lenfan and Pierre Frechrieu of Villefranche-de-Rouergue, and completed and delivered on August 2, 1497. It bears the stamps, P.F. (stamp of Pierre Frechrieu) and VILL (stamp of Villefranche-de-Rouergue).

PROCESSIONAL CROSS. About 1500. Silver parcel-gilt on a wood core. H. with shaft 8′ 7⅛″, h. of cross 70⅞″, w. 31½″. Treasury of the former Abbey Church.

pl. 224

The ends of the arms of the cross terminate in cinquefoil motifs adorned with silver-gilt balls. The arms are decorated on both sides with silver plaques stamped with a foliate design which are edged with a cable molding,

a plaited molding, and a second cable molding on which is soldered a crest composed of alternating buds and palmettes. Semiprecious stones, cabochons, and intaglios mounted in bezels decorate the two faces. The crossing of the arms is squared, with an acorn with a gilded shell at each of the corners.

pl. 225

In the center of the front face is a statuette of Christ with a cruciform halo. At the ends of the arms of the cross are figures of the Virgin and St. John; at the top, God the father; at the bottom, a rectagular window closing a cavity designed to receive relics. In the center of the reverse side is a statuette of St. Foy, and at the ends, the four Evangelists. All these figures are executed in repoussé, and their garments are gilded. The knop is in the form of an octagonal edifice covered with a roof decorated with an imbricated motif; each face, between buttresses crowned with pinnacles, presents a statuette of an Apostle: St. Peter, St. Andrew, St. Bartholomew, St. Matthias, St. James the Greater, St. Paul, St. Simon, St. James the Less. The cylindrical shaft is ornamented with spiral bands, some of which are original and are decorated with a foliate design, and others which date from the seventeenth century and are decorated with superposed palmettes separated by beading.

pl. 223

P. F. in Gothic characters, the stamp of Pierre Frechrieu, is on the piece; also that of Villefranche-de-Rouergue after 1498, namely, a Gothic V under a fleur-de-lis surmounted by an open crown.

50

THE GRANDSELVE TREASURY

The Abbey of Grandselve (*grandis silva*, great woods), was founded in 1114 by Géraud of Salles, a disciple of Robert of Arbrissel, who sent a few hermits to settle in a solitary, thickly wooded vale in the vicinity of Toulouse. The monastery was at first under the Benedictine rule, but soon became affiliated with Cîteaux. After the first building had become inadequate, a new church was erected between 1249 and 1253 and many altars were consecrated. The Abbey now became very important, and its influence grew throughout the thirteenth century, which saw the apogee of its power. During the whole of this period, Grandselve enjoyed the favor of popes and the protection of princes, many of whom honored it with their visits, and some of whom, like William IV, count of Montpellier, retired there permanently. The Abbey took an active part in the Hundred Years' War by sheltering the son of John the Good, who was imprisoned in London, and encouraging him to resist the English invaders; it was not, however, involved in the incidents of the wars of religion, which did not affect it. Nevertheless, Grandselve's decline, which began as early as the fourteenth century, was slowly to continue up to the Revolution, which administered the final blow. In 1791, there were only sixteen monks in an Abbey that had once housed 800, and on August 20th of that year it was sold to a judge of Toulouse for 100,000 francs. The buildings were destroyed. In 1799, only the church remained, and this was demolished in 1803.

Apart from a few capitals that were salvaged, the only things that remain from this great Cistercian Abbey of the Southwest are its treasures. They had been deposited in the college of St. Bernard in Toulouse in 1562, then returned to Grandselve one hundred years later. An inventory made in 1790 lists the pieces: five caskets and two reliquaries, one containing relics of the Holy Thorn and the Holy Shroud, the other embellished with silver and jewels. In February 1791, the caskets (one of the five seems to have disappeared) and the Reliquary of the Holy Thorn were deposited in the church of Bouillac, where they still remain, while the reliquary decorated with silver and jewels was transferred to Ardus, where it remains today, together with a disk reliquary of undetermined origin. This group has been studied in a recent article by M. Méras ("Le Trésor de l'Abbaye de Grandselve," *Les Monuments historiques de la France,* 1956, pp. 225–27).

BOUILLAC (*Tarn-et-Garonne*)

The four caskets are very similar: in the shape of a church with aisles and a transept and an octagonal two-storied tower at the crossing, in imitation of the brick towers of the Toulouse region.

CASKET OF THE CRUCIFIXION. 13th century. Silver, silver and copper gilt on a wood core. H. 24½", w. 21⅝", d. 11". Church of Bouillac.

pls. 228, 229

The tower, the triforium, and the crest of the roof are of copper gilt. The Crucifixion is represented on the principal face under a trefoiled arch decorated with filigree, gems, and intaglios. On either side, as well as on the short sides, are two figures of saints (one is missing on one of the sides) accompanied by two figures of abbots under rounded arches separated by colonnettes. The Virgin in Majesty is represented in the gable of the transept. The silver plaques of the roof have been worked to imitate tiles. The tower has pierced windows with round arches on the first story and pointed arches on the second and is surmounted by a crystal ball.

This casket, which is homogeneous in style, may be dated from the second half of the thirteenth century, the period when the altars of the Abbey Church were consecrated. Only the plaques in the gables of the nave are fifteenth century.

CASKET OF CHRIST THE LAWGIVER. 13th century. Silver, silver and copper gilt on a wood core. H. 17", w. 13⅜", d. 5½". Church of Bouillac.

pl. 230

The Casket of Christ the Lawgiver, and the Casket of Our Lady, are smaller than the Casket of the Crucifixion but constructed on the same pattern, with the important difference that the towers are not pierced. The Casket of St. Liberata (h. 23¼", w. 20½", d. 9") has no figures on it. These three caskets also date from the second half of

the thirteenth century, perhaps slightly later than the Casket of the Crucifixion, which is more archaic in character.

The reliquaries are very different in form.

RELIQUARY OF THE HOLY THORN. 13th century. Silver and copper gilt on a wood core. H. 21¼", w. 4", d. 4". Church of Bouillac.

pl. 226

pl. 227

fig. 51

The Reliquary of the Holy Thorn is in the form of a tower placed under a copper-gilt ciborium made up of four colonnettes supporting round arches, the whole topped by a conical roof ending in a ball. The tower is of silver and is decorated with three registers of filigree work windows with round arches filled with crystal plaques that protect miniatures painted on parchment. On the back is a plaque with an engraved inscription listing the relics enshrined in the reliquary. The neck, with a rock crystal knop, is in the form of a capital decorated with foliate scrolls and palmettes with silver inlays in copper, and resembles the Romanesque capitals of the Abbey which have survived. This reliquary could be carried on a staff in processions.

According to tradition, the reliquary was presented to the Abbey in 1251 by Alphonse of Poitiers, the brother of St. Louis, on his return from a crusade, but there is no recorded evidence to bear this out. In fact, we believe that this reliquary is of much earlier date than the caskets referred to above. The filigree work of the caskets, which is composed of regular windings of alternating foliate scrolls ending in buds or flowers, is characteristic of the mid-thirteenth century; we find it on the Nailly Cross in the Sens Treasury (p. 45), on the Casket of St. Taurinus of Evreux (fig. 30), etc. The filigree work of the Reliquary of the Holy Thorn, on the other hand, threading its way between large, conical, beaded lobes, belongs to a tradition that goes back to Ottonian precious metalwork (Cross of the Empire in the Vienna Schatzkammer, Evangeliary cover at Aachen). These characteristics, as much as those of its setting and the style of the miniatures, would seem to us to place the Reliquary of the Holy Thorn no later than the middle of the twelfth century.

LAMOTHE-CAPDEVILLE
(*Tarn-et-Garonne*)

RELIQUARY OF THE TRUE CROSS. 13th century. Silver plaques, copper gilt on a wood core. H. 26¾", w. 7½", d. 19¾". Church of Ardus.

pl. 231

The Reliquary of the True Cross, which at one time possessed two wings, is in the form of a panel surmounted by a gable. Two round arches stand out against the ground, supported by colonnettes with capitals. The arches, the frame, and the neck—a kind of volute composed of coiled palms and ears of corn—are of cast and gilded copper. The plaques of the ground, of silver gilt, are decorated with filigree, gems, and Antique intaglios. In the upper part, a plaque of modern glass shelters the relics of the True Cross. At the top is a ball of copper gilt which has been pierced, in which a modern cross has been placed. This is probably the reliquary referred to in the inventory of the Grandselve treasures made in 1790 as being "decorated with silver and precious stones." It was brought to Ardus by Dom Martin of Bellerive, sub-prior of Belleperche, a neighboring abbey, in 1791, and at his death was taken over by the Fraysines de Latour family, who gave it to the church in about 1825. It is worth noting that the decoration of this reliquary is very similar to that of the Reliquary of the Holy Thorn (pls. 226, 227), on which there is the same very unusual filigree work and the same motif of the palm and ear of corn on the handle. We are therefore inclined to believe that the two pieces originated in the same workshop and are contemporary.

DISK RELIQUARY. End of 12th century. Silver parcel-gilt on a wood core. H. 8¼", d. ¾". Church of Ardus.

51

52

The other reliquary preserved in the church of Ardus is in the form of a disk covered with plaques of nielloed silver. On one face, Christ is represented in a mandorla between the alpha and omega. On the other, six concentric inscriptions enumerate the relics enclosed in the disk. This reliquary could be placed on a staff, or even on another reliquary. It was brought to Ardus in 1791 by the sub-prior of Belleperche, and given to the church in 1895. The origin of this reliquary, which seems to date from the end of the twelfth century, is equally uncertain. Since it is not mentioned in the 1790 inventory of the Abbey of Grandselve, it has been surmised that it must have belonged to the Abbey of Belleperche.

pl. 233

pl. 232

PRUDHOMAT *(Lot)*

ARM RELIQUARY. End of 14th century–beginning of 15th. Silver and copper gilt on a wood core. H. 19¾″. Church of Castelnau-de-Bretenoux.

fig. 52

An arm reliquary is preserved at the church of Prudhomat whose owner was esquire of the right arm of St. Louis, who accompanied the king on his last crusade and was present at his death in Tunis in 1270. According to tradition, he returned with the right arm of the saintly king, and commissioned the reliquary. However, both the truth of the tradition and the authenticity of the relic are in dispute. The Reliquary consists of a silver hand, embossed and gilded, mounted on a wooden arm sheathed with strips of silver engraved with decorative motifs in which fleurs-de-lis alternate with rosettes; the cuff and base are decorated with cabochons set in bezels, which have disappeared in part.

OUST *(Ariège)*

RELIQUARY. 1542. Silver parcel-gilt. H. 18⅞″. Church of Oust.

pl. 234

The reliquary is in the form of a small rectangular edifice with four turrets at the corners and a pent roof; it bears an inscription in repoussé which gives the names of the consuls of Oust and the date of the gift, 1542. At the top of the roof, which is detachable and held by little

chains, is a cross between two small statuettes in long robes gathered at the waist, which are somewhat awkward in style. The monstrance rests on a base decorated with gadroons, as is the knop; figures of Apostles are on the stem, as well as on the long sides of the buildings where they alternate with small openings through which the relics could be seen. The reliquary bears the mark, IB, which might be that of a goldsmith of Toulouse.

SARRANCOLIN *(Hautes-Pyrénées)*

CASKET OF ST. EBBO. 13th century. Enameled copper gilt on a wood core. H. 18½″, w. 26⅜″, d. 10⅝″. Church of Sarrancolin.

fig. 53

The casket of St. Ebbo is decorated with figures of the Apostles, a bishop, a queen, and, on the short sides, SS. Peter and Paul, on a ground of blue enamel ornamented with a polychromed rinceau. The rear side, of copper stamped with rosettes, is decorated with six enameled medallions devoted to the infancy of Christ: on the roof, Annunciation to the Shepherds, Nativity, Two Magi; on the face, Annunciation, Virgin and Child adored by a king, Visitation. These charming scenes, treated with great delicacy of style, are on a ground similar to that of the principle face: blue enamel decorated with polychromed foliate scrolls. The medallions are edged with borders of red enamel with white dots.

pl. 235

The casket, which dates from the thirteenth century, disappeared for some years from the church, and was then found in the stream that runs past the bottom of the village.

SEIX *(Ariège)*

The church of Seix has two interesting pieces, both of which belong to the precious metalwork characteristic of Toulouse in the sixteenth century. One is a very fine ciborium of silver gilt decorated with spiral gadroons; the other is a reliquary monstrance.

MONSTRANCE RELIQUARY OF ST. STEPHEN. 1st quarter of 16th century. Silver parcel-gilt. H. 18⅛″. Church of Seix.

The reliquary consists of a multifoil base decorated with an undulating motif, from which rises a stem on which is a knop that supports a rectangular miniature temple with pinnacles, decorated both front and back with foliate scrolls and arabesques in Renaissance style. One of the faces is further embellished with figures of the Virgin and Child and the donor, placed on either side of a wide window through which the relics can be viewed. Two slender brackets rise from the central stem, on which are statuettes of angels that frame the monstrance.

This reliquary, on which the letter N can be made out, together with the letters T O L under a fleur-de-lis and the stamp of master IB, is attributed by Jean Thuile to the Toulouse goldsmith, J. Blaru, 1518.

SAINT-BERTRAND-DE-COMMINGES *(Haute-Garonne)*

The two most important pieces in the Treasury of Saint-Bertrand-de-Comminges are embroidered copes of English

53

origin, one of which, known as the Cope of the Virgin, is supposed to have belonged to St. Bertrand de l'Isle, bishop of Comminges, who lived in the eleventh century. This tradition is not sustained by stylistic analysis, and it is accepted that both copes were donated by Bertrand de Goth, archbishop of Saint-Bertrand from 1295 to 1300, under whose episcopacy the cathedral was rebuilt, and who was to become pope under the name of Clement V. Their presence at Saint-Bertrand coincided with the translation of the relics of St. Bertrand in 1309. The fact that Bertrand de Goth had previously been bishop of Bordeaux explains the English origin of these copes.

pl. 237

COPE OF THE VIRGIN. Beginning of 14th century. Red silk embroidered with gold and multicolored silk threads. L. 4' 6⅜", w. 9' 6¼". Treasury of the former Cathedral.

On the Cope of the Virgin, scenes from the life of the Virgin, the infancy of Christ, and the lives of the Apostles are embroidered on a red ground in multicolor silks, with green predominating. The scenes are enclosed in triangles and octagons created by vine scrolls and curious leaf masks reminiscent of those found on certain stained glass windows of the period, particularly at Saint-Ouen and Rouen. It is comparable with the Melk Chasuble (Österreichisches Museum für Kunst, Vienna), and is regarded as the earliest known English cope, with concentric arcades whose design recalls that of the rose windows.

COPE OF THE PASSION. Beginning of 14th century. White silk embroidered with gold and multicolored silk threads. L. 4' 6", w. 9' 6¼". Treasury of the former Cathedral.

pls. 238–239

The Cope of the Passion differs in treatment from the previous one in that it is highly sophisticated. The various

scenes of the Passion are described in many small, delicately conceived pictures, somewhat like miniatures, set in roundels surrounded by figures from a bestiary—birds and quadrupeds—of astonishing verisimilitude. The piece is very sumptuous, owing to the quality of the design and the use of gold thread mingled with silk.

TOULOUSE *(Haute-Garonne)*

The magnificence of the Treasury of Saint-Sernin of Toulouse, which throughout the Middle Ages was regarded as one of the richest in Christendom, is known to us from inventories which, from 1246 to 1657, describe the numerous pieces of precious metalwork that it contained. When ecclesiastical properties were confiscated in 1792, it contained no fewer than eighteen caskets, the finest of which were those of St. Saturninus, St. James, St. Exuperius, SS. Simon and Jude, SS. Philip and James; seventeen head reliquaries, among which that of St. James in a pilgrim's hat was especially remarkable for the sumptuousness of its decoration; a great number of arm reliquaries, statuettes, footed reliquaries, caskets of enameled copper, small ivory caskets, etc. Of all these precious objects, only a few were salvaged, among them three exceptional pieces: the great Cameo of Augustus, the Evangeliary commissioned by Charlemagne, and the Horn of Roland, which, with the head reliquaries of SS. Saturninus and Exuperius, were exposed to the view of the faithful during Holy Week. None of them, however, are now in the Saint-Sernin Treasury.

The Cameo, according to legend, had been found in the desert, then brought back from the Holy Land by Charlemagne. It was jealousy guarded by the canons and municipal magistrates of Toulouse until 1533, at which date Francis I appropriated it, and it took its place among the jewels of Marie de Médicis. It was deposited for safe-keeping in the Dominican convent of Poissy, then stolen during the wars of religion, and subsequently sold to the Emperor Rudolph II. In this manner it came to be included in the collections of the museum of antiquities in Vienna, where it has remained.

The Evangeliary of Godescalc, commissioned in 781 by Charlemagne and his wife, Hildegard, escaped the ravages of the Revolution thanks to the intervention of Baron de Puymaurin, who pointed out the value of the manuscript. In 1811, the municipality of Toulouse presented it to Napoleon, on the occasion of the birth of the King of Rome; the emperor deposited it in the library of the Louvre, and it was subsequently transferred to the Bibliothèque Nationale.

p. 49 below

Finally, the so-called Horn of Roland, an ivory oliphant of the Carolingian period carved with reliefs of birds, lions, and griffins which Swarzenski places in the twelfth century and attributes to the region of Salerno, is now housed in the Musée Paul-Dupuy in Toulouse.

Several objects, however, have remained at Saint-Sernin: the thirteenth-century crosier associated with St. Louis of Anjou; the white silk miter of St. Exuperius decorated with red and gray orphreys, also of the thirteenth century; and especially two casket reliquaries—the Casket of St. Saturninus and the Casket of the True Cross—which together with a Moslem textile known as the Silk of King Robert, are the best-known pieces in the Saint-Sernin Treasury.

In the course of the nineteenth century, several interesting pieces came to take their place alongside the aforementioned ones. Among them, we might mention two chasubles from the convent of the Jacobins in Toulouse, one of which, decorated with vine scrolls, peacocks, and pelicans, and known as the Chasuble of St. Dominic, could not, for reasons of style, belong to the thirteenth century, when that saint lived, but was probably, according to a recent study, a gift made by the family of Anjou and Sicily at the time of the translation of the relics of St. Thomas Aquinas to Toulouse, in 1369; the other, which is very simple, and of white silk, is known as the Chasuble of St. Peter of Verona, but may in fact have belonged to St. Dominic; also, liturgical gloves with their plaques, of the thirteenth century, and a small ivory casket of Arab workmanship.

RELIQUARY OF THE TRUE CROSS. Limoges, 13th century. Enameled copper gilt. H. 7⅞", w. 11½", d. 5½". Treasury of Saint Sernin.

pl. 240

The Reliquary of the True Cross is a very small casket covered with enameled copper plaques engraved with figures with applied cast heads which stand out against a blue ground strewn with red, light-blue, yellow, and dark-green rosettes. On the lid are represented traditional scenes from the life of Christ: Christ in Glory, the Annunciation, the Holy Women at the Sepulcher. On the casket itself, the Finding of the Cross by St. Helena, followed by the account of an incident especially connected with the history of the abbey, which is described as on a fresco or tapestry: before the city of Jerusalem, the abbot of the monastery of Josaphat offers a piece of the True Cross to Botardel, a Toulouse scrivener who had undertaken a pilgrimage to the holy places; Botardel embarks for home with the relic, then, upon his arrival in Toulouse, presents it to the abbot of Saint-Sernin, Pons de Montpezat, escorted by two canons; the latter then hand it over to Bishop St. Saturninus, while at the right are the outlines of the ramparts of a fortified city designated by its name: Tolosa.

The inventory of 1264 does not mention this very fine reliquary, which was expressly fashioned for Saint-Sernin by Limoges enamelers; it would seem to date from the middle of the thirteenth century. The cast copper caryatids which support the casket date from the sixteenth century.

SILK OF KING ROBERT. 12th century. Silk. In two pieces of 63⅜" x 56⅜" each. Treasury of Saint-Sernin.

pl. 241

The magnificent textile known as the Silk of King Robert is decorated with peacocks facing each other on either side of a horn, or stylized tree, at the foot of which stand two ibexes. This theme, which is treated here with

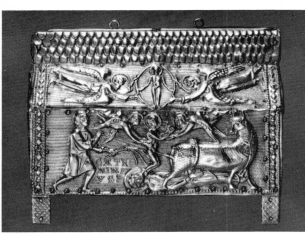

54

great style, is repeated in yellow and red on a black ground. Each row is separated by a horizontal band bearing the inscription, in Arab characters, EL BARAKA T EL KAMILAH (perfect benediction).

A recent study by M. Prin ("Les Vêtements liturgiques du Couvent des Frères Prêcheurs de Toulouse," *Mémoires, Société Archéologique du Midi de la France*, XXX, 1964, pp. 127ff) has made it possible to reconstruct the cope that was cut out of this fabric by comparing it with fragments preserved in the Musée de Cluny and the Victoria and Albert Museum which, technical analysis undertaken at the laboratories of the museum in Lyons has recently proved, were of identical manufacture. Some scholars, e.g., Falk (*op. cit.*, p. 21), believe it to be of Sicilian origin;

others, e.g., Kendrick (*Magazine of Fine Arts* [London], 1905, p. 124), attribute it to Hispano-Moorish workmanship. In support of the former theory we may cite the mosaics of the Palace of Palermo, where the peacock theme is similarly treated; in support of the latter, an ivory box originating in Cordova, now in the Victoria and Albert Museum, as well as a textile preserved in the Treasury of Salamanca. In that textile, however, the peacocks are back to back, with only the heads and beaks face to face. The matter, in fact, remains open. This type of textile, which was manufactured in the Islamized workshops of the West—in Sicily and Spain—and the art of which derived from that of the Sassanian workshops prior to the conquest, is a general type that is hard to localize, and of which other Eastern examples of the same period exist.

RELIQUARY OF ST. SATURNINUS. 13th century. Silver parcel-gilt on a wood core. H. 5", w. 25¼", d. 2¾". Treasury of Saint-Sernin.

fig. 54

The Reliquary of St. Saturninus is a small rectangular casket with a pent roof, sheathed with strips of silver gilt. Scenes illustrating the martyrdom and glorification of St. Saturninus are depicted in repoussé and engraving. The saint, whose name is indicated near his haloed head, bound and dragged between the hooves of a bull goaded on by a whip and a prong, breathes his last, while his soul (a nimbused, nude, sexless figure) is received by two angels. On the reverse face, on either side of a circular opening through which the relics may be seen, are represented two of St. Saturninus' most illustrious successors on the episcopal throne of Toulouse, SS. Honoratus and Eleutherus, their names indicated in an inscription; they are garbed in episcopal robes and are shown censing the remains of St. Saturninus and sprinkling them with holy water, each accompanied by an acolyte. On the slope of the roof, Christ is portrayed in Majesty receiving a mitered and nimbused St. Saturninus, who is presented by the Virgin. On the lateral faces, two angels are shown with lowered wings, carrying censers. The ridge is decorated with an imbrication motif; the bands at the sides, with lozenges between rows of beading. The legs and the bottom plaque are engraved with diaper work.

pls. 242–243

The reliquary is mentioned in the inventory of 1246, and has been attributed to the first half of the thirteenth century. It was at one time enclosed in a gilded wooden bust of St. Saturninus, and thus escaped destruction during the Revolution.

CASKET. Siculo or Hispano-Moorish, 12th century. Ivory. H. 3½", w. 6¾". Treasury of Saint-Sernin.

fig. 55

The small casket of engraved ivory, decorated with birds and quadrupeds in circles, with Arab tracery and characters, may be compared, among others, with those preserved at the cathedral of Apt at Sisco in Corsica; it may also, like the Silk of King Robert, be attributed to Moslem workshops in the Mediterranean West, perhaps those of Sicily, and presumed to date from the twelfth century. This casket, which was originally in the chapel of the college of Mirepoix at Toulouse, was not in the Saint-Sernin Treasury until the nineteenth century.

Roussillon — Languedoc

NARBONNE (*Aude*)

The Treasury of Narbonne, which is very rich in seventeenth- and eighteenth-century jewel work, also possesses several particularly noteworthy pieces from earlier periods, namely, a portable altar of serpentine and silver gilt, dated 1273, two very fine ivories, and a reliquary associated with St. Prudentius.

IVORY PLAQUE FROM THE COVER OF AN EVANGELIARY. Beginning of 9th century. H. 10", w. 6¼". Treasury, Cathedral.

pl. 245

One of the ivories is a plaque from an Evangeliary

55

cover given to the Cathedral of Saint-Just in 1850 which represents the Crucifixion. The beardless Christ is still in the Early Christian tradition. Under the branches of the cross, which is outlined by a beaded border and surmounted by the sun and the moon, saintly figures are grouped beside the men with the sponge and the lance, while at the foot of the cross the soldiers divide Christ's garments under a ball on a frame, representing the apparatus used for throwing dice. The remaining area is composed of four registers in which are depicted scenes from the Passion: the Last Supper and the Kiss of Judas, the Holy Women at the Sepulcher and the Incredulity of Thomas, and, at the top of the composition, at the left, the Ascension, where Christ, in a mandorla and bearing the Cross on his shoulder, is received by a divine hand, and, at the right, Pentecost.

pl. 246

This ivory may be placed at the beginning of the ninth century; it is an example of the Ada style, representing the Antique tradition developed in the Carolingian period in circles directly influenced by the imperial court.

IVORY BOX. 11th century. H. 4″, diameter 3″. Treasury, Cathedral.

pl. 247

The other ivory is a small cylindrical box with a conical lid, decorated with interlaces of stylized palmettes bordered by bands with geometrical designs of guilloche and beading. Around the base of the lid is a Kufic inscription whose characters form an ornamental band. The inscription has been translated as follows: "The blessing of God. Made in the city of Cuenca for the collection of Majeb Caïd." The reference is believed to be to Ismail Ibn Dhi 'n Nun, who was governor of Cuenca in the middle of the eleventh century.

RELIQUARY OF ST. PRUDENTIUS. 17th century. Engraved crystal, repoussé silver, painted ivory encrusted with intaglios of garnets and other precious stones. H. 15¾″, w. 22″, d. 15″. Treasury, Cathedral.

pl. 248

In the Reliquary of St. Prudentius we have an example of a secular piece finding its way into a church treasury. As at Vannes (pls. 80–81) the piece is a marriage casket, but whereas the importance of the Vannes piece lies in the charm of the painting that adorns it and not in the very simple and almost meager materials of which it is made, the value of the Narbonne piece lies in the preciousness of the materials used and the refinement with which they were used.

The casket is octagonal and the faces are made up of crystal plaques engraved with landscapes, seascapes, and figures representing the four seasons, Faith, and Justice. These plaques are framed by bands of repoussé silver which are in turn enclosed in bands of ivory painted with foliate scrolls. These ivory bands are set with a large number of garnets and some 350 antique intaglios. The base, supported on ten balls of cut crystal, is of two levels, the upper level including a small drawer. At the angles between the sides of the casket proper are small twisted colonnettes with capitals of enameled silver decorated

with flowers and fruit which support a cornice and balls of cut crystal. Crowning the piece is a small lion of rock crystal.

This precious casket is believed to have belonged to Marie de Médicis. It is probably of Italian origin, and may be compared—although it is perhaps later in date—with the so-called Albertine casket in the Reiche Kapelle in Munich, from the workshop of Annibale Fontana in Milan, who died in 1587. The original red leather case decorated with gilded motifs is still preserved.

PALAU-DEL-VIDRE (*Pyrénées-Orientales*)

CHALICE. 15th century. Repoussé silver gilt. H. 9″. Church of Palau-del-Vidre.

pl. 249

The silver-gilt chalice, which bears the Perpignan stamp, stands on a polylobe quadrooned base decorated with leaves. The knop, formed like a capital, supports two half-length cherubs, their hands crossed over their breasts, who stand back to back against the stem that expands into the leafwork of the outer cup. Such use of architectonic and plastic motifs, borrowed from the religious architecture of the period, makes this chalice unique among chalices known to have been produced in France. It may also be regarded as one of the earliest in the series of figured chalices; in the sixteenth century, however, such figures were to be treated in a different, more ornamental, style and placed under arcades.

RIGARDA (*Pyrénées-Orientales*)

MONSTRANCE RELIQUARY. 15th century. Repoussé silver gilt. H. 20⅞″. Church of Rigarda.

pl. 250

The monstrance is shaped like a building surmounted by a high, central gable, around the lunula that contains the Host, which rises between two little towers. This structure is held on a curvilinear triangle that rises from a hexagonal shaft composed of gables and pinnacles which, in turn, rests on a polylobe base supported by small lions. On either side, two brackets in the shape of volutes support two statuettes of angels with their long wings displayed. This monstrance, of skillful and elegant complexity, was one of the solutions found for dealing with the problem of presenting the Blessed Sacrament, instituted, as we know, in the fourteenth century. It is of repoussé silver gilt and bears the stamp of Perpignan.

pl. 251

SAINT-POLYCARPE (*Aude*)

Among the treasures of the Mediterranean Languedoc, those of Saint-Polycarpe are noteworthy for their rich jeweled work; they include two head reliquaries—of SS. Polycarp and Benedict—and a monstrance.

MONSTRANCE RELIQUARY. 13th century. Silver and copper gilt, cabochons. H. 13¾″. Treasury, Saint-Polycarpe.

pl. 252

The thirteenth-century monstrance reliquary belongs to the series of reliquaries with horizontal cylinders supported by two angels of which other examples occur, for instance, in the Treasury of Montpezat, at Egletons (Corrèze), where, exceptionally, one of the angels was replaced by the Virgin, or in Italy, at San Domenico in Bologna. On a rectangular base supported by lions, the two angels stand very erect, their wings falling vertically, and carry in their hands the ends of the cylinder which is crowned by two high towers. The ensemble is enriched with a number of cabochons set in bezels. There is no stamp. The piece is probably of southern origin.

HEAD RELIQUARY OF ST. BENEDICT. 13th century. Silver parcel-gilt. H. 11½″. Treasury, Saint-Polycarpe.

pl. 253

The head of St. Benedict, of repoussé silver, rests on a rectangular tray decorated with enameled medallions on which are the arms of the Bouteville family (azure, three shells or, three and one). The face is surrounded by a short beard of silver gilt; the hair and eyebrows, engraved in very delicate undulations, are also of silver gilt. The piece bears no stamp which would enable us to determine its origin; it would seem, however, to date from the thirteenth century, and should, according to J. Thuile (*Bulletin, Commission archéologique de Narbonne,* 1953–55, XXIII, part 2, p. 171), be attributed to a workshop of Languedoc.

QUARANTE *(Hérault)*

HEAD RELIQUARY OF JOHN THE BAPTIST. 1441. Silver parcel-gilt. H. 15″. Church of Quarante.

pl. 254   The head reliquary of John the Baptist is a fiercely realistic representation of the desert hermit, with emaciated features, hallucinated gaze, mouth parted to reveal the teeth, head framed in long, disordered hair and a beard that merges with the fleece covering the shoulders. This magnificent bust is believed to have been made at Montpellier during the priorate of Raymond III of Fabrègues (1413–59) by a goldsmith whom J. Thuile has identified as James Morel.

THUIR *(Pyrénées-Orientales)*

VIRGIN AND CHILD. 13th century. Lead, originally gilded. H. 21¼″. Church of Thuir.

pl. 255   The Virgin of Thuir is one of the rare examples of a Virgin in Majesty which is not of polychrome wood, like that of Saint-Denis, nor sheathed with precious metals, like those of Orcival (pl. 66) or Beaulieu (pl. 179). It is of lead, and was originally gilded. Roughly modeled, the figure is seated in a rigorously frontal position, as is the Child on her lap. Identical Virgins, cast in the same mold, exist in the Massif Central and in Catalonia, in villages that were stops on a pilgrimage route between these two provinces.

According to the legend, the Virgin of Thuir intervened miraculously to give Charlemagne the victory over the Moors at Monastir del Camp, a site near Thuir. The style, however, does not bear out the legend. In point of fact, the Virgin is not mentioned at Thuir until after the battle of Lepanto, in 1571.

VILLENEUVE-LÈS-AVIGNON *(Gard)*

VIRGIN AND CHILD. 14th century. Ivory. H. 17¾″. Collegiate Church.

pl. 256   This Virgin is one of the most celebrated productions of fourteenth-century Parisian ivory work.

In a charmingly maternal gesture, the Virgin arches her back and turns her head, which is veiled and crowned, as though better to admire her son, who stands on her lap and appears to be talking with her. The group is admirably well preserved, save for the Virgin's forearm, which is damaged. The original polychrome exists, chiefly on the clothes, which are bordered with blue and gold braid. The hexagonal wooden base, consisting of two levels joined by balusters, dates from the seventeenth century. This work, of exquisite grace and delicacy, is believed to have been given to the Collegiate Church of Villeneuve by its founder, Cardinal Armand de Via, the nephew of Pope John XXII.

BIBLIOGRAPHY

BABELON, J. *L'Orfèvrerie française.* Paris, 1946.

BRÉHIER, L. *L'Art en France des invasions barbares à l'époque romane.* Paris, 1930.

BRAUN, J. *Das christliche Altargerät in seinem Sein und seiner Entwicklung.* Munich, 1932.

BRAUN, J. *Die Reliquiare des christlichen Kultes und ihre Entwicklung.* Freiburg im Breisgau, 1940.

FROLOW, A. *La Relique de la vraie croix.* Paris, 1961.

LESNE, E. *Histoire de la propriété ecclésiastique en France: III, L'Inventaire de la propriété: Eglises et trésors des églises du commencement du VIIIe à la fin du XIe siècle.* Lille, 1936.

MÂLE, E. *La Fin du paganisme en Gaule.* Paris, 1950.

MARQUET DE VASSELOT, J.-J. *Bibliographie de l'orfèvrerie et de l'émaillerie françaises.* Paris, 1925.

MOLINIER, E. *Histoire générale des arts appliqués à l'industrie du Ve à la fin du XVIIIe siècle: IV, L'Orfèvrerie religieuse et civile,* Part 1, *Du Ve à la fin du XVe siècle.* Paris, 1896–1911.

SWARZENSKI, H. *Monuments of Romanesque Art.* London, 1954.

INDEX TO WORKS REPRODUCED
by location, according to city

PHOTOGRAPHIC ACKNOWLEDGMENTS

ARCHIVES PHOTOGRAPHIQUES 20, 21 bottom, 22, 25, 27, 30 above, 34 left and center, 35 below, 36 above, 43, 44 below, 45, 47, 50 left and right below, 51 right, 55, 56, 63, 66, 71–75, 78–81, 100, 105, 109, 112, 116, 119–21, 124–27, 132, 140, 141, 143, 156, 159–63, 166–69, 172–75, 181, 182, 184, 235, 237–39, 241, 255, 262 right, 263, 264, 272, 273 above, 275 below, 280, 281, 283 right, 284, 285 left, 286 below, 288, 300 right, 303   ARCHIVES PHOTOGRAPHIQUES–LUC JOUBERT 34 right, 35 above, 46, 48 left, 49 above, 50 center, 256   BALSAN 13, 14, 21 top   CENTRE INTERNATIONAL D'ETUDES TEXTILES ANCIENS, LYONS 190, 289 right below   CLEMENT 26   GIRAUDON 10. 17   HACHETTE 11, 16, 21 center, 23, 28, 29, 31, 33, 36 below, 37, 38, 39 below, 40, 41, 44 above, 48 right, 49 below, 50 right above, 51 left top, center, bottom, 52–54, 61, 62, 64, 65, 67, 69, 70, 77, 84–86, 88, 89, 92–97, 99, 101–3, 106–8, 110, 111, 113–15, 117, 122–23, 129–31, 133–39, 142, 144–45, 147–55, 157, 165, 170–71, 176, 177, 179, 180, 185–89, 191, 192–99, 201–34, 236, 240, 242–43, 245–54, 261, 262, 268, 269, 271, 275 above, 276–79, 282, 283 left, 285 right, 286 above, 287, 289 left, right above, 291, 293, 297, 298, 300 left, 301, 302   MUSEE LAMBINET, VERSAILLES 48 center,   JEAN-CLAUDE TOULOUSE 83, 87, 90, 91, 164, 183

The photographs on pages 30 below and 39 above are courtesy the author. The photographs credited to Hachette were taken especially for this book by Jean-Pierre Vieil.

CET OUVRAGE A ÉTÉ IMPRIMÉ
SUR LES PRESSES
DES IMPRIMERIES DE BOBIGNY - 65-388
FRANCE

DÉPOT LÉGAL N° 5033
3e TRIMESTRE 1966 - 23-81-1412-01